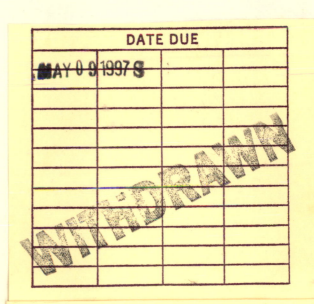

CrossCountry

No. 3/4

Special Issue: Montréal

NUMBER FOURTEEN   JULY, 1945

Contemporary

Verse

A Canadian Quarterly

ONE DOLLAR A YEAR
TWENTY-FIVE CENTS A COPY

do not drive on paved shoulder   Ramp speed 25

Beeeeeeeeeep   **bump**

left lane must exit

right lane must exit

alphabet

stop   maximum 30 ahead
                  maximum 30 ahead

rail ing cross way   rail cross ing way
rail ing cross way   rail cross ing way

radar enforced R*RrrRrrRrrr*Rrr
                RrrRrrRrrr

Construction zone ahead   RATA-RATA
RATATATA   Construction zone ends

No exit No stopping No left turn Do not pass No parking

YIELD

DELTA 20

(CANADA)

POETRY   •   ARTICLES   •   REVIEWS

New Roads To Peace

RESOLVED: That the next war should be fought on the moon.

RESOLVED: That atomic scientists should be transferred to work on love potions.

RESOLVED: That this poetry magazine be made required reading in all armies and military academies.

15 CENTS A COPY

FIRST
STATEMENT

CIV/n

6

APRIL., 1944   VOL. 2, NO. 6.

ANADIAN   PROSE   &   POETRY

THE CANADIAN
MERCURY

VOL. 1 No. 1   DECEMBER 1928

Holy Night
Jean Burton

The Problem of Canadian Literature
Stephen Leacock

On Funeral and Other Homes
B. K. Sandwell

25 Cents a Copy $2.00 a Year

BLEWOINTMENTPRESS
OCCUPATION
ISSEW

IF YOU REALLY   ARE AN EAGLE
YOU CAN FLY   THE COOP WITH ME

The Little Magazine in Canada 1925-80

The Little Magazine in Canada 1925-80

Its Role in the Development of Modernism and Post-Modernism in Canadian Poetry

Ken Norris

ECW PRESS

CANADIAN CATALOGUING IN PUBLICATION DATA

Norris, Ken, 1951–
  The little magazine in Canada 1925–80

Includes index.
ISBN 0-920802-53-2

1. Little magazines – Canada – History.
2. Canadian poetry (English) – 20th century – History
and criticism. * I. Title.

PN4914.L62N6 1984   051   C84-099176-2

The Little Magazine in Canada 1925–80 has been published with the help of a grant
from the Canadian Federation for the Humanities, using funds provided by the Social
Sciences and Humanities Research Council of Canada. Additional grants have been
provided by the Ontario Arts Council and The Canada Council.

Typeset by Imprint; printed by Hignell; cover design by The Dragon's Eye Press.

Published by ECW PRESS, 307 Coxwell Avenue, Toronto Ontario.

For Louis Dudek,
teacher and friend.

Contents

I

The Rise of Modernism
and the Role of the Little Magazine

Modernism is a development that came comparatively late to Canadian poetry and became the dominant mode in the 1940s, although there had been moderate intimations of it since 1914. By the time Modernism had fully established itself in this country, literature in most European countries and even in the United States had begun its "Post-Modernist" period. An attempt to see Canada within the context of development has led Robert Kroetsch to assert that "Canadian literature evolved directly from Victorian into Postmodern."[1] This is not true of Canadian poetry, whose Modernist evolution has been gradual and, at times, fragmented; it can also be argued that much of what is considered to be Canadian Post-Modernist poetry bears a strong resemblance to the work of the early American and European Modernists.

An understanding of the nature of Modernism is an essential aspect of a study such as this, yet a simple definition of Modernism is hard to arrive at. Modernism was a phenomenon that cut across all the arts almost simultaneously; literature represented one small branch of the tree. It seems difficult to reconcile movements such as German Expressionism, characterized by its passionate subjectivity, or Italian Futurism and its celebration of the machine and the liberation of typography, with the austere precision of the American and English Imagists; yet all of these are Modernist movements. They share an environment and certain common assumptions.

The Modernist artist felt very strongly a sense of the present, of living in a new age, of breaking with the past and its accumulation of traditions. In many respects, twentieth-century man has faced the greatest radical shift of values and of judgements about man's rôle in the world since the Renaissance. Beginning in the mid-nineteenth century, great philosophical and social upheavals were to indelibly change the face of the Western world; early-twentieth-century man faced a world radically different from that of his Victorian predecessors. Karl Marx's critique of capitalism began the assault on an economic system that had thrived in Europe and America for close to three hundred years; Charles Darwin's findings and theories brought western religions into question; Sigmund Freud provided man with a grammar with which to discuss the inner human process and began to bring to light man's dark, unconscious side; Albert Einstein's theory of relativity returned man to a Heraclitean world of flux and to a revalued sense of the nature of scientific objectivity. All of these endeavours represent severe and radical shifts in man's way of looking at himself and his world. Add to this other currents of thought like the philosophy of Nietzsche, the Suffragette and feminist movements, the discovery of primitive cave paintings in France and Spain, the invention of the electric light and other technological developments; the early twentieth century was a world totally transformed from the world of the Victorians. The old order was giving way to a new order, which had as some of its main components radical criticism, scepticism, reappraisal, dynamism, and doubt.

Artists also began to question the values and elements of their arts. This, too, is an essential property of Modernism: a concern with re-evaluating the rôle of art and investigating the elements that compose the medium. In the wake of the new discoveries made during this time, it is not surprising to find the artist using something like a scientific method in the analysis of art itself.

The Modernists held a variety of radical views about the value of the arts: the Dadaists were nihilistic in their attitude towards art, and concerned themselves with violating and debunking bourgeois values; for Marinetti and the Futurists one of art's purposes became the glorification of the machine age; the Surrealists desired to release the liberating and revolutionary powers of the unconscious; the Imagists were concerned with poetry as a precise art of charged visual depiction. The approach, in each case, was different, yet all the groups shared the urge to make art a vital life-force, destroying, celebrating, releasing, and crystallizing.

A central aesthetic concern in all the art movements is an investigation of the medium itself, or, as one critical summary puts it, "high aesthetic self-consciousness and non-representationalism, in which art turns from realism and humanistic representation towards style, technique, and spatial form in pursuit of a deeper penetration of life."[2] What results is that art itself becomes a category of human experience. Musicians investigate principles of tonality, painters of colour and perspective, sculptors of form, while writers investigate how language communicates through visual and auditory cues. In a sense the arts are brought under an aesthetic microscope for a study of their essential structure, and Modernism becomes a highly formalistic movement, diametrically opposed to the revolution of content represented by the Romantics. Although there is a consequent liberation of subject matter in Modern art, content often takes second place to the investigation of formal problems. As Louis Dudek notes in his essay "The Meaning of Modernism," formal analysis is evident in all of the Modern arts:

2

[W]e see that the Imagist method is as much an analysis and a dislocation of the elements of poetry as Cubism was in painting, or the atonal system was in music. The common principle of all these movements is that invariably the arts turn in upon themselves. Art for Art, which started the whole thing, has become art analyzing its own innards, or mechanically dismantling and reassembling itself in novel ways. Modernism is the disintegration of every art, after an expulsion of its subject matter.[3]

In locating the artist's concern solely in the artistic realm, relatively free of social implication, Modernism provided the artist with unprecedented freedom. As Bradbury and McFarlane put it:

[I]t set the artist free to be more himself, let him move beyond the kingdom of necessity to the kingdom of light. Now human consciousness and especially *artistic* consciousness could become more intuitive, more poetic; art could now *fulfil* itself. It was free to catch at the manifold — the atoms as they fall — and create significant harmony not in the universe but within itself....[4]

Implied in this new freedom was the possibility of achieving a new consciousness, one that was commensurate with the new modern world; in the Modernist phase, "modernity is a new consciousness, a fresh condition of the human mind."[5] Art must change to be a vital part of twentieth-century life; the formal order inherited from the Victorians does not serve the modern world. Victorian moral concern is now dated; the modern world, with all its dynamism, its novelty, is a world of uncertainty and chaos. These are elements that Modernism seeks to encompass, as Bradbury and McFarlane explain:

[I]t is the one art that responds to the scenario of our chaos. It is the art consequent on Heisenberg's "Uncertainty principle", of the destruction of civilization and reason in the First World War... of existential exposure to meaninglessness or absurdity. It is the literature of technology. It is the art consequent on the dis-establishing of communal reality and conventional notions of causality, on the destruction of traditional notions of the wholeness of individual character, on the linguistic chaos that ensues when public notions of language have been discredited and when all realities have become subjective fictions. Modernism is then the art of modernization — however stark the separation of the artist from society may have been, however oblique the artistic gesture he has made.[6]

3

The Modernist artist is intensely aware of living in a world catastrophically split from the past. We find, in Modernism, an intense historicity whose purpose, ultimately, is to tell us how different the present is from the past. For better or worse, the artist has been cut off from the great traditions that have developed in art; this separation is greeted by cries of joy or cries of despair. Part of the central dynamic of Modernism is the tension between artists celebrating their arrival in a brave new world and artists who lament the loss of the past. These extremes in vision and sentiment are perhaps best represented by the Italian and Russian Futurists, on the one side, affirming the present, and Eliot and all his followers, on the other, bemoaning the death of this great tradition. Looking at the Modernist arts, Bradbury and McFarlane find these two tendencies almost equally balanced:

> Modernism was in most countries an extraordinary compound of the futuristic and the nihilistic, the revolutionary and the conservative, the naturalistic and the symbolistic, the romantic and the classical. It was a celebration of a technological age and a condemnation of it; an excited acceptance of the belief that the old regimes of culture were over, and a deep despairing in the face of that fear; a mixture of convictions that the new forms were escapes from historicism and the pressures of the time with convictions that they were precisely the living expression of these things.[7]

The Modernist writer was aware of having been cut off from previous history, of finding himself not a product of a great past, but a fragment of a unique present. His art had also departed from "tradition" to express the new. Old forms could be employed, but they would need to be totally reconstituted to serve the modern sensibility. For most artists, the past had become "a heap of broken images." Artists surrendered to that vision of fragmentation and homelessness.

Before moving on to Modernist developments in English literature, and their interplay with the little magazine, we should consider, at least briefly, the so-called Post-Modernist phase of the movement. Despite the current description of Post-Modernism as a new artistic manifestation, examination reveals that it carries with it many of the earlier assumptions of Modernism; indeed, many of the Modernist artists are revered by the Post-Moderns. Post-Modernism is an elaboration of Modernist principles rather than a new anti-Modernist direction. Frank Kermode makes a case for the continuity between Modernism and Post-Modernism, which Bradbury and McFarlane summarize as follows:

4

Kermode (in an essay entitled "Modernisms") holds that the contemporary art of the random — the squaring out of a piece of space or time, the specifying and signing of an environment, as in Cage or Burroughs — is a blood-cousin to the earlier tendencies, though he draws a line across to distinguish early Modernism, which was much more formalist, or devoted to the paradoxes of form, from later Neo-Modernism, which is anti-formalist, though compelled to use form to subvert it.... Thus what Kermode calls Neo-Modernism and others have chosen to call Post-Modernism involves a change in what Harold Rosenberg calls the "tradition of the new" — a change falling perhaps around Dada — but it is still that same tradition.[8]

I am inclined to consider Post-Modernism as part of the Modernist tradition. The evolution of modern Canadian poetry is one of continued and continuing Modernist innovation, elaborations rather than radical departures from the Modernist tradition.

In English-language literature, as in most European literatures, Modernism first appeared as a repudiation of an exhausted Romantic tradition. This was particularly clear in the writings of the Imagist group, centred around Ezra Pound:

Pound, in part through Hulme's influence, denounced romantic emotionalism, vagueness, and sloppiness and preached the classical virtues of craftsmanship, economy, objectivity, precision. As he expounded it, the Imagist doctrine was primarily anti-Romantic, intended to produce hard, dry, classical verse.[9]

William Pratt observed that "the Imagist poem was both a beginning and an achievement" in modern verse, and that "taken as a whole, [Imagism] is modern poetry in miniature."[10] The three basic premises of Imagism, as stated by F. S. Flint in his essay "Imagisme," published in the March 1913 issue of *Poetry*, were to have an impact upon the way English, American and, ultimately, Canadian verse were to be written. These three principles were:

1. Direct treatment of the "thing," whether subjective or objective.
2. To use absolutely no word that did not contribute to the presentation.
3. As regarding rhythm: to compose in sequence of the musical phrase, not in sequence of a metronome.[11]

The flowery language of the Romantics and Victorians, brimming with adjectives, was to be replaced by a poetry of classical sparseness and precision; and the poem would no longer be held back by the trammels of end-rhyme and regularized metre — free verse would now become the accepted form. In essence, form and content were being set free. Poetry would no longer necessarily have to concern itself with the "higher truths" of existence; a red wheelbarrow would be as relevant as a Grecian urn. Poetic language would move closer to the patterns of human speech, abandoning the stilted metres of a previous age. This Imagist point of view was to have an effect on all the major poets writing in English at the time.

Imagism was, in many ways, one of the more conservative of the Modernist movements. The Imagists maintained that they were not doing anything that was radically new; rather, they were upholding the basic principles of good poetry. Yet we can see that the work of Aldington, H.D., Pound, Lawrence, Eliot, and Flint went against the grain of the day's literary conventions.

The unconventional work of the Imagists needed a specific forum. This forum was the little magazine. In magazines like *Poetry* and *The Little Review*, the essential program of the Imagists was given an airing; in other magazines, like *Blast*, *The Egoist*, and *The Exile*, Ezra Pound hammered home his ideas. The little magazine still exists today as an outlet for the development of Modernism.

The little magazine has a small circulation, usually no more than a few hundred readers. It serves as an alternative outlet for literature, usually "for the purpose of attacking conventional modes of expression and of bringing into the open new and unorthodox literary theories and practices."[12] This is from Hoffman, Allen and Ulrich, who have analysed the little magazine as a literary medium. Further, "one of the most significant contributions of these magazines to twentieth century literature is to give it an abundance of suggestions and styles which popular or academic taste scarcely could tolerate or accept."[13] The motivating force behind the little magazine is two-fold:

> [R]ebellion against traditional modes of expression and the wish to experiment with novel (and sometimes unintelligible) forms; and a desire to overcome the commercial or material difficulties which are caused by the introduction of any writing whose commercial merits have not been proved.[14]

Louis Dudek has elaborated on the relationship between the little magazine and the commercial press. Modernism and the little magazine

...are characterized by opposition to the dominant character in our society—to the popular press, the advertising economy, and all those pressures which would reduce the individual to stark uniformity as producer-consumer of a mechanized super-state; on the other hand, both modern literature and its experimental magazines are characterized also by the effort to rehabilitate literature as living communication, to halt its decadence as the cultural property of an academic or a genteel minority. The new literature and the new magazines, therefore, are open to attack both from the side of popular taste of the great majority, and from the side of the conservatively-traditional educated class.[15]

The little magazine is, in its turn, free to criticize its two attackers: the first for their lack of a civilized aesthetic sensibility, and the second for clinging to the traditions of the past. Dudek connects the appearance of the little magazine with the new poetry of Modernism. The little magazine has served well as the primary vehicle for modern poetry. In 1946, Hoffman, Allen, and Ulrich could summarize the importance of the little magazine:

[T]he best of our little magazines have stood, from 1912 to the present, defiantly in the front ranks of the battle for a mature literature. They have helped fight this battle by...first publishing, in fact, about 80 per cent of our most important post-1912 critics, novelists, poets, and story-tellers. Further, they have introduced and sponsored every noteworthy literary movement or school that had made its appearance in America during the past thirty years.[16]

Hoffman, Allen, and Ulrich consider the motivation of the little-magazine editor: one who prints a magazine of small circulation, who is prepared to lose money, and who is essentially a rebel against the literary standards of the time.

Such a man is stimulated by some form of discontent...with something he considers unjust, boring, or ridiculous. He views the world of publishing and popularizers with disdain, sometimes with despair. If he is a contributor and wishes to be published, he may have to abandon certain unorthodox aesthetic or moral beliefs. Often he is rebellious against the doctrines of popular taste and sincerely believes that our attitudes towards literature need to be reformed or at least made more liberal. More than that, he generally insists that publications should not depend upon the whimsy of conventional tastes and choices.[17]

The little magazine is always a reflection of the orientation and poetic politics of its editor or editorial group, and can only be as good as this editorial judgement permits:

> For the most part, each magazine serves its separate purpose before it dies: that purpose generally is to give finished form and some degree of distribution to the personality and the convictions of its editor or editors. Often these convictions are given editorial form. The editorial statement may be simply an expression of generosity to those who are akin in spirit; it may be (or become) a program or platform; and it may very well be (or become) the expression of some school of political or aesthetic thought which uses the magazine as its voice.[18]

We will see the unique progression and evolution of Modernism in Canada as it is reflected in the contributions, editorial concerns, and debates in little magazines from 1925 to the present. The development of Canada's little magazines is different from that of England or the United States, since Canadian magazines contain a specific branch of Modernism. This development reflects the social and cultural conditions that are particular to Canada. The crisis of western culture that was so apparent in Europe from the beginning of the twentieth century was not so evident in a country that was still evolving from a frontier community. The world war that tore apart Europe touched Canada much less significantly; though soldiers were sent to fight, Canada was not a battleground. And, because of physical distance, the English-Canadian community could maintain a Victorian sensibility long after that sensibility had been considerably altered in England itself.

It must also be noted that Modernism arrived quickly in countries that had well-established literary traditions. Yet it was only with the activities of the Canadian Authors' Association in the early 1920s that a general interest in Canadian writing began to develop. Two Confederation poets, Charles G.D. Roberts and Bliss Carman, had to leave Canada to make their literary reputations, while Archibald Lampman, Duncan Campbell Scott, and others remained to languish in relative obscurity in Canada. Reminiscing about his return to Canada from Oxford in 1923, F.R. Scott noted that there "was very little culture coming out of Montreal at that time."[19]

Louis Dudek argues that little magazines are "the embattled literary reaction of intellectual minority groups to the commercial middle-class magazines of fiction and advertising which had evolved in the nineteenth century."[20] But in Canada there was little of an intellectual majority to rebel against. F.R. Scott, A.J.M. Smith, and Leo Kennedy took the first tentative steps towards a Modernist poetry, and they were able to level criticisms at the

Canadian Authors' Association and the Confederation poets; but they themselves had to establish a national setting in which their writing could be presented. The Canadian magazines of the 1920s were not very bohemian when compared with their English parallels, *Blast* or *The Egoist*, and the commercial magazine was not very strong in Canada in 1920. Magazines available to the educated middle class were likely to be American products such as *Harper's*, *The Atlantic Monthly*, and *Scribner's Magazine*. Canadian periodicals that attempted to compete with these publications in the late nineteenth century, such as the *Dominion Illustrated Monthly*, *Massey's Magazine*, and *Our Monthly*, could not match the American magazines' financial resources, and quickly disappeared. A notable exception was *Canadian Magazine*, which lasted for three decades.[21]

Modernism, then, had a slow and tentative start in Canada. It would not be until the 1940s that Modernism, equipped with embattled little magazines, would re-enact the cultural drama in Canadian terms. It can also be argued that it was not until the 1960s that avant-garde literary magazines began to appear in Canada — some fifty years after the outburst of radical European Modernism. In Canada, Modernist evolution went through a series of gradual shifts, beginning with very moderate experiments, proceeding through stages of radical political and aesthetic development, until the entire range of the modern revolution was explored. This will be our story.

2

The Beginnings
of Canadian Modernism

In 1914, a book of poems by Arthur Stringer, entitled *Open Water*, was published. As Dudek and Gnarowski put it:

> This book must be seen as a turning point in Canadian writing if only
> for the importance of the ideas advanced by Stringer in his pre-
> face.... Stringer pleaded the cause of free verse and created ... an early
> document of the struggle to free Canadian poetry from the trammels
> of end-rhyme, and to liberalize its methods and its substance. Strin-
> ger's arguments become even more striking ... if we recall that in 1914
> free verse was still in the experimental stage, and that the famous
> notes of F. S. Flint and the strictures of Ezra Pound on *imagisme* and
> free verse had appeared less than a year before this, in the March 1913
> issue of *Poetry: A Magazine of Verse* (Chicago).[1]

In 1914, the ruling style in Canadian verse had been established by the poets of the Confederation — Charles G. D. Roberts, Bliss Carman, Archibald Lamp-man, and Duncan Campbell Scott — and was still very much the offspring of English Victorian verse. Most Canadian poets were to cling to this traditional mode until the 1940s. But a few poets began to infuse the Modernist spirit into Canadian poetry.

In 1920, F. O. Call published a book of verse entitled *Acanthus and Wild Grape*. Like Stringer's book, its preface was more important than its poetry. New ideas began to appear on the scene before any successful Modernist Canadian poem had been written. Assessing Call's book, Dudek and Gna-rowski say that

> Call took up the cudgels in the cause of free verse, and argued with
> more than passing eloquence and conviction for the rejection of the
> hackneyed limitations imposed by end-rhyme. His message was iden-
> tical to that of Stringer and he pleaded for a hearing and a chance to

get poetry moving once more in the direction of a technically freed and spontaneous expression.[2]

But neither poet wrote any striking poetry to prove his case. W. W. E. Ross, R. G. Everson, Raymond Knister, and Dorothy Livesay wrote in the Imagist mode in the twenties, experimenting with free verse. Their activity was individual and unrelated; their poems appeared in American and English literary publications. "A scattering of Canadian literary writers, in no way organized or identified with any Canadian literary magazine, already reflected the changes taking place in the early 1920s."[3] It was only with the rise of the little magazine that a local setting for Modernism would be provided.

> The little magazine in Canada has been the most important single factor behind the rise and continued progress of Modernism in Canadian poetry. The history of the little magazine covers a period of some forty years and closely parallels the development of modern poetry itself from the mid-1920s to the present time. All the important events in poetry and most of the initiating manifestoes and examples of change are to be found in the little magazines.[4]

On 21 November, 1925, the first issue of *The McGill Fortnightly Review* was printed. Two of the prime movers behind the founding and editing of the review (1925–1927) were A. J. M. Smith and F. R. Scott, two graduate students then attending McGill University. In 1924, Smith had edited the *McGill Daily Literary Supplement*. F. R. Scott, recalling how he first met Smith, reviews the events that led to the founding of the periodical:

> He [Smith] was running the *McGill Daily Literary Supplement* and every Wednesday you opened it up and there was an insert with some bright poems, a few articles, and book reviews. This delighted me when I was a law student because the lectures were usually so dull that you had to read something during them. I sent the *Supplement* a translation of an old French chanson and Smith published it. To my delight at the end of the year I received a letter from a man signed A. J. M. Smith, whom I had never met, asking me to join the editorial board. Of course I accepted. Then we heard that the students' society had decided not to give any money to publish the *Literary Supplement* because it contained no advertising; the frustrated editors decided to found a new independent student journal, which we called the *McGill Fortnightly Review*.[5]

The periodical was not strictly a "little magazine"; it was very much a student publication. It was not started so that it could battle the literary conventions of the time (although with succeeding issues the battle did begin). The name was modeled on a prestigious nineteenth-century magazine, published in London since 1865, *The Fortnightly*. The editors sought to ally themselves with accepted traditions and institutions. Their first editorial praises a series of lectures given by Bliss Carman at McGill. Four years later, Scott would write a sharp critique of Carman's verse in *The Canadian Mercury*. *The McGill Fortnightly's* first editorial is not militant; in the course of editorial comments about student council meetings and McGill varsity games, the magazine defines its editorial policies:

> *The Review* is an independent journal and, as such, it has a right to an independent opinion of its own on all matters. The Editors will express that opinion in the Editorial columns. But this emphatically does not mean that we shall suppress the contributions of those who disagree with us. We shall be glad to receive and publish articles taking any attitude whatever. We reserve only that they shall be of sufficient literary merit....[6]

In most ways, *The McGill Fortnightly Review* was a typical student publication. It mixed literature and opinion with the general concerns of university students. It was not, as Michael Gnarowski has pointed out, "a truly self-willed little magazine. Its historic value lies in the fact that it brought a group of promising poets together, gave them editorial experience and finally pointed them in the right direction, thus starting a literary movement on its way."[7] The McGill group, as it has come to be known — Scott, Smith, Kennedy, and, later, Klein — put forward some new ideas that pointed to Modernism, and it did begin the debate about Canada's backward literary condition. F. R. Scott recalls the group's working principles and policies:

> When we founded the *McGill Fortnightly Review* we were protesting against the literary standards of the time — particularly against the poetic standards; A. J. M. Smith organized this group around the *Fortnightly* because he felt that things were happening to modern literature which students here didn't know anything about. He wanted to begin a magazine with experimentation in new verse, which was then called modern verse; that led to a different approach to the idea of literary composition, and we were primarily concerned of course about poetic composition.[8]

The *Fortnightly* aimed its criticism at the literary temper of the times, at the Canadian Authors' Association, and at the quasi-Victorian verse of the twenties. The McGill group took pot-shots at the CAA through *The McGill Fortnightly Review* and through *The Canadian Mercury*. As well, *Fortnightly* attempted to define Modernism in articles and in poems. Both sides of the program — attack and definition — were taken up in the *Fortnightly*'s second issue:

> Whatever sympathy one may feel for the aims of the Canadian Authors' Association and however eagerly one may hope for the creation of a worthy national literature, it is impossible to view the excesses of "Canadian Book Week" in a favourable light. Publicity, advertising and the methods of big business are not what is required to foster the art and literature of a young country such as Canada, while the commercial boosting of mediocre Canadian books not only reduces the Authors' Association to the level of an advertising agency but does considerable harm to good literature. After all, it is not so much Canadian books that we should like to see the public buy, as *good* Canadian books; and as there are not very many of these latter yet, we should be very well content with a public that would buy merely good books, regardless whether their writers are English, American, German or Japanese.[9]

The McGill group expressed a natural antipathy for "mediocre Canadian books," that is, poetry weighted down by a transplanted Victorian tradition living out a protracted decadence in Canada. In its stead, these poets offered as models the new modern poets — the Imagist group and W. B. Yeats and T. S. Eliot.

> A. J. M. Smith himself was studying and liking Yeats; Eliot was beginning to write in England, and D. H. Lawrence was beginning to become known.[10] The changeover from the Georgian poets to the modern poets came mostly through the influence of the American writers and Smith was just soaking up this new American approach to poetry and its philosophy; he wrote an article for the *McGill Fortnightly* pointing out what was happening to science in the world and the changing industrial conditions, and it was ridiculous to go on in old poetic form.[11]

Smith, in a series of articles, was the theoretician of the new poetry; he would define for Canada the rôle of poetry in the modern world. His first article, "Symbolism in Poetry," appeared in issue number two. He argued that symbolism was necessary in modern writing, and provided some theoretical and historical background for symbolism. In the final paragraph he quoted Yeats on the rôle of symbolism in modern poetry; it is, he says, opposed to the poetic indulgence of the previous fifty years. Symbolism means "a casting out of descriptions of nature for the sake of nature, of the moral law for the sake of the moral law, a casting out of all anecdotes and of that brooding over scientific opinion that so often extinguished the central flame in Tennyson, and of that vehemence that would make us do or not do certain things...."[12] The excesses of Victorianism are also the excesses of the Canadian poets of Confederation, who too often were caught up in descriptions of nature and in extended moralizing. In the 1920s both Carman and Roberts received high praise from the CAA and from critics; the McGill group felt it was necessary to get beyond this maple-leaf school of poetry. As Scott has recently observed, "when we were on the *Fortnightly* there was not a single Canadian poet we paid much attention to, certainly not an old poet like Bliss Carman, Charles G. D. Roberts, Archibald Lampman or Duncan Campbell Scott."[13]

Yeats and Eliot, on the other hand, meant a good deal to Smith and Scott. Smith's second article on modern poetry in the *Fortnightly*, "Hamlet in Modern Dress," provided an adept analysis of Eliot's difficult poem *The Waste Land*. Smith reveals his preference for the Yeats–Eliot axis of Modernism, rather than for that of Pound and Williams (who were to loom large with later generations of Canadian poets). Scott, too, has declared that *The Waste Land* "had a terrific effect upon me as a poem."[14]

But it was in his article "Contemporary Poetry" that Smith defined most clearly his view of the purpose and quality of the modern.

> Our age is an age of change, and of a change that is taking place with a rapidity unknown in any other epoch.... Our universe is a different one from that of our grandfathers, nor can our religious beliefs be the same. The whole movement, indeed, is a movement away from an erroneous but comfortable stability, towards a more truthful and sincere but certainly less comfortable state of flux. Ideas are changing, and therefore manners and morals are changing. It is not surprising, then, to find that the arts, which are an intensification of life and thought, are likewise in a state of flux.[15]

This "erroneous but comfortable stability" was to be replaced by a new order of life and art. Smith argued that the new poetry "must be the result of the impingement of modern conditions upon the personality and temperament of the poet."[16] The poet could enthusiastically welcome the birth of a new age and new prospects for the individual, as Modernists like Lawrence and Williams did, or he could lament modern man's divorce from the traditional world of values and culture, as Yeats, Eliot, and Pound did in their poetry. But "the peculiar conditions of the time forced them all to seek a new and more direct expression, to perfect a finer technique."[17] Experiment in the arts was a marked feature of the 1910s and 1920s; Smith saw the experiment not as a conscious choice but as a condition virtually forced upon the writers. The artist who had his eyes open could not help but see the disparity between the modern world and the world reflected in Victorian and fin-de-siècle works. New poetry could provide a change in form—free verse—although Smith thought the greater part of modern poetry would be "infused with the new spirit... written in the traditional metres and with the traditional rhyme schemes."[18] This was certainly true of his own poetry.

But the new poetry also reflected a change in poetic diction. "The deems, forsooths, methinks, the inversions for the sake of a rhyme, the high sounding pomposities and all the rhetorical excesses which make so much Victorian poetry seem overdressed and slightly vulgar—all these have been ruthlessly removed from the diction of contemporary poetry."[19] To support his view he quoted Harriet Monroe, then editor of the little magazine *Poetry*, which had played a rôle in the development of early Modernism.

> The new poetry strives for a concrete and immediate realization of life; it would discard the theory, the abstraction, the remoteness found in all classics not of the first order. It is less vague, less verbose, less eloquent than most poetry of the Victorian period and much work of earlier periods. It has set before itself an ideal of absolute simplicity and sincerity—an ideal which implies an individual, unstereotyped rhythm.[20]

The concrete realities of modern living would spark modern verse. This idea naturally led to conflict with the writers dominant in Canada at the time.

Scott and Smith wrote most of the poetry in *The McGill Fortnightly Review* under their own names and under such pseudonyms as "Brian Tuke," "Michael Gard," and "Vincent Starr." Often their formal experiments or their satirical verse appeared under the pseudonyms. Their poems usually were not written in free verse, but adhered to some principle of metre and rhyme; this is especially true of Smith, who worked with traditional metres, in the manner of Yeats, and infused the old metres with "passionate speech." He always was a highly formal poet. Scott also worked closely with rhyme and measured metres. It is only in their poetic diction that both poets began to show a Modernist orientation. Their poetry was written in an approximation of the modern idiom and strove to move away from the conscious poeticisms of the Victorians and their epigones. Early versions of some of their more successful poems appeared first in *The McGill Fortnightly Review*: Smith's "The Lonely Land" and "Epitaph" (volume one, number four), Scott's "Below Quebec" (volume two, number three), as well as his broadside at the CAA, "The Canadian Authors Meet," in the last issue.

The McGill Fortnightly Review ceased, at the end of the spring semester in 1927, because its editors had moved beyond the university. A year later they would launch *The Canadian Mercury*, a more ambitious enterprise. In retrospect, *The McGill Fortnightly* appears as very much a student publication, and the contributions of Scott, Smith, and Kennedy, for the most part, were in line with work characteristic of university publications. In *The McGill Fortnightly* Smith tested his critical theories, and the poets brought out their first tentative work. In the pages of *The Canadian Mercury*, which had no connection with the university, they made a more vigorous stand for the principles of Modernism in poetry.

The Canadian Mercury began publication in December 1928 and ran for seven issues before it terminated with the great economic crash of 1929. Lou Schwartz, who had been the business manager for *The McGill Fortnightly*, served as *The Canadian Mercury*'s financial sponsor. *The Mercury* enjoyed considerable freedom. Its editorial board consisted of Jean Burton, F. R. Scott, Leo Kennedy, and Felix Walter. A. J. M. Smith sent in his contributions from the University of Edinburgh, where he was attending graduate school; Leon Edel was in Paris, whence he filed reports on literary activity. Liberated from the trammels of university concerns, the editors devoted themselves to the problems of literature. *The Mercury* contained more poetry and fiction than *The McGill Fortnightly Review*. The McGill group also appears to have become a tighter organization, for the magazine is marked by the appearance of a consistent outpouring of poetry and other writings from a well-defined group of writers. This spirit of new confidence and independence is given voice in the opening editorial:

> *The Canadian Mercury*, with nothing between it and the eyes of the judiciary but an ingenious and rather ribald colophon, appears, determined to preserve its policies in spite of all reactionary opposition; intent on offering the more thoughtful Canadian public the best available matter on subjects immediately concerning that public; demanding, as we have said, a higher and more adequate standard of literary criticism in Canada, and striving to contribute in

so far as it is possible to the consummation of that graceful ideal, the emancipation of Canadian literature from the state of amiable mediocrity and insipidity in which it now languishes.

To change the image, Canadian Literature is a lusty but quite inarticulate brat constrained in too-tight swaddling: you will know him by his red Mounted Policeman's jacket, and his half-breed guide's raccoon-skin cap. He has been sired by Decorum out of Claptrap … and we are not resigned. He has not the faculty of self-expression which may be found in his adolescent American cousin; he has not reaped the benefits arising from an extensive immigration policy. He has retained the stifling qualities of Nordic consciousness and is likely, by present symptoms, to become idiot. We do not approve of this, and therefore gather behind our colophon, which at least symbolizes vigour and a modicum of intellectual health.

We must add that we have no affiliation whatsoever: we owe no allegiance to the Canadian Authors' Association, The Canadian Manufacturers' Association, the Young Communist League of Canada, the IODE, the YMCA, the UF of A or the CPR.

In brief, it may be said that with the exception of a spinster aunt in London and a wild uncle in America, neither of whom would claim relationship, *The Canadian Mercury* is individual…and again we revert to our hobby. We have no preconceived idea of Canadian literature which we are endeavouring to propagate; our faith rests in the spirit which is at last beginning to brood upon our literary chaos. We believe that an order will come out of the void, an order of a distinct type, reflecting, as modern Canadian painting has begun to do, a unique experience of nature and life.

Above all, *The Canadian Mercury* is intended primarily for the younger writers in this country. The editors are all well under thirty and intend to remain so. We seek to ally with ourselves all those whose literary schooling has survived the Confederation, and whose thought and verse is not afraid of being called free.[21]

The first issue of *The Canadian Mercury* shows the full scope of the editors' new commitment to Canadian literature. Included in the issue is an article by Stephen Leacock called "The National Literature Problem in Canada." Leacock prefers Canadian qualities in Canadian literature to clinging to English-American models; regarding the "boostering" of Canadian writing, he is firmly an anti-nationalist, in the sense of being anti-isolationist. He concludes that Canada cannot close its eyes to the literature of the rest of the world. Also contained in the issue are poems by Smith and Scott. Smith's "Proud Parable" is an early version of the poem now known as "Like An Old Proud King In A Parable." Though predisposed to rhymed, metrical verse, Smith's Modernist sensibility can be glimpsed in the directness of his diction and prosody. Scott's "Vagrant" is a more visibly "modern" poem, although it, too, incorporates metre and rhyme.

Issue number two contained a story, "Heat," by Dorothy Livesay, a long poem of uneven quality, "The Haunted House," by Abraham M. Klein, and Leon Edel's "Montparnasse Letter," which discusses the periodical *transition* and the current literary atmosphere of Paris. The third issue of *The Canadian Mercury* includes the poem "Sequel" by Leo Kennedy. This poem, like Smith's, is highly formal in structure. (In his preface to the reprint edition of *The Shrouding*, Kennedy says of his poems of the late twenties and early thirties that they "were written when the world was more formal and poets thought a lot about scansion and almost as much about rhyme. Like the farm boy who learned to make love by mail order, I had no proper tutor and learned my trade if I learned it at all by imitating every poet I liked in the Oxford Book of English Verse and Louis Untermeyer's Modern American Poetry."[22]) Smith's essay, "A Note On Metaphysical Poetry," also appeared in the third issue, with two poems by Scott, "Spring Flame" and an early version of the beautiful "Old Song." Issue number four contained an early version of Smith's poem "Good Friday" and a positive review of Stephen Vincent Benet's *John Brown's Body* by F. R. Scott.

The first article in issue number five–six of *The Canadian Mercury* is Leo Kennedy's "The Future of Canadian Literature," a polemic directed at the Canadian Authors' Association. According to Kennedy, the Association fosters everything that is wrong with Canadian writing and promotes archaic, transplanted Victorianism, which is judged by purely parochial standards. Kennedy maintains that "the least attractive aspects of Victorianism still hold licensed Canadian creative writers firmly by the gullet. In poetry the Tennysonian and Wordsworthian traditions still rule, and are bolstered by none of the genius and technical ability of those poets."[23] This Victorian sensibility is sustained by

> the highly respectable protestantism of a past era, coupled with a firm belief in Empire and the indelicacy of sex psychology and human anatomy...a pronounced Anglo-Saxon self-approval, a distrust of Latin influence (the naughty Frenchmen!) and new ideas....[24]

Kennedy expresses the conviction that Canadian literature "will not readily be written by Canadian Authors,"[25] meaning, of course, the partisans of the CAA. He recognizes that the future of Canadian literature resides in the sceptical young writers, who discuss Joyce, Hemingway, Shaw, Pound, and Aldous Huxley rather than the Canadian poets of the Confederation and their third-rate imitators. Kennedy speculates about the future:

> Concerned then with writing something which is true and enduring, desiring to declare what is fine and not necessarily best-selling, they will commence, and come in time to express themselves with gratifying clarity.... [T]hey will learn the lesson of all precursors, discovering in a western grain field, a Quebec *maison*, or in a Montreal nightclub, a spirit and a consciousness distinctly Canadian. Just as the writers of the United States today are inclined to segregate...so I believe these younger Canadians...will embrace this practice, and write each of the soul and scene of his own community.[26]

Until its termination, *The Canadian Mercury* continued its attack upon the old currents that were still dominant in Canadian writing. The final issue includes a satirical poem entitled "God Bless the CAA," which, it seems, came from an anonymous source in Toronto, and a review by F. R. Scott of Bliss Carman's latest book of verse, *Wild Garden*. Scott observed that "Carman's technique and form is undiluted 1880; he seems impervious to change. He has no conception of rhythm, but only metrical accuracy."[27] The review amounts to a wholesale condemnation of an archaic poetic.

The McGill group knew what was wrong with Canadian poetry in the 1920s, and they knew where to find the remedy: in the English and American experiments that began sometime around 1909 and crystallized in Ezra Pound's Imagist movement. The movement had cleared the ground for T. S. Eliot and the later Yeats, both of whom served as models for the McGill group. In rejecting Canadian verse, the McGill group cleared the ground for Canadian Modernism. Although their magazines were not, in the strictest sense, little magazines, they played an important part in Canadian literary history by bringing the new literature to Canada. An assessment of this Modernism is given by Peter Stevens in his book *The McGill Movement*:

> Their poetry was in the nature of a critical rejection of overblown romanticism in Canadian verse taken over from late-Victorian and Edwardian sources. Poets throughout the 1920s with one or two exceptions were writing a kind of Canadian equivalent, I suppose, of the English Georgian Movement. The McGill poets drew much of their material and methods from imagism and its development, particularly in the work of Eliot. This interest lead them to the French

symbolists, Metaphysicals and Yeats, and to all the trappings derived from Eliot's poetry and criticism.[28]

The poetry was still derivative and occasionally imitative. But working with a new sense of form and an extended range of subject matter, these poets began to carve out a poetry adapted to the age.

The age, however, was in a state of rapid change. The atmosphere of the twenties was quickly shattered by the Depression. The crash of the stock market brought a quick end to *The Canadian Mercury*, and the Modernist movement had to start from scratch in the thirties. As Joan McCullagh has aptly noted:

> The brand of modernism produced by the Montreal group was largely derived from Yeats and Eliot — an exciting antidote to the excesses and irrelevancies of romanticism in the twenties, but quickly rendered obsolete by cultural changes and new trends in British and American poetry in the thirties.[29]

The McGill group and other Modernists published little in the thirties; decadent romanticism prevailed. No little magazines firmly dedicated to the purpose of Modernism appeared. (*The Canadian Poetry Magazine*, edited by E. J. Pratt, began publication under the auspices of the CAA in 1936; Pratt merely humoured the idea of writing in the modern vein, and the magazine was solidly conservative.) The publications of the Canadian moderns — including the McGill group — were sparse; when they appeared, the Modernist qualities of their verse were "tentative and uncertain."[30] Leo Kennedy published his only volume, *The Shrouding*, in 1933. Scott, Klein, and Smith appeared with Kennedy, Robert Finch, and E. J. Pratt in the slim anthology *New Provinces*, published by Macmillan in 1936. The only other volumes of verse by poets of Modernist inclination published in the thirties were *The Roosevelt And The Antinoe* (1930), *The Titanic* (1935), and *The Fable Of The Goats* (1937) by E. J. Pratt; W. W. E. Ross's *Laconics* (1930) and *Sonnets* (1932); Dorothy Livesay's *Signpost* (1932); L. A. MacKay's *Viper's Bugloss* (1938); and Anne Marriot's *The Wind Our Enemy* (1939).[31]

The tussling over the publication of an anthology, *New Provinces*, illuminates the lack of unified purpose that kept Modernism in its tentative state during the thirties. In letters to Scott concerning the anthology, Smith insisted that Dorothy Livesay be included, arguing the need for left-wing political poetry. Scott managed to pass over Livesay, saying she would be included in the second edition — an edition that was never to see the light of day. Smith was also aware of the necessity of putting in permanent storage the bulk of

Canadian poetry, which he saw as "romantic in conception and conventional in form."[32] Conventions that were thirty years dead still haunted Canadian poetry, Smith wrote in a proposed preface to the anthology. But Smith's preface was countermanded by E. J. Pratt, by Robert Finch, and by Hugh Eayrs, of the Macmillan Company of Canada; all three objected to the "nose-tweaking" Smith was giving to the Roberts–D. C. Scott crowd. A nondescript statement written by F. R. Scott and Leo Kennedy, and left unsigned, replaced Smith's preface; the poems were left to speak for themselves. On their own, they did not speak in a voice loud enough, or clear enough, to elicit much interest. In its first year, the anthology sold only eighty-two copies. (F. R. Scott purchased ten.)

Smith was not the only poet who felt that a change in the current of poetry was necessary in the thirties. In an article published in *New Frontier* in June of 1936, Leo Kennedy renounced the metaphysical and mythological basis of early Modernist work in favour of a realism that was more relevant to the times. He also took a few well-aimed shots at the poets who dealt in romantic conceptions:

> It is my thesis that the function of poetry is to interpret the contemporary scene faithfully; *to interpret especially the progressive forces in modern life which alone stand for cultural survival.* And it is my private recommendation that, setting theory aside, middle class poets had better hustle down from the twenty fifth floor of their steam-heated janitor-serviced Ivory Tower, and stand on the pavement and find out and take part in what is happening today, before the whole chaste edifice is blasted about their ears and laid waste!...
>
> We need poetry that reflects the lives of our people, working, loving fighting, groping for clarity. We need satire — fierce, scorching, aimed at the abuses which are destroying our culture and which threaten life itself. Our poets have lacked direction for their talents and energies in the past — I suggest that today it lies right before them.[33]

Unfortunately, despite Kennedy's theoretical statement, even the Modernist poetry of the time lacked realistic substance. But Kennedy was correct: the direction for modern poets lay "right before them" in the mundane realities of life, in worldly situations. It would take the outbreak of World War Two to move a whole generation in the direction of real social concern. The thirties pointed towards social realism; but the political and humanitarian poetry being written in England by Auden and Spender found no opportunity to germinate in Canada until the forties.

3

The Social Realist Movement
in Canadian Poetry

In the forties, Canadian poetry needed "new roots...new shoots that could produce a rough, socially relevant, indigenous poetry."[1] This poetry would require a forum. During the forties several little magazines emerged and took up the cause of social realism, but it was Alan Crawley's *Contemporary Verse* that served as the first sign of this new poetic growth, beginning in the fall of 1941. Crawley's magazine served as a meeting ground for all the concurrent "schools" of the time, and spanned the decade with a long record of regular publication. The new poetry became a truly national endeavour.

The idea of *Contemporary Verse* began in the spring of 1941, when Dorothy Livesay visited Floris McLaren's house in Victoria, British Columbia. With Doris Ferne and Anne Marriott, Livesay and McLaren discussed the possibility of starting a magazine that would encourage the new poetic techniques, engage itself with a poetry of social relevance, and give young writers a place to publish and be heard. In a CBC radio talk, McLaren described the events that led to the starting of *Contemporary Verse*:

> Dorothy Livesay said we could start a poetry magazine ourselves. I said, "That's a nice pipe dream." Dorothy said why? Then we began to talk. We knew nothing about the publication of a poetry magazine, we knew nothing about the financial problems involved, but we talked of it. Someone said who would edit...and the three of us answered together, "Alan Crawley!" Dorothy agreed to talk to him when she went back to Vancouver and tell him of this suggestion.[2]

Crawley, a former lawyer who had been struck by blindness in the early 1930s, was passionately interested in modern poetry. After giving the proposition some consideration, Crawley agreed to edit the magazine.

Crawley proposed a working arrangement which was accepted by the committee. The board of founders—Alan Crawley, Floris McLaren,

22

Dorothy Livesay, Anne Marriott, and Doris Ferne — would decide matters of policy and management; the editor would read all manuscripts submitted and "have the sole right of rejection or acceptance."[3]

The working committee discussed printing costs and solicited subscriptions and manuscripts. Regarding editorial policy: "Crawley believed that the work of a poetry magazine was to publish poetry, and he had no particular literary approach to eschew and no axes to grind. He wanted to encourage and publish poetry that was alive and fresh and relevant; poetry that was sensitive and honest and of the best possible quality."[4]

Louis Dudek has described *Contemporary Verse* as a magazine that "was not a fighting magazine with a policy; it was concerned only with publishing 'good poetry' — which, in itself, can embody an affirmation — but it did not in addition work out any program of ideas which this poetry could fire."[5] The affirmation *Contemporary Verse* embodied was that it published, of those who were writing in Canada at the time, "every modern poet with the exception of W. W. E. Ross and Patrick Anderson."[6]

Contemporary Verse is an important publication because of the breadth of social-realist poetry it printed in the forties. Its first issue was totally exemplary of the path it was to take: it included poems by Earle Birney, P. K. Page, Floris Clark McLaren, Leo Kennedy, Dorothy Livesay, A. J. M. Smith, Doris Ferne, and Anne Marriott. These poets were spread out across the country and represented different schools or non-schools of poetry. The issue contained a simple foreword by Crawley:

> During a recent winter of forced inactivity my reading was limited to the books on my own shelves, poetry by the great writers of the past from Shakespeare to Whitman, all within easy reach of my hand. In the following year I spent more than two hundred hours reading poetry published in the preceding twenty years in Great Britain, Canada and the United States. It took about half as many hours in libraries and book shops and in searching through current magazines to find and get together these poems. Conviction was added to my belief that beauty and truth is not all told; that there are many writers of our own times who can speak to us in words and images and forms that interest and appeal; and that, for most of us, their writings are too hard to come by. A small group of readers and writers, sharing these feelings, send out this first issue of *Contemporary Verse, A Canadian Quarterly*, in high hope that it and succeeding numbers may play a worthy part in the building of Canadian literature.[7]

What came closest to a statement of intention and general editorial policy was expressed in Crawley's editor's note in issue number four:

> A glance at the notes on contributors at the back of this number shows that *Contemporary Verse* is not the chapbook of a limited or local group of writers. The contents of each number will at once dispel any charge that it exists to press political propaganda, particular social readjustment or literary trend. The aims of *Contemporary Verse* are simple and direct and seem worthy and worthwhile. These aims are to entice and stimulate the writing and reading of poetry and to provide means for its publication free from restraint of politics, prejudices and placations, and to keep open its pages to poetry that is sincere in thought and expression and contemporary in theme and treatment and technique.[8]

Contemporary Verse was a little magazine totally devoted to modern poetry. Unlike *The McGill Fortnightly Review* and *The Canadian Mercury*, it made no attempt to be a journal of liberal opinion; unlike *Preview* and *First Statement* it printed no fiction. It was a magazine filled with poetry and the occasional review of anthologies, chapbooks, and volumes by individual authors. Much of the criticism was written by Crawley and is laudatory and easy-going; any reviews with bite were written by Dorothy Livesay.

Contemporary Verse published thirty-nine issues, from September 1941 until winter 1952, thus bridging the entire forties period and reflecting the poetic explorations of that generation of writers. As A. J. M. Smith observed about the era:

> The poetry of the forties grows out of a sense of being involved in the whole complex of life of our time — its politics, its society, its economics — and of being involved in it in a deeply personal way that touches the sensibilities, the mind, and the physical being of the poet. This is perhaps the common attitude which unites all the very individual poets into a single recognizable school.[9]

This "sense of being" was expressed in the poetry of the early forties in various ways — in verse forms and in the differing sense and use of rhythm and metaphor — but the poetry of the forties seemed to share three common qualities: "a lyric approach, an overriding social concern, and the focus of the war."[10]

As Joan McCullagh noted, the poetry of the forties developed in two stages. From 1940 to 1946, the war held precedence in the minds of all Canadians. This period saw the birth of *Contemporary Verse* and the literary feuds of *Preview* and *First Statement*. The young poets were writing with a strong awareness of politics and psychology and were aware of W. H. Auden, Stephen Spender, and Dylan Thomas. This first stage was anthologized by John Sutherland in *Other Canadians* (1947). But *Other Canadians* also marked the beginning of the second, more amorphous phase, which Sutherland interpreted as the failure of the movement.

> How suddenly it all changed! The First Statement Press had no sooner published *Other Canadians*, "An Anthology of the New Poetry in Canada, 1940–1946," which I furnished with a bristling defiant introduction, than the whole purpose and driving spirit of the "new movement" were in a state of decay. We had barely rushed to the side of this challenger of tradition, holding up his right — or rather his left — hand in the stance of victory, when the challenger laid his head upon the block and willingly submitted to having it removed. What were the causes? Not *Other Canadians*, or my introduction to it; it went deeper than that. With the end of the war, there came a realization that, in the world at large, Russia and the United States were not in a state of undeclared brotherly love, and that, at home, the Canadian socialist movement had very shallow roots. It would be foolish to base a literary judgment of this movement on the value of its political ideas: but there is no doubt that one of the reasons it lost part of its momentum was because it lost its political faith. There were, of course, other factors involved in its marked if temporary decline: for example, the slowing down of the tempo everywhere by the return from war to a partial peace; the tapering off of the Canadian movement of expansion; and, last but not least, the poor durability of the poetic talents.[11]

Joan McCullagh's assessment of this time is quite different:

> The late forties' poetry... is cooler and more personal than that of the earlier years. The anger, indignation, and political panaceas of the earlier poetry are gone and so (largely) is the gaucheness. The emphasis on specifics and the here-and-now of the "aggressively realistic poetry of early modernism" has given way to more universal concerns — the search for enduring patterns of myth, religion, the cycles of nature which would give coherence and meaning to life.[12]

Poets no longer approached poetry from the same vantage point; poetry began to reflect a wider variety of subjects. Poets such as Dorothy Livesay, Earle Birney, P. K. Page, Miriam Waddington, and Louis Dudek, whose work had appeared in *Contemporary Verse* during its first five years, continued to appear within its pages; they were joined by several post-war poets. James Reaney made his first appearance in *Contemporary Verse* in issue number eighteen (July 1946). Issue number twenty-three was devoted to the poetry of Dudek, Reaney, and Raymond Souster, three poets who, with Irving Layton, would dominate the poetry of the 1950s. Issue number twenty-seven marked the first appearance of Jay Macpherson. In the fifties, Macpherson and Reaney would provide a remarkable new direction for Canadian poetry.

In the fall of 1951, Alan Crawley compiled the thirty-sixth issue of *Contemporary Verse*; the issue marked ten years of publication. All the poets who had contributed to the first issue were called upon to submit material for this issue and were joined by a few others, notably F. R. Scott and E. J. Pratt. In a foreword, Alan Crawley spoke of the original aspirations of *Contemporary Verse* and its hopes for the future. Also contained in this foreword were the seeds of doubt that were eventually to lead to the demise of the magazine. Crawley indicated that of late he had "been wavering and distrustful" of his decisions.[13]

The last paragraph of the foreword attempted to strike a note of affirmation and to affirm a continuance of purpose:

> There is a job for *CV* in presenting the best of Canadian poetry written in the 1950s as it has presented that of the last ten years. If such poetry is written, then so long as it is possible, Floris McLaren and I will get out *CV* in very irregular order and with as great interest and pride in what we are doing as we have done for thirty-six times. The place occupied by *Contemporary Verse* has not yet above it a sign TO LET.[14]

In just another year *Contemporary Verse* would close its files. Crawley's doubt as expressed in his foreword to the anniversary issue continued to plague him; this, complicated by the scarcity of submissions of good material, led Crawley to the belief that *Contemporary Verse* had declined from "its peak of usefulness."[15] The end of *Contemporary Verse* signalled an end to the movement of the forties. (*Northern Review*, edited by John Sutherland and also concerned with the forties' movement, continued for another few years.) As Joan McCullagh put it:

> Alan Crawley was a forties' man. He grew up on modern poetry from England and the United States, and he was on hand, an enthusiastic

welcomer and supporter, when modernism settled in Canada in the forties and took over Canadian poetry. Crawley was one of the main sponsors of this new poetry through his magazine *Contemporary Verse*, and no one worked harder than he to help get it naturalized in Canada. But just as he was sensitive to the beginning of this trend in 1941, he recognized its ending in the early years of the fifties and chose to close down his magazine with the termination of this distinctive period in Canadian poetry.[16]

Raymond Souster began publishing *Contact* as *Contemporary Verse* folded, and *CIV/n* began publication a short time later. A new period had already begun. But *Contemporary Verse* had provided the movement at large with a place to grow. Although *Preview* and *First Statement* provided much of the fireworks, *Contemporary Verse* provided a fixed stage for the movement that spanned the decade. "In this manner *Contemporary Verse* fulfilled one of the most important tasks of a little magazine, which is that of attacking conventional modes of expression by bringing into print the results of new theories and practices in Canadian literature."[17]

The Modernist writings of the forties were composed of various elements and influences. In Montreal, two groups with different approaches to poetry came into being in the early forties and centred their activities around two magazines, *Preview* and *First Statement*. For three years these magazines co-existed somewhat contentiously; then they merged briefly into *Northern Review*. Both *Preview* and *First Statement* were militant in their political and aesthetic programs. Behind each stood a single personality who shaped the magazine, *Preview*'s Patrick Anderson and *First Statement*'s John Sutherland.

Preview made its initial appearance in March 1942. Patrick Anderson was an Englishman who had come to Montreal from Oxford; his poetic fathers were British writers who had come to prominence in the thirties: W. H. Auden, Stephen Spender, and Louis MacNeice. The magazine was neatly mimeographed, and a list of permanent contributors appeared on the front cover. Those listed were the *Preview* group. The magazine lasted for three years, from 1942 to 1945. The first issue listed F. R. Scott, Margaret Day, Bruce Ruddick, Patrick Anderson, and Neufville Shaw on the cover. The first page carried a statement of intention:

This is no magazine. It presents five Montreal writers who recently formed themselves into a group for the purpose of mutual discussion and criticism and who hope, through these selections, to try out their work before a somewhat larger public.... [C]reative and experimental

27

writing must be kept alive and there must be no retreat from the intellectual frontier—certainly no shoddy betrayal, on the lines of Archibald MacLeish, Van Wyck Brooks, and others, of those international forces which combine in a Picasso, a Malraux or a Joyce.... [T]he poets amongst us look forward, perhaps optimistically, to a possible fusion between the lyric and didactic elements in modern verse, a combination of vivid, arresting imagery and the capacity to "sing" within social content and criticism.[18]

Preview attempted to combine "arresting imagery" with "social content." Often, in the attempted "fusion between the lyric and didactic elements," the didactic took precedence. The poetry in *Preview* was clearly in the "cosmopolitan" tradition, and much of it is formal, stiffened by a rather elevated British diction. The writing is often highly metaphoric and metaphysical. This is precisely what the poets in *First Statement* found artificial and unacceptable.

Despite *Preview*'s statement that "this is no magazine," the publication was very much a little magazine in format and intent. It presented the work of a small group of writers who held some common beliefs about politics and art. It presented writing that generally adhered to stated aesthetic and political principles. In spite of its hard line, however, the magazine did open its pages to other writers. Poems by A. M. Klein (later a contributing editor), Raymond Souster, Kay Smith, Miriam Waddington, Ralph Gustafson, Anne Marriott, Denis Giblin, and James Wreford appeared; even *First Statement* contributors were occasionally welcomed to the pages of *Preview*. There were changes in the list of permanent contributors: P. K. Page was added with issue number two, Margaret Day was dropped with issue number four; Neufville Shaw was dropped with issue number sixteen, Klein added with issue number nineteen. The editor's note in issue number twenty welcomes James Wreford as a contributing editor, though he was never listed on the cover. F. R. Scott, P. K. Page, Bruck Ruddick, and Patrick Anderson were the nucleus of the magazine. Anderson contributed poetry, prose, and editorial statements. Ruddick contributed articles and fiction, while Scott and Page were represented by poems as well as reviews. Patrick Anderson was very much the centre of the magazine.

Much of the poetry that appeared in *Preview* reflected a social consciousness and an awareness of the war and a concern for its larger implications. Patrick Anderson defined what he saw as the literary task of the Canadian writer during times of war:

Our task is clear: not only to help in the winning of the war by our literary work and our vivid enthusiastic embodiment of the issues for which it is being fought, but also to supply something of the personal, the graceful and the heroic to this half-empty Dominion.[19]

The outstanding characteristic of the work printed in *Preview* is a dedication to the economic and political issues raised by the Depression and the war. This political consciousness is reflected in most of the articles about poetry that appeared in *Preview*. In issue number eight, P. K. Page provided an assessment of Canadian poetry in 1942 based upon politically motivated notions:

> Today with three new magazines — *Contemporary Verse, First Statement* and *Preview* — the poet is no longer silent. He has yet to come to grips with himself and stop crying "Help" from the prairies and woods and mountains. If instead he will hitch-hike to the towns and identify himself with people, forget for a while the country of his own head, he may find his age and consequently his belief.[20]

The overwhelming presence of the Canadian Authors' Association had not been dispelled during the 1930s. The productions of CAA members had far outweighed those of the Canadian Modernists during the Depression era. In the ninth issue of *Preview* (November 1942), F. R. Scott reviewed the anthology *Voices of Victory* — put together by the Toronto branch of the CAA — in an article called "A Note on Canadian War Poetry." Scott notes that "by this volume, nothing has altered in the realm of poetry or politics since 1914. Needless to say there is no new style or diction, no venture in original modes of expression."[21] The most significant idea in the essay appears in the opening paragraph:

> A live movement in poetry will reflect and often foreshadow the creative movements in its social environment. Poets sensitive to the growing forces of their age will give symbolic expression to those forces and will become a potent instrument of social change. The more revolutionary their epoch the more markedly will their writing differ from that of their predecessors, for they will be obliged to experiment with new form and imagery in order to convey their new ideas.[22]

The *Preview* poets were highly conscious of themselves as "instruments of social change." (This was the position of the majority of Modernist poets in the forties. Dorothy Livesay and Raymond Souster, for example, were engaged with the sociological and political implications of the war, yet remained outside the *Preview* orbit.)

The year 1943 saw the first edition of A. J. M. Smith's *The Book of Canadian Poetry*. The anthology attempted to discern a Canadian poetic tradition and to trace it from before Confederation to the 1940s. (Smith discerned two traditions in Canadian poetry, what he called the "native" and the "cosmopolitan.") The anthology generated much discourse and reaction.

In *Preview*, the anthology was reviewed by Neufville Shaw in an essay entitled "The Maple Leaf is Dying" (number seventeen, December 1943). Shaw considers the quality of Canadian poetry, and finds the pre-Confederation work highly derivative from English models. His criticism of the Confederation poets is marked by a political undercurrent:

> The newer "Golden Age" poetry was written in an age which was determined to find the gold and little else. While expanding Canadian industry was merrily chasing the dollar across a thousand miles of prairies, the poets drearily painted golden sunsets or found Pan and Eurydice under every Maple Leaf.[23]

Shaw is also highly critical of the work of Pratt, Finch, and Smith. He does not agree with Smith, who viewed Pratt as the greatest of the contemporary poets. Shaw is not impressed by the grandeur of Pratt's epic narratives. He considers Finch and Smith to have written "glittering inconsequentials."[24] He does, however, find a validity and real contact with life in Klein's writing.

In the writings of the *Preview* group, Shaw finds an affirmation of a new Canadian poetry tradition.

> It is the verse of Scott, Anderson, Page and Wreford which makes us quite contentedly proclaim the death of the Maple Leaf for here we find a complete disregard for a dictated chauvinism and a didacticism which, while not constituting a political directive, is a ruthless analysis of social falsehood. It is on this tide of affirmation that the future of Canadian verse rests for it is by a union with the great wave of social protest which is, at present, sweeping the country that a universalized statement can be made which carries within its scope all the proud and sweeping ramifications of mankind itself.[25]

Shaw is correct in viewing the poetry of social protest and social realism as the death of the "Maple-Leaf" school. The socially conscious movement of the forties established itself as the mainstream of Canadian Modernism. The movement was not limited to Scott, Anderson, Page, and Wreford; it incorporated almost all of the Modernist poets of the time. The poetry published in

Preview, First Statement, Contemporary Verse, and *Direction* supplanted the Roberts–Carman tradition.

The twenty-first issue of *Preview* is particularly interesting. It is called "An Explanatory Issue," and the poets supply comments on their poems. The comments are fascinating, but even more remarkable is the explanatory statement Patrick Anderson provides for the issue as a whole. He poses a list of aids or questions whereby modern poetry should be judged:

> 1.   Is the language vital and original? Are the epithets and images exact and fresh without being forced or overexotic for the general coherence of the subject? Is the poem emotionally evocative? If the poem passes this test you can say that you have at least the *makings* of a good poem.
> 2.   Does the poem hang together? Does it seem to spring from a genuine experience? Is its development coherent, so that it seems to be all of one piece? Does it throw light upon the matter it treats? If the answer to all these questions is yes, then you can safely say you are faced with a good poem.
> 3.   Does the poem show a general awareness of life and its problems? Does it help you to understand what it describes within a general system of relationships? Here we are on more dubious ground, of course.
> 4.   How does the poem tie in with other poems by the same author? What architectural expression do you get from his work as a whole — from the range of his subjects and the degree of general understanding he shows? This, like the preceding point, is less easy to establish exactly but one can be pretty sure that points three and four, or others like them, make the basic difference between the minor and/or occasionally good poet and great master. Between, shall we say, the poet of restricted range and the poet of wide human understanding.[26]

Anderson's criteria for the making of a good poem were reflected in the writing in *Preview*. The striving for originality in language and image often led to the overexotic. Anderson insisted that poetry spring from genuine experience; this is exactly the ground of the realist movement. What also emerges from the thirties influence in this push towards realism is a clarity of meaning and intention. The obscurities of Eliot and Yeats, which involved the inner realms of psychology and myth, have been replaced by the reality of political and social systems.

In the final paragraph Anderson defines what he sees as the state of poetry in Canada, and the ultimate function of the poet and poetry:

> I believe that there are good poets in Canada and I believe that the poet has a real function to play in our society, particularly when social and economic progress is getting ahead of the cultural and "spiritual" development. I think that this is obvious when we reflect that the forces which are progressive politically are sometimes little more than reactionary culturally. Whether we define the role of the poet as being to stress the importance of the economic and psychological individual or to build up a rich associational background for our increasingly collective age or simply as a means for interesting the middle-class in social change, or all these things and more, I feel that he has an important part to play. He can be a humanist leader of the modern movement.[27]

Preview published twenty-three issues, from March 1942 until 1945 (the last issue carries no date), before merging with *First Statement* to create *Northern Review*. The quality of its poetry was high; it was highly polished as well as politically committed. It was a more formal poetry than that produced by the *First Statement* group. John Sutherland would admit, in his introduction to *Other Canadians*, that, "judged by the pure aesthetic standard, the English colonial poets [the *Preview* poets] are producing the best work."[28] But he saw in the group that had collected around *First Statement* "something of more significance for the future."[29]

If Patrick Anderson was the guiding spirit of *Preview*, John Sutherland was even more truly the controlling force behind *First Statement*. Wynne Francis explains the origin of *First Statement*:

> The central figure, if not the leader, of the "First Statement Group" was John Sutherland. John came to Montreal from Saint John, New Brunswick, in 1941 to attend McGill University after a three year bout with tuberculosis. During his illness he had spent much time reading, writing poems, and corresponding with writers and editors of literary magazines both in Canada and abroad. By the time he arrived in Montreal, he was well acquainted with the Canadian literary scene and with modern American and British poetry. Shortly after arriving, he determined to launch a little magazine of his own and to this end he engaged the help of several undergraduates including R. G. Simpson and Mary Margaret Miller, and Audrey Aikman who later became

his wife. Together, in 1942, these new friends turned out the first six or seven issues of an eight-paged mimeographed sheet which they named *First Statement*.[30]

One story has it that Sutherland was prompted to start *First Statement* when some of his poems were rejected by *Preview*, and he drew much of his early energy from his argument with *Preview*. What type of magazine Sutherland wanted *First Statement* to be seems at first unclear.

Louis Dudek argues that it isn't easy to explain the differences between *Preview* and *First Statement*.

> It's a highly complicated question because John Sutherland, for example, who was the editor of *First Statement*, had a kind of affinity with the *Preview*-ites. He admired their work, he published P. K. Page at the very beginning in his own magazine; he published Patrick Anderson...I feel Sutherland really admired the *Preview* group greatly — more, probably, than he did in fact the people in his own group. The editor of *First Statement* was essentially a *Preview*-ite. That complicates the question of opposition between the two parties. There was some opposition, however, because at the head of *Preview* stood Patrick Anderson, and he was a visiting Britisher in Canada ...one magazine, *Preview*, was associated with what I think of, historically, as the colonial attachment of Canadian literature... whereas the *First Statement* people were more related to contemporary American poetry...you had in these two magazines...a significant confrontation between the colonial pull toward British literature and the new native strain that would come right out of Canada.[31]

In many respects, *First Statement* went through three periods. The pull toward twentieth-century American poetry occurred when the magazine hit its second phase, when Layton and Dudek became involved with it, and the magazine became the outlet for a specific group.

At the beginning, Sutherland put forward *First Statement* as something of a gesture. He wrote in the magazine's first editorial:

> Someone will say that we will be talking in a vacuum, to ourselves alone, and be making gestures that have reference to nothing. It does not seem to us an unreasonable criticism. In the present stage of Canadian literature, a gesture would appear to be more important. A display of activity may symbolize a future, and plant a suggestion in someone's mind. The religious ceremonies which thrived many cen-

turies ago must have arisen from a belief in the newness of living and the youth of the race. What had happened seemed rare, and it was not certain that it would happen again. Bread was broken to express the hope that bread would be granted again. We intend to go through the ceremonies, in our Canadian literary youth.[32]

From the very beginning, *First Statement* was "A Magazine for Young Canadian Writers," as the cover indicated. Sutherland offered a forum for such writers even before he had found the writers he wanted to publish. The early issues of the magazine presented material by Sutherland, Robert Simpson, and Audrey Aikman — members of the magazine's editorial board — as well as members of the *Preview* group. (P. K. Page, Patrick Anderson, and Neufville Shaw all appeared in the first seven issues.) With issue number five, *First Statement* combined with a new west-coast publication, *Western Free-Lance*, and the work of Dorothy Livesay and Anne Marriott appeared. Sutherland seemed to find his first "discovery" in Kay Smith, a writer who made her first appearance in the third issue of the magazine.

The second issue included a statement that the magazine would be eclectic, that it would "contain as varied a representation of Canadian literature as possible." Sutherland states, "We shall try to exhibit the art of various groups of writers in Canada, rather than express any opinions of our own."[33]

The early issues of the magazine are generally unspectacular and do not seem to show any definite direction. Sutherland spent much of his time picking at flaws in *Preview*. In the first issue of *First Statement* he wrote about Bruce Ruddick's short story, "Vi," which appeared in *Preview*. Sutherland questioned the doctrinal approach he saw in *Preview*, maintaining that words are not mechanical, utilitarian, or convenient modern tokens to be used for putting across a message, but that language contains a certain magic. "Before an artist has any other creed, he has religious faith towards words."[34] Sutherland was taking a stand for the autonomy of literature.

In the third issue of *First Statement* Sutherland argued for a variety of literary approaches. He insisted that a Canadian literature does exist, and he said his magazine would provide a forum for Canadian writers: "Hence our desire to exhibit without discriminating against any, the various modes and types of writing as we find them in Canada. We would like to become the mirror of this variety, and so provide the Canadian reader with the freedom of choice that he requires."[35] In light of these early editorials, Dudek's contention that "Sutherland had always wanted a nice, solid, intellectual magazine like *Northern Review*, not a fighting rag like *First Statement*"[36] seems convincing. Sutherland seemed more inclined toward a non-partisan literary forum than a militant magazine.

In the early issues of *First Statement*, Sutherland opened the magazine to every variety of writing—although there is no trace of the Roberts–Carman tradition. Sutherland continued to criticize *Preview*, but not in a hostile manner. In the eighth issue, Sutherland argued that the *Canadian Poetry Magazine* should shake itself out of its doldrums, and that *Preview* should produce a magazine for readers, not for writers.

It is in the ninth issue of *First Statement* (late December 1942) that we begin to see a marked change in the magazine. This change is introduced by the appearance of three poems by Irving Layton, whom Sutherland had just met. The issue also contains a review by Sutherland of Earle Birney's collection *David & Other Poems*. In the review Sutherland reprimands Scott, Smith, Klein, and Kennedy for excluding all sense of the Canadian landscape in their writing. It is the first indication of the full-scale assault Sutherland would later mount against the "cosmopolitan" tradition.

Layton knew Louis Dudek; three of Dudek's poems appear in issue number ten. The eleventh issue carried work by Miriam Waddington and Raymond Souster. With the tenth issue, *First Statement* also changed its subheading: it was now "A Canadian Literary Magazine."

Sutherland was at last finding the native Canadian literary youth he had been looking for. With the twelfth issue, which included work by Layton, Dudek, and Kay Smith, the magazine began to hit its stride. In an editorial, Sutherland notes that Layton, Dudek, and Smith have been ignored by the critics and the public.

> Yet each one is producing work that may appear, in the future, as a valuable contribution to Canadian poetry.... What I should like to stress about all three poets, Dudek included, is their common interest in nature... since Canada is an agricultural country it is hardly possible for the poet to avoid contact with nature. Nature not only rules great sections of our country, but it also invades a metropolis. It enters the heart of Montreal and sits down in the form of Mount Royal. We compared Kay Smith to Dorothy Livesay, and I think that her identification with nature partly explains one's feelings that Miss Livesay is so essentially a Canadian poet. Neither she nor Miss Smith nor Irving Layton are giving us nature pure and simple; or absorbing for other purposes a peculiarly Canadian landscape, as Earle Birney does. But their link with nature is inescapably a part of their experience of living in Canada.... Here are three poets, not lacking in imagination or intellectual power, who are producing work that is much more honest and wholesome than that of our Modernist school. What they write is essentially readable, and it is valid and real as poetry.[37]

Sutherland has found in them what he considers to be a real alternative to the *Preview* – A. J. M. Smith axis. He sees in their work a writing that has imagination and intellect, and, at the same time, has a greater realism than the work of the *Preview* writers, for it is readable and real rather than erudite and put up. Reading the poems themselves, one finds that Sutherland's enthusiasm is, perhaps, more for a premonition of what they will write in the future than what they were writing at this time.

The new energy level is apparent in issue thirteen. The magazine, subtitled "A National Literary Magazine," carried an editorial that announced the formation of *First Statement* groups around the country for the creation of a consciousness of Canada and of Canadian literature. And the magazine boasts a new staff:

> *First Statement* is produced by the following group: John Sutherland, Betty Sutherland, Irving Layton, Glyn Owen, Audrey Aikman and Louis Dudek.[38]

Energies were gathering. The fifteenth issue, dated 19 March, 1943, stated that *First Statement* was in the process of securing a printing press.

Issues twelve to twenty, the last mimeographed issues, represent the fighting *First Statement*. Once the magazine came to be printed it began to change, gradually ceasing to be what Dudek has termed "a fighting rag." Issues sixteen, nineteen, and twenty carry articles that dispute the *Preview*-ites' programme. Dudek's article "Geography, Politics and Poetry" appears in issue sixteen. Dudek maintains that poetry should register an honest reaction to first-hand experience. He saw, however, examples in the *Preview* group's work that went against the grain of this contention:

> There seem to be, however, three tendencies in modern writing which war against the simple truth of the above argument. These three tendencies are hostile to the natural desire of poets to "react honestly... first hand"...
>
> The tendencies, in order, are: (a) a clever aptitude for exploiting the unreal universe of language; (2) a pedantic absorption in the second-hand universe of books, literature, and erudition; and (3) a falsified devotion to a special universe of ideas, chiefly, sociological and political ideas.[39]

In stating that poets desire to "react honestly... first hand," Dudek is quoting the American poet Hart Crane. We see that the *First Statement* group was influenced by the American impetus rather than the British. The group preferred the earthy quality of poets such as Whitman, Masters, Sandburg, and Crane to the eloquent sonics of an Auden or a Dylan Thomas. They began to approach the American sensibility that William Carlos Williams would later define as a basic principle of poetry: "No ideas but in things." As Wynne Francis puts it:

> *First Statement* poets prided themselves on writing a masculine, virile "poetry of experience"—their own experience. They would not write of the phoenix and the hyacinth but of Berri Street and De Bullion. Scorning the artifice of metaphor and symbol, they preferred to shout huzzahs and hurl insults, to fight, spit, sweat, urinate and make love in their poems, and did so in a deliberate defiance of *Preview*. They eschewed all abstractions and swore that "words" would not come between their poetry and life. "Celebration, not cerebration" as Layton was later to phrase it.[40]

Dudek also argued against the social preaching he perceived in *Preview*:

> In short, what is wrong with today's social preaching in poetry is that it is likely to be falsified preaching. It is likely to show the influence of an "upper class," higher-cultured, intellectual spirit. Its writers may not be aristocrats, but they have learned the separateness, subtility, and love-of-culture of the aristocracy. They are simply not plebeian enough. We have in Montreal a magazine, *Preview*, in which much of the work illustrates exactly this point.
>
> By way of correctives, *First Statement* can suggest three slogans for the poet's masthead. No polyglot displays. No poetry about poets and poetry. No high party politics.[41]

Dudek's article is followed by a satiric poem of Irving Layton's, "The Modern Poet," which is directed against the "Modernism" the *Preview* poets represented:

> Since Auden set the fashion,
> Our poets grow tame;
> They are quite without passion,
> They live without blame
> Like a respectable dame.[42]

The *First Statement* writers saw themselves as "working-class poets."

The art of the poison pen was also being refined in *First Statement*. In issue sixteen there was an exchange of letters between Patrick Waddington and Irving Layton concerning Waddington's criticism of Layton's work; Layton's letter is early practice for the letters he would come to be known for in later years. The nineteenth issue contains the article "The Writing of Patrick Anderson," written by John Sutherland, which led to a libel suit from Anderson. Sutherland says that "a sexual experience involving two boys"[43] lies behind Anderson's perceptions and influences much of the metaphor of his writing. Sutherland, claiming knowledge of some homosexual encounter in Anderson's past, says that one "would rather have wished that Anderson had employed his energies...to a direct description of abnormal sex."[44] (Issue twenty was delayed because of the threatened libel suit. When it appeared, the issue carried a retraction of the statements in Sutherland's article.)

The first printed issue of *First Statement*, subtitled "Canadian Prose & Poetry," appeared in August 1943 and looked like a conventional small literary magazine. In the thirteen printed issues that followed, the magazine became less militant and opened its pages to contributors from outside the group.

In the fourth issue of the second volume of *First Statement*, an editorial entitled "Literary Colonialism" is John Sutherland's first full-fledged criticism of A. J. M. Smith's introduction to *The Book of Canadian Poetry*, Sutherland's new literary target.

> A. J. M. Smith, in the introduction to his *Book of Canadian Poetry*, makes a distinction between a "native" and a "cosmopolitan" tradition which he defines in these terms: "The one group (the native) has attempted to describe whatever is essentially and distinctly Canadian and thus come to terms with an environment that is only now ceasing to be colonial. The other (the cosmopolitan) from the very beginning has made a heroic effort to transcend colonialism by entering into the universal, civilizing culture of ideas." I don't know whether this distinction has been made before, but it is a valuable one, and it throws a good deal of light on Canadian poetry of the past and present. But are the characteristics of the two traditions correctly defined by Mr. Smith?
>
> Can Mr. Smith ignore the colonialism that stamps the work of Canadian poets, particularly the writers of the cosmopolitan group? As his scholarly and well-balanced anthology makes abundantly clear, no poetry movement has ever taken place in Canada that did not depend, in the matter of style, upon the example of a previous movement in some other country. In this respect, those modern poets who continue the native tradition also waited for the go-ahead signal

to come from England and America. Those poets who continued the cosmopolitan tradition were acclaiming the work of Spender and Auden, Barker and Thomas. Mr. Smith, who apparently sees a special virtue in importing other people's ideas and literary forms, believes that the future belongs to the cosmopolitan group, because they respond to every change of fashion. Yet he argues that this group, the leaders of which did not leave England until they were in their twenties, is making "a heroic effort to transcend colonialism."

As he fails to understand that a poet preaching politics in the guise of Auden may be just as colonial as a member of the CAA praising Britain in the metres of Tennyson, so he fails to see what Canadian poetry of the future might be. It will not be a poetry that is exclusively occupied with Canadian subjects, or is anxious to express a patriotic pride, or even to discover a form and an idiom that are adaptable to Canada. Primarily, it will be a poetry that has stopped being a parasite on other literatures and has had the courage to decide its own problems in its own way. Regardless, therefore, of the fact that the native tradition has so far failed to establish its independence, writers with the objective simplicity of Knister and Ross or the vitality of Pratt, Livesay and Marriott indicate much more hope for the future than do the writers of the cosmopolitan tradition.[45]

Sutherland was essentially correct in his view that the "native" tradition promised more for the future than the "cosmopolitan." It was a position he would later repudiate, when he found himself unable to accept the changes that were leading poetry out of the forties into a new era. In 1943, however, Sutherland was beginning a campaign for the native tradition that would lead Smith to change his point of view significantly.

The April 1944 issue (volume two, number six) presented more criticism of A. J. M. Smith. Dorothy Livesay was critical of Smith's *News Of The Phoenix*, claiming that Smith was working in a limited area. "It means that the poetry is dated as of the twenties and early thirties; that it is cosmopolitan, without a grain of native, salty flavour; and that it speaks to a coterie of Eliot and Yeats devotees."[46] She concluded: "[I]n the present mood of the world, such poetry will not give sustenance nor direction."[47]

In a formal review in the same issue, Sutherland disputes Smith's contention that it is the "cosmopolitan" tradition that will supply the future of Canadian poetry:

Dr. Smith, in his haste to prove that the future belongs to the cosmopolitan writers, fails to see the native tradition in its proper perspective. He fails to see precisely what the native qualities consist of, and he does not take into account the cosmopolitan elements in the modern writer of the native group. Not only is the distinction, as he has made it, a vague one, but it is hardly possible to imagine a Canadian Literature of the future that lacks either native qualities or cosmopolitanism of outlook. The editor's thesis is not convincing because it does not notice a blending of the two traditions already taking place in Pratt and in Livesay, and in a group of younger writers who have recently appeared in Canada.[48]

Subsequent issues of *First Statement* include interesting work and editorials. The April and May issues of 1944 contain a two-part article by Sutherland on Nietzsche. The May issue has an article by Layton, "Let's Win The Peace," calling for political unity between the Allies. The editorial in the August issue maintains the standard of art over the political context of the work. The issue includes Dudek's article "Academic Poetry," in which he takes note of the large number of poets attached to the universities throughout North America and calls for a revolution in thinking that would liberate poetry from the limitations of the academic environment.

Issue number ten of the second volume is noteworthy for two poems, Souster's "Go To Sleep, World" and Layton's "The Swimmer." Number eleven carries an advertisement for Layton's book *Here & Now*, just published by First Statement Press; the magazine had started to publish books as well.

Issue number eleven also contains a favourable review of E. J. Pratt's *Collected Poems*. Sutherland finds in Pratt a truly individual poet of merit. This is the first sign of Sutherland's devotion to Pratt and the start of his dedication to Pratt's work, a task which was to occupy him in the last years of his life.

The next-to-last issue of *First Statement* (volume two, number twelve) begins to point towards the merging of *First Statement* and *Preview*. The issue includes a Patrick Anderson poem, "Adam," and an advertisement for Anderson's *A Tent For April*, the second book from First Statement Press. The most impressive piece in the final issue is from a writer on the *Preview* masthead, A. M. Klein. His "Portrait of the Poet as a Nobody," later retitled "Portrait of the Poet as Landscape," is one of the finest Canadian poems written during this period.

The new magazine *Northern Review* would unite *First Statement* and *Preview* in an uneasy marriage. It was not a relationship that was to last. The imagined conflict between *Preview* and *First Statement* had done much for the young *First Statement* poets, defining a direction for them. Much of the work that appeared in *Preview* had had a totally English influence; the young

First Statement poets, on the other hand, saw the American branch of Modernism as the more positive. It was a working-class tradition, unrefined and unpolished, filled with a sense of the land, as opposed to the British tradition still clinging to aristocracy and the principle of art as artifice.

The *First Statement* poets began the second wave of Canadian Modernism. Layton, Souster, and Dudek would point the way to the fifties and sixties. In the process John Sutherland, very much a forties man, like Alan Crawley, would be left behind; through *Contact*, *CIV/n*, and *Delta*, the Cerberus threesome would push Canadian poetry into new realms. As Neil Fisher describes it in his short history of the magazine:

> The major achievement of *First Statement* lies...in the issue of modernism. The group and the magazine appeared at an opportune time. A number of talented individuals came together, and their belief in themselves and in the direction that modern poetry should take was strengthened by their sense of group feeling. The magazine offered encouragement and stimulation through publication and competition. As a result, the most vital poetry of the period appeared in its pages. *Canadian Poetry Magazine* with its lack of taste and direction pales in comparison. The intellectual exercises of *Preview* seem to be the last limpid laps of the first wave of modernism. *Contemporary Verse* surges positively, especially in the early issues, but it lacks the character and variety of *First Statement*.
>
> It was the poets of *First Statement* who represent the second wave of Modernism in Canadian poetry, a wave which has proven to be of tidal consequences.... The honesty of both poetic and critical experiences, the anti-intellectual element present, and the North American bias have formed the basis for the development of contemporary poetry in Canada.[49]

The last of the little magazines to appear in the early forties was *Direction*, edited by Raymond Souster, William Goldberg, and David Mullen, who were all in the service at the time. The magazine lasted for ten issues, from November 1942 until February 1946; it was produced on a Gestetner machine in the various locations where its editors were stationed. Like *Contemporary Verse*, *Preview*, and *First Statement*, *Direction* was fully dedicated to the cause of Modernism in Canada. The magazine took its impetus and name from a quotation from Henry Miller:

> This may sound confusing but actually it is very clear and very simple. Everything that lives, that has being, whether it be a star, a plant, an

animal or even a human being, "Even God Almighty" has direction.
...Along the road which each of us is travelling there is no turning
back. It is forward or dead stop, which is living death.[50]

On the front page of the first issue is a reproduction of a letter written to "Ada"
by William Goldberg, under the heading "The Beginning," which describes
how the magazine came into existence:

> Let us make a declaration of our fighting faith.
>   Let us denounce the Canadian Authors' Association, including Sir
> Charles G. D. Tradition. God, they're dying on their feet... Ray says:
> "This has to be a blast. It *doesn't* have to be logical or sensible... We
> must attack, attack and attack. Let us call it the Mag, the Attack or
> Sperm, anything that will shock the dull witted Canadian imagina-
> tion out of its lethargy."[51]

Although the editors of *Direction* agreed with the trend of Modernist little
magazines in Canada, they were not entirely satisfied with the achievement of
those magazines. In the first issue of *Direction*, Souster offered his judgement
of their performance:

> *Contemporary Verse* of Vancouver has published much good, but
> little fresh and vital poetry. *Preview* of Montreal serves us with a
> rehash of Spender, Auden and MacNeice brought up to date with a
> Canadian setting, and any future claim to fame it may make will rest
> upon the fact that it first published Patrick Anderson... *First State-
> ment*, also of Montreal, has been the most experimental, and perhaps
> for that reason, the least successful. But its experimentation is healthy
> and it has less interest in names and more of literature than its
> contemporaries.[52]

Direction served as a forum for the work done by its editors and other service
men, with occasional contributions from outside. Poems by Irving Layton and
Miriam Waddington appeared in the second and third issues; a story by
Patrick Waddington was printed in issue number six. Issue number seven
presented a Canadian first, "The Paris of Henry Miller," excerpts from *Tropic
of Cancer*, which was on the lists of banned pornography.
    Direction published prose and poetry. Much of the prose was written by
William Goldberg; Souster also wrote some prose, but his main contribution
consisted of poetry. Much of the writing is directly concerned with the

war—stories about soldiers on furloughs and poems about the distance between lovers as the poet sits alone and melancholy in his bunk.

Like Souster's later magazines, *Contact* and *Combustion*, *Direction* pointed towards an American connection that would become increasingly important to Canadian poetry. (The second issue contains a piece by Souster entitled "A Debt," a tribute to Henry Miller and Kenneth Patchen. Both writers are praised for their uncompromising courage and honesty in writing the truth about our civilization.)

Canadian literature was also examined. The castigation of the "Sir Charles G. D. Tradition" was published in the eighth issue, in an article by John Sutherland, "Great Things & Terrible." Sutherland illustrated Roberts's short-comings and attempted to show that Roberts's inclinations towards grandeur were what "prevented him from raising his writing up from the level of verse to that of poetry."[53] He also denounced Roberts for trying to use poetry as a pedestal on which to elevate himself. Then, in the last issue (number ten), Souster wrote an appreciative assessment of the writing of Raymond Knister. *Direction* put down the "native" tradition of the Confederation poets and picked up on the later "native" strain represented by Knister and the realists.

A letter from Souster to William Goldberg was reproduced in *Direction* number six. The letter was prompted by the return, "from a well-known Canadian publishing house," of Souster's manuscript "together with a letter (well-intended of course) which revealed in its contents what seems to be pretty well the accepted slot into which all Canadian poetry must fall if it is to be tolerated at all."[54] In his reply, Souster disputes the criticism of his work. He denounces discipline and restraints, the suppression of freedom, vitality, frank-ness, and ideals in poetry. His closing paragraph represents the attitude of the entire forties generation towards the last vestiges of Victorianism, as they saw it, which were still cluttering the Canadian literary scene:

> No, poetry cannot be healthy or even possible as long as such ideals are cherished and held up for future generations to follow. They must be stamped out, if need be, ruthlessly. It will be the pleasure of a few of us to fight this challenge and defeat it.[55]

Direction helped to defeat the remnants of the Roberts tradition, and to create a new poetic approach.

Northern Review began publication in the post-war period. Theoretically *Preview* and *First Statement* were merged, but in actual fact it would seem that *Preview* was absorbed by *First Statement* under the new banner, since *First*

Statement had more energy—and also happened to own a printing press. Louis Dudek, who was then in New York, later assessed the new magazine:

> [A]s I understand it, the merger came about because *Preview* was going down anyhow. It could not have continued. It didn't have the people willing to take the responsibility for production and editing and so on, and Sutherland was therefore in a sense absorbing the other magazine. The easiest way to do that sort of thing is for everybody to get together at first and sing about the great union. But gradually you find that there is only one magazine and the other has vanished. Certainly after two or three years there was no *Preview* and there was only *Northern Review*.[56]

He sees *Northern Review* as a continuation of *First Statement*. The politics that had fired the social-realist movement began to cool down in the post-war period; it soon became apparent that, despite high hopes, socialism was not coming to Canada. *Preview* had been inspired by the socialist movement. *Northern Review*, however, continued the forties movement with a broader forum. The editorial board in the first issue was a fair balance of the *Preview* and *First Statement* groups. John Sutherland is listed as managing editor, with F. R. Scott, A. M. Klein, Irving Layton, Patrick Anderson, A. J. M. Smith, Audrey Aikman, R. G. Simpson, and Neufville Shaw on the board. The magazine also had regional editors, P. K. Page, Dorothy Livesay, James Wreford, and Ralph Gustafson. In theory, the differences between the two magazines were to be buried on behalf of a greater good, Canadian literature. The first editorial does not argue for a sharply defined school of writing or for any political commitment; it simply offers the magazine as a forum for the serious writer:

> *Northern Review* represents the amalgamation of two wartime literary magazines, *Preview* and *First Statement*, but its editorial board has been fortified by writers from distant points and its scope is national; it aims to print the best work being done in Canada. Its purpose is to present Canada to itself and abroad as a country where political and economic changes have not taken place without a real, though as yet not a quantitatively comparable, literary and artistic advance.
>
> We shall try to fulfill the classic function of the "little magazine"— to afford a means of expression for the serious writer who, without a reputation and without the advantages of commercial publicity, is

nevertheless determined to make no concessions to the slick, the theatrical, and the popular. Canadian magazines, Canadian publishing houses, and even some government agencies, aided occasionally by the New York book supplements, are manipulating copious and superficial Canadian authors into the ranks of the "great." The "unknown country" is in danger of becoming a lucrative province in the empire of the publisher's blurb and the Book of the Month Clubs. We wish to provide a place where the young writer who has something true and unpleasant to say can say it without fuss or frill. We hope to maintain a critical and artistic standard that in Canada exists only in the quarterlies — and there only spasmodically. Valuable as the universities are in the field of history and scholarship they have only rarely shown themselves capable of sympathetic and intelligent understanding of the aims and accomplishments of our younger poets and story writers.

It is admitted that our standards cannot be perfectionist but they must be rigorously enforced; all work printed will be examined to the best of our ability not in the light of a dubious nationalism or regionalism, not in obeisance to "big Canadian names" or so-called national traditions, but in respect to that general cosmopolitan culture to which we all adhere.[57]

It is clear from this editorial that much of the fire of the two earlier magazines had been lost. *Northern Review* was not to be the militant production of a small group; instead, the editorial points in the direction of the eclectic periodical. It is also odd to note that the material in the magazine would be judged "in respect to that general cosmopolitan culture to which we all adhere." Sutherland's opposition to the principles of cosmopolitanism had, for the time, been dropped. (In conversation, F. R. Scott said that the initial editorial may have been drafted by Patrick Anderson, with changes from other *Northern Review* editors.) The "cosmopolitan" attitude was given further support in an article by A. J. M. Smith, "Nationalism and Canadian Poetry," in which he argues that the universal element in Canadian poetry provides for a more vital art than a poetry filled with nationalist concerns. Smith holds that "the claims of nationalism are less important than those of universality and that a cosmopolitan culture is more valuable than an isolated one."[58] Clearly, at this time, the cosmopolitan *Preview* editors were making their presence felt.

The quality that had prevailed in the later issues of *First Statement* continued in the pages of *Northern Review*. As Dudek noted, Sutherland always wanted a quality literary review rather than a fighting magazine.

Sutherland in his editorials in *First Statement* was always aiming at a larger audience, at the time the responsible middle-class reader, and something of the quarterly-review look and tone that *Northern Review* came to acquire. That type of magazine is *Tamarack Review*; later, it's *Encounter* or the *London Magazine*, the big ones — it's not *Blast*. You see, *Northern Review* was no longer the type of mag that, to me, is the holy ground of modern poetry, where new battles are fought out on the aesthetic, intellectual front, programs that really mean a change in the shape of literature.[59]

Northern Review was initially dedicated to the written arts; later it dealt with other aspects of Canadian culture. It was a respectable cultural publication. The first five issues featured articles on the writing of Rilke and Karl Shapiro by Patrick Anderson and A. M. Klein; F. R. Scott's fine poem "Laurentian Shield"; an evaluation of P. K. Page's poetry by John Sutherland; four poems by the young James Reaney; a consideration of Kafka; and an article by Ralph Gustafson on the poetry of Archibald Lampman. Although much of this work is interesting, it is not pointed in any definite direction; there is no real centre to these issues of *Northern Review*.

In the sixth issue of the first volume, dated August–September 1947, Sutherland published a rather vitriolic review of Robert Finch's book, *Poems*, which had just won the Governor-General's award. Sutherland's critical spirit, which had been so evident in *First Statement*, flared up. But the article had explosive consequences: the tenuous "merger" was dissolved. The seventh issue presented a rather abbreviated organization: Sutherland remained managing editor, and his associates were Audrey Aikman, R. G. Simpson, Irving Layton, Mary Miller, and John Harrison. A notice appeared at the back of the issue:

> Certain changes have taken place in the editorial board of *Northern Review*, effective from the last issue. The following editors have resigned: Neufville Shaw, Patrick Anderson, A. M. Klein, F. R. Scott and A. J. M. Smith. Two regional editors, P. K. Page and Ralph Gustafson, have also resigned.
>
> The reason for these changes was a difference of opinion about editorial policy, particularly concerning criticism and reviews. The immediate occasion for disagreement was a review of Robert Finch's poems by John Sutherland, which appeared in the last issue. The editors who resigned maintained that this review, and similar pieces of criticism, were too harsh and unjust for publication, while the present editorial board held that criticism of this kind was badly

46

needed in Canada. Our readers can form their own opinions in the matter.

Elsewhere in this issue we have printed a short letter from P. K. Page, at her request, stating that she was ignorant of the review on Finch. Perhaps we should mention that our regional editors never saw contributions to the magazine before they were printed and were not entitled to vote on them.

The present editors are John Sutherland, R. G. Simpson, Mary Margaret Miller, John Harrison, Irving Layton and Audrey Aikman. We intend to carry on *Northern Review* in its present form. We hope that the concentration of responsibility in the hands of a smaller editorial board will result in greater efficiency and a more interesting magazine.[60]

The new editorial board may have produced "greater efficiency" but it certainly did not result in a more interesting magazine. Editors quit one by one, and more of the control of the magazine came to lie in the hands of Sutherland, who eventually ran the magazine with the aid of his wife, Audrey Aikman. Sutherland's gradual abandonment of the Modernist position of the forties turned *Northern Review* into a magazine that literally worked counter to Modernism in Canada. The magazine ceased publication in 1956, with Sutherland's death; by then, *Northern Review* had moved totally outside of the mainstream of Canadian poetry.

Within the pages of *Northern Review*, Sutherland waged a consistent war with what he felt was the shoddiness of Canadian criticism. He held firmly to the belief that a literature cannot advance unless its progress is facilitated by a competent criticism. In his article "Critics on the Defensive" (October–November 1947), he stated his main complaints: that Canadian critics continually took a defensive stance when writing about Canadian writing; that they had a tendency to praise Canadian writing for purely nationalistic reasons; and that they tended to emphasize elements of tradition and traditional values in their critiques. "These critics are on the defense," Sutherland wrote, "because they cling to a past world in order to deny the existence of the present one. [They are] a drag on the vital movements of our poetry."[61] Among the critics he cited were E. K. Brown, W. E. Collin, and A. J. M. Smith.

Northern Review went through further changes in format and organization. The July–August 1948 issue (volume two, number two) contains poetry, film, painting and drama criticism, and reviews. This issue is also the last in which Irving Layton is listed as a member of the editorial board. Two of his poems appear in the September–October issue; they are the last of Layton's work to appear in *Northern Review*. Sutherland was turning away from the members of the group he had praised in *First Statement* and *Other Canadians*. The April–May issue of 1949 (volume two, number five) features four poems by Patrick Anderson. Most of the issue is taken up by a critical article on Anderson's work, in which Sutherland argues that Anderson's influence upon Canadian poetry has been significant, in that he has influenced not only the members of the *Preview* group but also poets such as Layton and Dudek.

With the October–November issue of 1949 (volume three, number one), *Northern Review* forsook the ground of the little magazine and became a review of cultural opinion. The issue contained stories and poetry, and film, radio, stage, music, painting, and book reviews. Sutherland wrote in the editorial:

> The vital approach to Canadian art lies between the extreme of "cosmopolitanism" and of sentimental nationalism...We need the kind of Canadianism, cosmopolitan in its breadth of outlook that Lorne Pierce has expressed for us in "A Canadian People": "No nation can achieve its true destiny that adopts without profound and courageous reasoning and selection the thoughts and styles of another..." It is in this spirit that our criticism should approach what is its most important problem: the relationship of the arts in Canada to the English tradition... We believe that this is the logical critical approach to Canadian art in its present tentative state of development, and that, in fact, it represents the best practical way of understanding and employing our cosmopolitan background.[62]

Having once rejected Smith's notion of "cosmopolitanism," Sutherland picked up the term himself and used it favourably. (Contrast the programme of searching out a "native" tradition, which he had expressed in his introduction to *Other Canadians*.) As well, he was concerned with the relationship of Canadian art to the English tradition. Sutherland gravitated more and more towards the achievements of specific English writers. Paradoxically, he continued to speak at the same time of native Canadian work. Dr. Pierce's comment struck a responsive chord with Sutherland; it was printed on the back cover of every subsequent issue of *Northern Review*.

Convinced that the social-realist movement of the forties had been a failure, Sutherland began to look for other writers. The December–January (1949–1950) issue featured poems by E. J. Pratt and James Reaney, a new poet whose work continued to appear in *Northern Review* until the magazine's termination.

The work of Anne Wilkinson also began to appear in *Northern Review*. Kay Smith, whose work had begun to take a religious turn, was the only original *First Statement* poet whose work continued to appear on a regular basis.

48

Dudek's and Souster's work appeared infrequently until *Contact* and *CIV/n* began publication, when their work no longer came out in *Northern Review*. (Dudek has pointed out that they stopped sending work to Sutherland because they disapproved of the trends evident in *Northern Review*.)

The shift in Sutherland's orientation can be seen quite clearly in the publication list of First Statement Press. The titles printed in the forties had been Layton's *Here and Now*, Anderson's *A Tent For April*, Miriam Waddington's *Green World*, Souster's *When We Are Young, Other Canadians*, and Layton's second book, *Now is the Place*. First Statement printed two books in the fifties, Kay Smith's *Footnote to the Lord's Prayer* and Wilkinson's *Counterpoint to Sleep*. Sutherland seemed to be searching for something to replace what he felt was the failed movement of the forties, and he found glimmerings of this in the "mythy" writings of Reaney and Wilkinson, in the religious work of Kay Smith, and in the epic narrative of E. J. Pratt.

In the December–January issue of 1951 (volume four, number two), two articles, "Number Ten Reports" by Harold Horwood, editor of *Protocol*, a Newfoundland magazine, and Sutherland's "The Past Decade in Canadian Poetry," attempted to evaluate the writing of the forties. Horwood thought that "Canadian poetry is in a bad way."[63] He commented on the poets of the forties:

> [W]ith their obvious virtues their faults lay thick as dust. Not the least of their faults was the brevity of their artistic lives....[O]ne reason would be common to all—the discouragement which must have assailed most sensitive persons when the war was won and the peace was destroyed at the same mad moment of history. Political disillusionment is a powerful force. Most of the young writers were socialists of various colours. And they sensed, after their first passion for reforming the world had spent itself, that socialism was not coming to Canada in the foreseeable future. This tendency to be ephemeral was only one fault. Others were intellectualism at the expense of emotion, and a habit of using rather clotted symbolism at the expense of the image.[64]

This sense of failure of the forties is given fuller treatment in Sutherland's essay, where he attempts to give a credible historical account of the workings of the movement. Sutherland notes that the political theme had been announced in the thirties in Canada, in the writings of such poets as Dorothy Livesay and F. R. Scott, but gained full expression only in the forties.

The large group of poets who appeared then—James Wreford, P. K. Page, Louis Dudek, Raymond Souster, Patrick Anderson,

Miriam Waddington, Ronald Hambleton and several others—were all concerned, to a greater or less extent in individual cases, with the problems which they believed then arose from class divisions in society. Nor was the difference between the thirties and the early forties simply a quantitative one: there were also important differences in technique and in the approach to the political theme. The most clear-cut political group of the thirties—Birney, Livesay, and Marriott—was mainly concerned with the land and with the fate of an agricultural class: the new poets of the forties—nearly all of them residents of the East—saw the class issue in urban and industrial terms. The political poets of the thirties were essentially pragmatic in their outlook, prepared to adopt a cause and to devote their talents directly to its realization: the poets of the forties saw the contemporary world in psychological as well as political terms, and relied as much on Freud as Marx. The older poets had felt the impact of the English Marxist poetry of the thirties, but were relatively little influenced by the technical experiments of Auden and Spender or by those of Dylan Thomas and George Barker—while endeavouring to preserve the burden of the political theme. These main differences, and others that might be enumerated, make it clear that a new kind of Canadian poetry was being written in the early forties.[65]

Sutherland saw the forties as an exciting time in Canadian poetry. But the termination of the war brought change.

How suddenly it all changed! The First Statement Press had no sooner published *Other Canadians*, "An Anthology of the New Poetry in Canada, 1940–1946," which I furnished with a bristling, defiant introduction, than the whole purpose and driving spirit of the "new movement" were in a state of decay.[66]

Sutherland insists that the publication of *Other Canadians* had nothing to do with the failure of the movement. But perhaps the very process of formalizing a literary movement contains the seeds of that movement's dissolution or obsolescence. A movement that has been defined is limited to a set of precepts, which any writer in the process of development is sure to outgrow.

The failing political impetus had perhaps caused some people to cease writing. Sutherland talked of those who continued to write.

The new poets have come back, if not always to religion, at least to a soul-searching which has strong religious implications, and to an attitude of mind more in harmony with that of earlier Canadian poets. In their writing they no longer attribute the present state of the world to class oppression, but to a guilt which makes no class distinctions and which involves every individual, including the poet. They speak now in a more personal way, exhibit a willingness to bear their share of the universal guilt, and seem to imply that the puritanical fury with which they once attacked the "middle class" was really a blustering way of hiding their own feeling of guilt. They look back to the poetic traditions, strive for a greater simplicity, and try to sing rather than to bluster forth protests.[67]

Sutherland evaluated the state of Canadian poetry at the beginning of 1951.

> This, then, is a general picture of how the movement of the forties developed and of its present condition. What, you may ask, is the value of the recent poetry, as compared with that produced in the early forties, and what is its development likely to be? I will answer the second part of the question first: I believe the present religious trend may become more marked; if not, I believe there will be a reaction against it.... As for the first part of the question, it seems obvious to me that the recent work of the younger poets is inferior to their work in the early forties, but that, nevertheless, the principles behind this recent work are potentially better principles for poetry. It is generally better for the poet to accept than oppose the values inherent in his society; it is better for him to aim at simplicity than to perpetuate the obscurity which is gradually killing off the respect for poetry in the minds of intelligent readers; and it is better for him to use and not oppose the traditions of poetry — and for the Canadian poet not to completely ignore his relation to the traditions of poetry in Canada.[68]

When he saw the change in direction of Canadian poetry, Sutherland took it as a sign that the social-realist movement had failed; he could not see it as another stage in the evolution of Canadian Modernism. He denounced what he considered the remnants of the failed movement, and looked for a revival of religious thought and traditional intention in Canadian poetry.

Northern Review began to carry more poetry by English writers, and to publish articles about them. The December–January (1951–1952) issue was a special English issue; the poetry of Roy Campbell appeared in the April–May issue of 1953 (volume six, number one). George Woodcock's "Recollections of George Orwell" appeared in the August– September issue of that year (volume six, number three); Sutherland's article on "The Great Equestrians" appeared in the following issue, with an article on Wilfred Owen by Dennis S. R. Welland and more poems by Campbell.

Later issues also reflect Sutherland's conversion to Roman Catholicism. The August–September issue, 1953, carried an article called "An Excerpt from Poetry and Dogma" by Malcolm Ross. It was an examination of the use of Christian symbolism in poetry. Issue five of volume six (December–January, 1953–1954) ran the article "Towards a Christian Aesthetic" by Dorothy Sayers. The Spring 1955 issue (volume seven, number two), the first issue in which *Northern Review* became a quarterly, was published from Toronto and included an article called "The Religious Basis of Art" by Wladimir Weidle, as well as numerous poems dealing with Easter and Christian symbolism. Much of the poetry was religious in tone and content.

Sutherland became a fervent supporter of the work of E. J. Pratt. The February–May issue of 1952 (volume five, numbers three and four) is mainly concerned with Pratt's work. As the cover stated: "This issue is devoted almost entirely to E. J. Pratt. It is published in the belief that Pratt's significance has been misinterpreted and that he deserves to be ranked as a major poet."[69] Pratt's long narrative "The Great Feud" is included, along with a lengthy critique by Sutherland, "E. J. Pratt: A Major Contemporary Poet," where Sutherland cites the themes of power, and compassion in the face of power, as the primary basis of Pratt's work.

Sutherland's repudiation of Modernism is expressed in his article "The Great Equestrians."

> There is not the slightest doubt that modern literary development is now on its death-bed. All that was fathered by Joyce and Pound is obviously on the verge of complete extinction. As Edward Dahlberg phrased it in a recent issue of *Poetry Chicago*, "By now James, Pound, Eliot, Joyce are dowds, jades, and trulls of Parnassus, and we are weary of them. It may be that they will be curious again in some other time, but now they do not provide the spectacle of remoteness so significant in literature." What is to follow this debacle of the moderns? There are increasing signs that the younger generation, weary as it is of a rabid experimentalism, is turning back to the School of the Great Equestrians. The Equestrians have provided one of the few oases in the wasteland of our times. While the rest of the literary world has been standing on its head, they alone have been seated firmly in the saddle. They have been virtually the one healthy vein in a diseased and corrupt body. As the twilight of the "moderns" deepens into darkness, we can anticipate the moment when these apostles of Equestrianism will come riding towards us over the sunny, dew-

besprinkled meadows of the dawn. It will be a glorious dawn—
perhaps one of the most glorious in the whole of literary history.[70]

These "equestrians" were G. K. Chesterton, D. H. Lawrence, Roy Campbell, and C. S. Lewis.

Though Sutherland turned his back on it, Modernism did not go away. In Canada, the third stage of Modernism was developing in the pages of *Contact* and *CIV/n* while Sutherland was dancing upon its grave. Unable to understand what had happened to the movement he had so militantly put forward in *Other Canadians*, disappointed because the poets had not fulfilled his prophecies, he turned against social realism and Modernism and tried to encourage a new movement, rooted in religious belief and the English poetic tradition. Most of what Sutherland published in the last five years of *Northern Review* was peripheral to the evolution of modern poetry in Canada. If anything, *Northern Review* served as a lesson for poets like Layton, Souster, and Dudek; it represented what they did not want their magazines to become.

Several other little magazines appeared after the war. *Reading*, edited by Allan Anderson, Ronald Hambleton (editor of the anthology *Unit of Five*), and Lister Sinclair, originated in Toronto in 1946 and ran for several issues. *Reading* gave its emphasis to prose, featuring short fiction as well as commentaries on film, drama, music, radio, art, people, and books. Though resembling the little magazine in format, it did not follow through with any decisive content. Its opening editorial took pains to describe the publisher's and printer's unsuccessful attempts to find egg-shell-style paper on which to print the magazine. Although the magazine served mainly as a tasteful guide to culture, it did print poems by Birney, Souster, Smith, Hambleton, Page, and Anne Wilkinson—an assortment of poems without any particular direction.

The periodical *Here And Now* was also based in Toronto. Edited by Catherine Harmon, it ran for four issues, from December 1947 until June 1949. It was the most impressively produced magazine of the forties, with expensive printing and layouts in sharp contrast to the other little magazines of the time. Although its appearance gave it the sheen of a literary review, its opening editorial sought to place it in the stream of little-magazine experiment:

> At the present time there are, in England and in the United States, a number of excellent Little Magazines which play a very considerable part in the culture of these countries. Ever since the nineties of the last century, they have, with varying degrees of popularity, presented the greatest writers and artists of the time. That Canada has played a relatively small part in this movement is the result less of its being a

"young country" than of a preconceived notion that Canada does not possess enough *avant-garde* writers and artists to warrant such publications. With the exception of *Canadian Poetry Magazine* and *Contemporary Verse*, two poetry magazines of a very high order, which have for many years been attempting to disprove this, there is no publication whose primary aim it is to provide an outlet for the wide variety of Canadian art that does exist.[71]

It is not in error that the editorial cites *Canadian Poetry Magazine* and *Contemporary Verse* as models of little magazines "of a very high order": *Here And Now* followed in the tradition of eclecticism that these magazines displayed. *Here And Now* published a wide assortment of poetry and prose, as well as articles on Canadian art and photography. It opened its pages occasionally to work from outside Canada, on the grounds that Canadian writing could "not exist apart from the underlying literary currents"[72] of the day. The first issue included "A Greeting" by E. J. Pratt, an article by Northrop Frye on "The Eternal Tramp" (Charlie Chaplin), prose fiction by James Reaney and P. K. Page, an article by H. Reid MacCallum on "*The Waste Land* After Twenty-Five Years," sections of art and photography, and poems by P. K. Page, Patrick Anderson, Colleen Thibaudeau, Earle Birney, Roy Daniells, James Reaney, Ralph Gustafson, and W. W. E. Ross. The magazine served as an open forum for good writing.

Here And Now placed emphasis on prose writing. Its second editorial took up the question of popular fiction, looking at the ways writers and readers were cheated by literature's Tin Pan Alley. The issue also featured samples of fiction by Ethel Wilson and James Reaney. Poetry was treated seriously in Reid MacCallum's "Coal and Diamonds," an article on the patterns of sound and sense in poetry. Northrop Frye offered an appreciation of painter David Milne as well as literary comment. Poetry by Page, Gustafson, Reaney, Souster, A. J. M. Smith, and Stephen Spender also appeared in the second number.

The third issue included prose fiction by Roy Daniells and Ralph Gustafson, Jean Cocteau (in translation), an article by A. M. Klein on the complex structure of the "Oxen of the Sun" chapter in Joyce's *Ulysses*, and poems by R. A. D. Ford, Margaret Avison, Colleen Thibaudeau, Ralph Gustafson, Robert Finch, Robert Choquette, Louis Dudek, A. M. Klein, Roy Daniells, and Anne Wilkinson.

The fourth and last issue was the most ambitious. Most of the pages were devoted to criticism. The editorial pointed out the geographic difficulties of finding an audience, the difficulty of getting published, the threatening proximity of American mass culture; it took a swipe at the rise of creative-writing courses, arguing that they could not teach creative writing because they failed to teach creative reading. The critical concerns of the articles were varied. W. E. Collin's "The Literary Renascence of 1934 in French Canada" discussed the founding of the French periodical *La Relève* and considered Francois Hertel, Saint Denys-Garneau, and Robert Charbonneau. A. M. Klein wrote a general critique of criticism and criticism conferences. Robert Weaver presented "A Sociological Approach To Canadian Fiction." Harry Roskolenko's "Post-War Poetry In Canada" was a review of most of the significant books of verse published in the post-war period up until June of 1949. The issue also included a section of Cocteau's *Le Grand Ecart* in translation and poems by Dudek, Page, L. A. MacKay, Malcolm Ross, Anne Wilkinson, Earle Birney, E. J. Pratt, and Alfred G. Bailey.

Here And Now attempted to reflect the literary climate of the times, and to a degree it accomplished its purpose. In format and orientation, however, it strayed from the basic premises of the little magazine; it foreshadowed a periodical like *Tamarack Review* rather than continuing the true little-magazine tradition carved out by magazines like *Preview*, *First Statement*, and *Direction*.

Other ephemeral publications were started in the post-war period. In Montreal, *Elan*, "A Magazine For Young Writers," appeared in February of 1946. In spirit, this was a sister publication to the early *First Statement*; Phyllis Aikman, Audrey Aikman's younger sister, was on the editorial board. The magazine was eclectic in spirit. It printed work of writers within and around McGill University. *Index*, "A Guide to Good Reading," was edited by R. G. Simpson, and first appeared in March of 1946. In contrast to the coterie magazine, *Index* was intended as "a publication for the reader...not for the writer or publisher."[73] The magazine hoped to "do something to encourage a greater volume of more pleasurable and more constructive reading."[74] These publications, as well as *P. M.*, which originated in Vancouver, *Impression* from the mid-west, and *Protocol* from Newfoundland, had little to do with the central poetic struggles and innovations of the time. At most, they fleshed out the literary and cultural atmosphere of the forties. *Fiddlehead*, an exception, originated at the University of New Brunswick in 1945 and continues to this day; it has maintained an eclectic, fairly non-partisan position.

4

Social Realism's Second Phase

The McGill Movement and the poetic activity of the thirties provided the first tentative step in establishing Modernism in Canadian poetry. In the 1940s the spirit of Modernism prevailed and became the mainstream of poetic sensibility. But as a leftist movement the poetry of the forties failed to sustain itself. The reaction to the movement's faltering, in the late 1940s, was best exemplified by John Sutherland in *Northern Review* from 1949 to 1956. Many of the poets Sutherland included in *Other Canadians* stopped writing or ceased to produce valid work: Patrick Anderson slowly slipped out of the limelight, finally leaving the country in the early 1950s; Denis Giblin, Guy Glover, Mark Edmund Gordon, Ronald Hambleton, David Mullen, Bruce Ruddick, Neufville Shaw, and Sutherland himself (as a poet) quickly slipped into obscurity; Kay Smith never really went beyond the 1940s sensibility. But a handful of the poets included in *Other Canadians* were to make an important impact upon Canadian poetry, and to push it on to a new stage of Modernist development in the 1950s. Louis Dudek, Raymond Souster, and Irving Layton were involved in the organizing and running of Contact Press, and provided the most solid foundation upon which the work of the fifties was built. In a different way, Margaret Avison, James Reaney, and Miriam Waddington (all published in *Other Canadians*) contributed to the new poetic environment of the 1950s and 1960s.

Layton, Souster, and Dudek were coming into their prime years in their writing and in their attempts to define a new aesthetic. Souster provided the initial spark for a new push; in a letter to Dudek in 1951 he expressed his dissatisfaction with the current state of things:

> I think you are probably as fed up with *Contemporary Verse* and *Northern Review* as I am, and I know there are plenty of others who feel the same way. I give them credit for publishing competent publications in the face of every obstacle and I support them but if we are going to move on something will have to take place. We need an

outlet for experiment, and a franker discussion of the directions poetry is to take, not articles on lampman [sic] and the movies. What we need is in short a poetry mag with daring and a little less precious an attitude.[1]

When he received the letter, Dudek was living in New York, but planned to return to Montreal in September. He agreed with Souster that a new magazine was needed, but urged Souster to wait; he thought he would be able to influence Sutherland, to get him back on the right track. Souster decided against Dudek's suggestion and, in October of 1951, announced his intention to produce a new little magazine:

...we plan to bring out the first issue of a new mimeographed magazine of verse to be called *Contact* in February. We want to feature translations, experimental writing from Canada and the USA, the odd poetry review, the emphasis on vigour and excitement. MAKE IT NEW is our unofficial slogan.[2]

Dudek was quick to support Souster's idea for an experimental mimeographed magazine. Anne Wilkinson and George Nasir were slated to be involved with the magazine's production, but they both dropped out of the project. Dudek became Souster's main source of moral support, and a main link in the development of *Contact*. Dudek had lived in New York for seven years, where he had become familiar with some American writers and had established a correspondence with Ezra Pound. As Michael Gnarowski notes:

It was this set of Dudek's connections with American writers and poets, to say nothing of his pre-occupation with Ezra Pound, which urged *Contact* along the road of literary internationalism — both North American and European. The pressure of this influence coincided neatly with Raymond Souster's own desire for a magazine with a policy of wider orientation, and placed *Contact* in diametrical opposition to the specially defined and circumscribed nationalism of John Sutherland and *Northern Review*.[3]

When he was one of the editors of *Direction*, Souster demonstrated an interest in American writing and showed admiration for Henry Miller and Kenneth Patchen. During the summer of 1951 Souster and his wife visited Montreal and met with Dudek. One incident was to have a major influence on Souster's poetic development. As he relates it:

57

I'll always remember the day at the farm on the Little Jesus River, with Louis Dudek throwing the first two issues of Cid Corman's *Origin* down on the picnic table and saying "this is typical of what the nuts in New York are doing these days." I remember casually flipping through both copies and then giving them back to him—I was not yet ready for Charles Olson and Robert Creeley. But the next year something led me back to those two issues, and then Louis came to Toronto in May and left me as a gift *The Collected Later Poems of William Carlos Williams*. From that time on my world of poetry assumed largely its present shape.[4]

Souster would, in time, establish literary relationships with the *Origin* group, and also with W. C. Williams. In particular, Corman, Creeley, and Olson would have a significant impact upon *Contact*.

The first issue of *Contact* appeared in January 1952. It contained poems by Layton, Dudek, A. G. Bailey, Kenneth Patchen, and others. Souster wrote a short review of Layton's *The Black Huntsman*, which had been privately printed, and he reproduced the title poem. The other piece of significant prose was Dudek's opening editorial/article, "Où Sont Les Jeunes?" The first paragraph sounded the call for a new beginning in Canadian poetry:

Poetry in Canada needs a new start. To the young, the field is wide open. Our younger poets are getting grey about the temples. The work of the forties is by now old and yellow: it was a good beginning, but not yet the real thing. There is now a ready audience for any young writer with something fresh and bouncing to say, someone with a new technique, a vision, or a gift for making art out of matters of fact. But where are the young? Where is the "new" generation?[5]

A new generation *would* emerge out of the middle 1950s, a diversified group, including Leonard Cohen, Avi Boxer, Alden Nowlan, D. G. Jones, Phyllis Webb, Gael Turnbull, Eli Mandel, Henry Moscovitch, and Daryl Hine. Yet one gets the feeling that the generation Dudek was looking for was not this group. Rather it was the "New Wave Canada" explosion of the 1960s that would fulfil such expectations, and then Souster was the editor willing and eager to define the New Wave.

Within the pages of *Contact* we do not see the emergence of a new generation; rather we see the forward movement of several poets who had begun and been trained in the forties, and who now were ready to move ahead. Layton, Souster, and Dudek sought to fulfil what Dudek defined as the needs of Canadian poetry: "Canada needs poets who will have learned from the experimental and realistic writing of the last ten years and who will go on from there."[6] In the course of his article Dudek notes some of the elements of this forward-moving poetry: raw imagination, an ability to write social realism, a knowledge of the craft of free verse, a concern with the concrete rather than the abstract, and a poetry that is alive with energy and thought. He avers: "Poetry today aims at making the major integration of life."[7]

In the course of their correspondence, Dudek had suggested that Souster contact Cid Corman, the editor of *Origin*. Souster sent Corman a copy of the first issue of *Contact*, and asked that Corman put him in touch with young writers Corman thought promising. In his reply, Corman indicated his dissatisfaction with the material in *Contact* but approved of the energy behind the magazine and promised to relay some of the writers in the *Origin* group to Souster. Corman was critical of the Canadian content in the second issue as well, finding it somewhat amateurish; he stepped in to influence the direction of *Contact* and to provide it with much of its "international" flavour. Gnarowski has assessed Souster's position after two issues of *Contact*:

> The alternatives were obvious. If Canada was not producing the kind of work that was needed, then *Contact* could either settle for second best, or go to the United States and Europe for more impressive material. And here, Corman really came into his own. Not only did he impress the importance of Charles Olson and Robert Creeley on Souster, but his own far-ranging interests "internationalized" *Contact* to an extent to which no other Canadian little magazine had ever aspired. Corman supplied translations of the work of Gottfried Benn, George Forestier, Octavio Paz, Rene de Obaldia and Guillaume Apollinaire. More translated material would be forthcoming from other sources, so much that by the time *Contact* ceased publication, the magazine had featured selections from Jacques Prévert, George Seferis, Jean Cocteau and Anna Akmatova, providing in the case of the latter one of the rare occasions when her work found its way into English translation.[8]

The third issue of *Contact* contained a significant number of poems by members of the *Origin* group. William Bronk, Vincent Ferrini, Charles Olson, and Samuel French Morse appeared in the company of Irving Layton, Avi Boxer, and Phyllis Webb. Souster never contributed poetry to *Contact*, but he wrote the occasional comment or article. In the third issue, in an article titled "A Note on *Origin*," he introduced the readers of *Contact* to Corman and his group. Summarizing the work of *Origin*, Souster noted:

[Charles] Olson is the key figure in this resourcing of creative effort. His distinction lies in his having assimilated the richest part of Pound's and Cummings' achievement and then adding his personal intelligence, a most penetrating and widespread intelligence to a driving passionate voice. He has recognized that poetry derives from the speech we use; that that is its norm and no other. Poetry becomes the voice's most articulate strategy.[9]

Souster calls Olson's essay, "Projective Verse," a "brilliant article" and quotes from it several paragraphs dealing with speech and language. Comparing Olson's verse with Souster's, it is difficult to see the bearing of the one upon the other, or where the relation, if any, resides; we note, however, that the great liberating principle implicit in Olson's "Projective Verse" is the notion that poetry derives from human speech in its common form. This approach to poetry is apparent in Souster's easy, colloquial style. (One might even argue that Souster, in his poetry, is more true to the language as it is spoken than Olson in some of his more syntactically complex moments.)

Corman was judging *Contact* by an international standard, and finding it wanting. But it was also possible to look at *Contact* in light of what it provided for Canadian poetry. In this context, the Canadian content was not second-rate; rather, it was perceived as a great improvement on what was being printed in Sutherland's *Northern Review*. Above all, the purpose of *Contact*, and Contact Press, was to revitalize the flagging Canadian poetry scene. In *Northern Review*, Sutherland sought to place the sickly Canadian poetry in a closed oxygen tent; Souster seemed to think that what it needed, above all else, was a transfusion.

Despite Corman's criticism of Canadian writing, Souster continued to publish Canadians as well as international contributors. The fourth issue presents a blend of international and Canadian content: it contains work by George Seferis and Rainer M. Gerhardt, along with poems by Eli Mandel, Malcolm Miller, Louis Dudek, and Irving Layton. It also includes sections of Layton's and Dudek's prefaces from *Cerberus*. Dudek makes the point that "Language is the great saving first poem, always being written; all others are made of it."[10] Layton attacks the "gentility," "propriety," and "respectability" that have overtaken Canadian poetry; as an alternative, he proposes Whitman's "barbaric yawp." Layton's attack is seconded, in volume two, number one, by Charles Olson, in his short poem "These Days." The poem reiterates an approach to poetry that was begun in Canada with the *First Statement* group, and that has become the abiding trend since the early sixties:

```
        whatever you have to say
leave the roots on, let them
dangle
And the dirt
                    just to make clear
                    where they came from[11]
```

With the members of the *Origin* group, Dudek and Souster shared their primary poetic sources, the joint masters of the Canadian and Black Mountain group — Ezra Pound and William Carlos Williams. The directives of these two poets, "Make it new" and "No ideas but in things," were guiding principles for these young Canadian and American poets. Pound had made a terrific impact on Dudek and on Olson; yet, in many ways, Dudek and Olson were worlds apart. And so it was with the others. Far from forming a united front or super-school of North American poetry, the *Cerberus* group and the *Origin* group merely appeared side by side in *Contact*; they never became, in any sense, a collective unit. In September 1952, seeking a greater internationalism, Corman suggested the merging of *Origin*, *Contact*, and an English little magazine, *Window*; this move was resisted by Dudek and Souster. As Gnarowski puts it, "Dudek had practical objections as well, but worry about the work and influence of *Contact* being diverted from the Canadian scene was of prime importance."[12] Souster refused to become part of an international cooperative; at the same time, he resisted Dudek's suggestion that Dudek and Layton take a greater part in the running of *Contact*. Despite the influence of Corman, of Dudek, of Layton, and despite suggestions from Robert Creeley, *Contact* was very much Raymond Souster's magazine. Although he accepted advice, the final editorial decisions were always his own.

Souster wanted a magazine that would break national and provincial boundaries. For too long, Canadian writing had been shut in upon itself and had looked at itself in a mirror of its own making. As Sutherland had pointed out, the Canadian critic was too quick to praise Canadian writing *because* it was Canadian. Such criticism had led to the promotion of much second-rate material. Sutherland began, however, to judge Canadian writing in relation to what he considered to be the established Canadian and English poetic traditions.

The eighth issue of *Contact* featured a quotation from William Carlos Williams: "Think of 'English' and 'American' as one language among us called the 'old' and the 'new' language."[13] Canadian poetry was more related to new American writing than to the old, worn-out traditions and verbal machinations of the English bards. Another instructive note is included in the same issue, this one from Ezra Pound, taken from his correspondence with Dudek:

> naturally to HELL with Canadian or any other parrochial pt/ of view... BUT a live review/not merely one of these art-shop fly leaves/ has got to be based on understanding of LIFE.... "NOT trying to get a teaparty or suppress data in favor of pink punks".... "Hell No/git yr/eye off Canada and onto internat/criteria/"[14]

Clearly, with *Contact*, Souster was trying to place Canadian writing in the context of international writing and to have it judged on the basis of its inherent value rather than upon its significance to a burgeoning national literature. Articles on writers who were not Canadian (George Seferis, W. C. Williams, and Gottfried Benn) appeared in the pages of *Contact*. As well, certain Canadian books were reviewed by the *Origin* group. Cid Corman's assessment of *Canadian Poems 1850–1952*, edited by Dudek and Layton, appeared in the sixth issue of *Contact* (February–April 1953). Creeley's "A Note On Poetry" (volume two, number two) is a comprehensible explanation of the general ideas outlined by Olson in "Projective Verse," and his "A Note On Canadian Poetry" (number eight) is an impressionistic recounting of a Frenchman who had written poetry while making the voyage to this continent with Champlain. Following an idea proposed by Pound to Dudek—"A periodical runs by getting a lot of contacts/NOT by isolation in a circle of diminishing purists or devotees of some one idea"—the magazine ran upon its "contacts."[15]

In his account of the history of the magazine, Gnarowski maintains that Dudek, Corman, and Creeley lost interest in the magazine, and this led Souster to cease publication. In fact, several things happened concurrently. Dudek, in 1953, became involved with the running of *CIV/n*, a new magazine in Montreal; Corman seemed more concerned with *Origin* as his effect on Souster waned; and Creeley was beginning to teach at Black Mountain College and to edit the *Black Mountain Review*. Souster's time was also taken up with the operation of Contact Press, which was becoming the most vital small press in Canada. In February 1954 Souster contacted Dudek, Creeley, and Corman to inform them that *Contact* number ten was to be the last issue. The cover of that issue carried the following notice:

> *Contact*, an international magazine of modern poetry...wishes to thank both readers and contributors for the support they have given it over the past two years. They regret having to give up the magazine,

but find it impossible to continue it with the limited free time at their disposal. The companion magazine of Contact Press, *CIV/n*, is however still very much alive, and we know that many of our readers and poets will support this outstanding quarterly, which is now also international in scope and welcomes a wider range of material.[16]

In its two years, *Contact* presented an alternative to the conservative policies of *Northern Review*. "Contacts" had been made. Ironically, the *Origin/*Black Mountain poets were to have a much greater impact on the poetry of the sixties. The "Black Mountain" poetic would literally revolutionize Canadian poetry and stimulate the "new wave" of the sixties. Souster, completely sympathetic to this development, would anthologize the revolution in his Contact Press anthology *New Wave Canada*. The shift in alliance from British to American influences would finally be achieved; *Contact* played an extremely important part in this shift.

Souster's attempts, through *Contact*, to counter the effects of *Northern Review* were bolstered by the appearance of *CIV/n*, a magazine that originated in Montreal early in 1953. *CIV/n* ran for seven issues; the last two were published after the demise of *Contact*. Louis Dudek has recounted how *CIV/n* came into being:

> It was a mimeographed magazine for the first five numbers, printed for the last two. The initial move to start the magazine came from the Editor Aileen Collins. She had with her two close friends and assistants who completed the nominal editorial board, Stanley and Wanda Rozynski, a married couple.... When Miss Collins, however, put the suggestion for a magazine before me, I offered help and advice, and proposed that manuscripts be read by a larger group including Layton and myself, and that Aileen Collins and the Rozynskis edit the magazine in the light of our group discussions. There was always a tactful solicitude on the part of Layton and myself not to interfere with the editorial freedom of the actual editors. We read the poetry before a group at Layton's house, enjoying free comments and debate over the poems, but we made no decisions and left the final choice of what was to go into the magazine up to the Editor.[17]

Despite Dudek's contention that he and Layton tried to stay in the background, their presence was very much felt. The title of the magazine itself came from Dudek, who took it from a statement of Ezra Pound's: "CIV/n not a

63

one-man job." The production work and distribution were handled by Aileen Collins and the Rozynskis, but much of the energy expressed in the magazine stems from Layton and Dudek, and particularly from Dudek.

Like *Contact*, *CIV/n* started out as a Canadian production and gradually worked towards a broader orientation. By early 1953 *Contact* had already started to include international content, as Souster was influenced by Cid Corman and the *Origin* group. *CIV/n*, at first, resisted this pull. The first issue featured a selection of Canadian writers from the forties and fifties: poems by Phyllis Webb, Dudek (who also contributed under the pseudonym "Alexander St. John Swift"), Avi Boxer, Layton, Souster, D. G. Jones, E. W. Mandel, and Patrick Anderson. The issue contained no editorial. On the first page, below the somewhat cryptic title, appeared the explicit statement "Civilization is not a one man job." The poems contained in the issue reflect a certain social consciousness and show a concern for the prospects of civilization in Canada.

The second issue continued in the style of the first, and included poems by Layton, Gael Turnbull, Souster, Avi Boxer, D. G. Jones, Ralph Gustafson, and Alexander St. John Swift. There was also a section called "Views & Reviews," which contained three reviews: one by James Boyer May of *Canadian Poems 1850–1952* (which was edited by Dudek and Layton); one of Kenneth Rexroth's *The Dragon and the Unicorn* by Dudek; and one of *Cerberus* by Neil Compton. In his review, Dudek argued that poetry needed vitality:

> *The Dragon and the Unicorn* may serve as an example of what can be done to give poetry the guts it needs, to win it back from the pasty sold-out intellectuals and critics and place it in the centre of the fight for reality and reason.[18]

This fight for reality and reason is reflected in Compton's evaluation of *Cerberus*, the first publication of Contact Press, which contained prefaces and poems by Dudek, Layton, and Souster. As Compton sees it, the fight is for a vital language and literature. In his short review, Compton concentrates on the common ground to be found in the poems included in *Cerberus*.

> As Dudek says, "We three in this book share the same affirmations and therefore the same negations in the face of the present." More than that, they constitute a recognizable school in Modern poetry. All three are confident of the social value of art, and agree that the hatred of art which characterizes official culture in Canada is symptomatic of our social sickness; all three are non-conformists and iconoclasts of that most dangerous type (to flabby conformity) which finds its ideal subversive expression in the uninhibited *yawp* of positive affirmation:

each manages to equate a healthy contempt for things-as-they-are with a (perhaps illogical) confidence in the possibilities for the future.[19]

In its poetry and critical views, *CIV/n*, with *Contact*, represented an opposition to the reactionary trends of *Northern Review*, just as Layton, Dudek, and Souster provided an alternative to writers such as Douglas Le Pan, James Wreford Watson, and Charles Bruce. Yet, despite this, Ezra Pound (who was incarcerated at St. Elizabeth's Hospital in Washington, DC and who maintained a correspondence with Dudek) did not look favourably upon the work *CIV/n* was doing. In a letter received by Dudek in late April 1953, Pound, in response to the second issue of *CIV/n*, remarked that "surely among all these bright young things yu OUGHT to be able to find the makings of at least one polemical writer."[20] Pound also wanted the magazine to be international. Dudek himself assessed Pound's criticism:

The magazine was in fact extremely "polemical," but Pound only recognized as rightly polemical and "useful" those magazines which parrotted his little program to the letter.... We were very much for Pound, but we could not possibly serve him in the way he wanted. In fact, *CIV/n* had its own ego-personalities, and a very locally focussed Canadian program, so that it could not be entirely subordinated to Pound's internationalist ideas.[21]

Despite Pound's criticism, *CIV/n* continued to be primarily "locally focussed." The third issue featured poems by Waddington, Gustafson, Souster, Aileen Collins, Layton, Phyllis Webb, Gael Turnbull, and Dudek. Three poems by George Seferis appeared in translation; a poem and an article by Melech Ravitch were translated from the Yiddish by Layton. Also included was an article by Dudek on two books by H. A. Innis and one by Marshall McLuhan, *The Mechanical Bride*. Dudek was highly critical of these two writers for "compounding with Madison Avenue instead of making a radical criticism of illiterate culture; and also [for] turning away from the major arts to an exaggerated concern with the vaporous media, treating them, rather than the traditional arts, as the shaping forces of society."[22]

In response to the third issue Pound wrote: "CIV/ V [sic] o.k. for local centre / question whether D / has contact with anyone or any means interest in mag / standing for maximum awareness."[23] Pound also forwarded a statement, signed by ten university professors, that argued (in Poundist fashion) about the alarming state of the humanities. This was reprinted in *CIV/n* number four.

The fourth issue reflects an expansion in the scope of the magazine: work by members of Corman's *Origin* group is included. The issue contains poems by Webb, Dudek, Creeley, Layton, Boxer, Leonard N. Cohen, Corman, Souster, and D. G. Jones. The bulk of the prose writing is concerned with Pound. Dudek's review of Pound's translations looks at Pound's skills as a poet and translator. There is an "editorial" of sorts, written by Dudek, titled "Why is Ezra Pound Being Held in St. Elizabeth's Hospital, Washington, DC?" Dudek asks to have Pound set free; two quotations from writers in Ireland also call for Pound's release. Finally, there is an article by Camillo Pellizzi, translated from the Italian, called "Ezra Pound: A Difficult Man," which presents a personal view of Pound by someone who knew him in Italy during the war years. Pellizzi maintains that Pound never committed treasonable acts against the United States. Although *CIV/n* may not have followed Pound's criteria for what a magazine should be, it certainly took up his political cause in this issue.

Also in the fourth issue is an article by D. G. Jones called "The Question of Language Prostitution." Jones contrasts the way language is used in literature — in the cause of truth — and in advertising — in the cause of sales. A concern with the media was quite noticeable in *CIV/n*. The magazine's contributors, particularly Dudek, were sensitive to the development of post-war media and saw in the media a serious threat to literary language and to literature. (Dudek was completing his book *Literature And The Press* at this time.)

In the fifth issue of *CIV/n*, Aileen Collins wrote a column called "Letters From The Editor." She comments on what she calls "Canadian Culture":

> Culture...is the main topic today, for CBC radio talks, letters in *Saturday Night*, etc, etc, etc....
>
> Now, to me, it doesn't matter half a damn whether we ever achieve a "Canadian Culture" — or not. Nothing will be done until we start concentrating on producing *poetry* without qualifications as to nation. But a poet in Canada is forced to write with maple syrup on birch bark (which will insure his being included in any later anthologies edited by Birney, probably under the classification "Natural Resources").
>
> The kind of poetry we want will be a vital representation of what things are, done in strong language (if necessary) or any language, but it will force the reader to see just what the world around him is like.[24]

Collins's call for a realistic and vital poetry allies *CIV/n* to *First Statement* in the requirements set for Canadian poetry. Issue number five also announces the demise of *Contact*.

The fifth issue strengthened the relationship with the *Origin* group. Robert Creeley appears in company with Layton, Turnbull, Dudek, Cohen, Souster, and Anne Wilkinson; there is an extended review by Dudek of books by Paul Blackburn, Charles Olson, and Robert Creeley. Olson, who was the main theorizer of the Black Mountain group, is today considered the poet, among that group, of the greatest poetic achievement. Dudek's review reveals why the Canadian *Cerberus* trio and the Black Mountain/*Origin* group never formed a unified movement. Dudek is critical of Olson's method of composition; he argues that "One can see the private-monologue-in-private-shorthand menacing us all along the way from 1915,"[25] and he finds this shorthand in Olson's writing. Olson, he says, is an imitator of Pound, and has also been influenced by the poetic theories of William Carlos Williams. Commenting on the theory of Projective Verse, Dudek notes:

> The theory, bluntly, is that poetry is not an art form: it is a lump of coral that grows onto the living substance of life, or personality, and contains the shape and rhythm of reality. The test is authenticity.
>
> But when life itself has lost all shape — as the right flank, directed by Eliot, has long ago made clear — you cannot make art out of the literal record. A vivid picture of the city dump, or of the private dump of one's own conscious or unconscious, makes no poem. Everyone knows that: but we are often heading more or less toward that last stand.[26]

Dudek argues against Olson's approach — that is, composition by field. His criticism, however, is followed, in the issue, by Creeley's "A Note On Poetry," which is an affirmation of the Black Mountain poetic approach.

The last two issues of *CIV/n* continued to develop the contact between the American and Canadian groups. The sixth issue presented the work of Jacques Prévert, Creeley, Jonathan Williams, and Charles Olson, juxtaposed with poems by Aileen Collins, F. R. Scott, Gael Turnbull, Phyllis Webb, Anne Wilkinson, D. G. Jones, A. J. M. Smith, Dudek, Layton, and Souster. The magazine was still very much rooted in the context of Canadian poetry, but this third stage of Modernism in Canada had its eyes open to the possibilities of poetry beyond national and regional boundaries. Canadian poetry would no longer be viewed in provincial terms or limited to parochial perspectives.

The seventh issue featured characteristic work by the young Leonard Cohen, and also work by Dudek, Layton, and Creeley. Layton was the prime essayist. In "Shaw, Pound, and Poetry," he agreed with George Bernard Shaw and Ezra Pound that power in our time is founded upon money; he also wrote a piece on Souster's *Crepe Hanger's Carnival*. Both essays lashed out against some force or group that Layton saw as oppressors of poetry; in the Shaw–Pound essay it is the bourgeois class that leads to the perversion of art and morality; in the Souster article the enemies are "pompous ignoramuses"[27] — the critics. Layton contended that the monopolies of these groups must be broken.

In its time *CIV/n*, like *Contact*, both resisted the regressive tendency in poetry that stemmed out of the late forties and also pushed poetry forward to a condition of Modernism resting on the most solid of foundations. Although the socialist verse of the forties had suffered a defeat, social force and consciousness were still necessary in verse, as were moral integrity and commitment to language. The narrow tradition that held Canadian poetry in the forties had to be broken, and this process was begun in the pages of *Contact* and *CIV/n*. Layton, Souster, and Dudek appeared side-by-side with Olson, Creeley, Corman, and others of the Black Mountain group because they all shared a tangible commitment to poetry, to keep it moving ahead and to write it in the real language of the day.

The Montreal magazine *Yes* appeared in 1956, and the spadework that had been done by Souster and Dudek in *Contact* and *CIV/n* was taken for granted. There was no need to chart a new course for Canadian poetry: a positive direction had already been established. Edited by three young Montreal poets — Michael Gnarowski, Glen Siebrasse, and John Lachs — *Yes* first appeared in April of 1956 and quickly established itself as an eclectic magazine that continued the tradition of social realism and its early-fifties aftermath. The founding editorial stated no hard-line program; rather it defined what the editors felt was the function of the little magazine, and affirmed literary expression:

> A new magazine has come to Montreal. Perhaps the thought of a city that could clothe its people in the periodicals it sells does not make this seem an impressive accomplishment. Yet a distinction must be made here; for the professional efforts that roll their paper like two-legged beavers are quite apart from the phenomenon known as the "little magazines." These productions, such as Fredericton's "Fiddlehead," are not devoted to making money (heaven forbid), but rather to providing a stimulating and indispensible literature. Especially in such fields as poetry, which is not commercially attractive, is this need fulfilled. Their other important contribution lies in the fact that they give encouragement to new talent by allowing them a medium in which to present themselves; people who, one day, might add weight to our cultural progress.

Unfortunately the little magazine movement in Canada has shown a tendency to lapse in recent years. It is to be hoped that this mimeographed effort will initiate a new phase of activity in this field so as to provide a suitable outlet for the commencing Renaissance of Canadian Writing.

Our magazine is called *Yes*. This is its attitude. It has been created for the writing of the second half of the twentieth century which we believe will once again be the expression of positive values. The world is a yes place — let us then say so.[28]

In saying yes to literature of the twentieth century and yes to quality, the editors of *Yes* were also saying yes to the direction that had been established by the social-realist movement. They felt no need to define a new direction for poetry. This was to be the mark of the Montreal poets of the sixties: their utter willingness to follow in the path that had been established by Souster, Layton, and Dudek. Glen Siebrasse and Michael Gnarowski would later ally themselves closely with Dudek; eventually, they participated in Dudek's Delta Canada, a small press that published books. At the time of the founding of *Yes*, however, the editors were resistant to Dudek's prodding that editorial policy be more definite than a mere yes to contemporary writing. In an editorial in the third issue, they defended their intention to remain free of any declared editorial policy:

In a letter to the editors Mr. Louis Dudek suggests that we come forward and state our views — advance an editorial, a policy. It seems to be an accepted custom with intellectuals since the days of the Marxian incarnation in 1848, to prepare at regular intervals manifestos in which humanity is neatly divided into two camps, the world interpreted in terms of Manichaean struggle of light and darkness, opinions are stated, policies outlined. A similarly incisive declaration of allegiance is demanded of all others, to aid the enterprise of cut and dried classification in the proper filing cabinets of the mind. People who talk little are not well liked; one does not know what to expect of them....

In our view it is not absolutely essential for a magazine devoted to publishing contemporary writing, to be factional and consequently to be unavailable to the majority of poets, who are then considered "outsiders." This is especially the case in Canada, where poetry has only just come to life a decade or so ago and where unfortunately so few little magazines serve the young poet.[29]

The editors made a strong avowal of their eclecticism, and maintained it for most of the magazine's life. Significantly, however, Dudek began a new magazine, *Delta*, nine months after *Yes* was started. *Delta*'s first editorial included some words on the need for sometimes saying no. An open-door policy in little magazines makes them valuable only until another magazine with a pertinent policy emerges and reveals the need for a clear line of progression. It is for this reason that *Yes* exists as a minor accomplishment as compared with *Delta* and *Tish*, two of its immediate contemporaries.

The editorial in the first issue of *Yes* made it clear that the magazine was to be a medium for new talent, although the new talent, at first, was that of the editors themselves. Gnarowski was honing his academic and poetic skills; poems by Siebrasse and Lachs appeared regularly. In addition, there were old and new Montreal poets: Dudek, Layton, George Ellenbogen, Daryl Hine, Henry Moscovitch, Lionel Tiger, F. R. Scott, Milton Acorn, and Al Purdy. Over several editorial shake-ups and moves Gnarowski maintained control. Lachs dropped out after issue number nine (he left to teach in Maryland, and to publish books of philosophy there); Siebrasse disappeared from the masthead for two issues and was temporarily replaced by an American editor, Donald M. Winkelman. Then Winkelman vanished and Siebrasse returned, with Hugh Hood in tow in the role of associate editor, for issues twelve to fourteen. From the fifteenth issue until the magazine's termination, the editors were Gnarowski and Siebrasse. The magazine also changed location several times as Gnarowski changed academic posts; it moved from Montreal to Port Arthur, Ontario, then to Pierrefonds, Quebec. Perhaps because of these moves, the magazine never came to encompass the burgeoning Montreal scene of the sixties. (*Cataract*, edited by Seymour Mayne, K. V. Hertz, and Leonard Angel, was perhaps more successful.)

As an eclectic magazine, *Yes* hit its stride with issues thirteen to sixteen. The editorial in issue number thirteen recounts the latest developments in the early sixties Dudek–Layton feud. The issue also features a section of Layton's poems with an introduction by Gnarowski, and includes interesting work by Souster, Hood, Fred Cogswell, Milton Acorn, and Siebrasse. Number fourteen contains sections from Dudek's *Atlantis* as well as notebook entries, and poems by Everson, Gustafson, Douglas Barbour, and A. J. M. Smith. Issue fifteen features John Glassco, along with poems by Barry McKinnon, Tom Marshall, Michael Harris, Don Gutteridge, Souster, and Dudek. The sixteenth issue of *Yes* contains work by Purdy, Victor Coleman, Tom Marshall, Joan Finnigan, Michael Ondaatje, John Wieners, Henry Beissel, and Alden Nowlan. *Yes* seemed to be fulfilling its original aims by 1967. But a two-year silence ensued after issue number sixteen; when number seventeen appeared in October of 1969, an editorial announced a turnabout in policy.

A question which has been much on our minds and one which needs raising in connection with the revival of this magazine concerns the sum total of what has been happening to poetry in the last few years.

When we started *Yes* in 1956 we believed that the directions for poetry in this country were clear. We believed that the poem had to be rooted in real experience; we believed in a style and content which would be of this country but which would also recognize its North American contact. Furthermore, ours was a literary fundamentalism which saw the poem as deriving from an artistic and reassuring faith in the creativity of people, and we believed that literary values and aspirations had been democratized. We believed that popular art could be great; we did not know that great art could not be popular. For us the line of descent was clear. From Whitman and along lines laid down by the man from Idaho. Since we believed in Walter Whitman more than in Professor Henry Wadsworth Longfellow, it followed that we would believe more in Raymond Souster than in Professor Arthur James Marshall Smith. The spirit of the man... damn it...it was the spirit of the man that was close to us. Had Whitman not — in a style which would become the hallowed modus operandi of little presses and their people, of First Statement and Contact — had he not designed and published his own first edition of *Leaves of Grass*? Therefore, Masters and Sandburg and Williams were good and important. Therefore, Sutherland's position (which was ours and we don't give a damn about the Pratt bit) — Sutherland's position formed on the left with Layton and Dudek and Souster. Therefore, there was no need for manifestos in 1956...just a shift from the social realism of the First Statementers to a sharper urban focus and a greater interest in the possibilities of the image the new context was beginning to provide. But it didn't work out. If we had valued the hard-edged directness of the colloquial poem, we saw it become amorphous and formless. If we believed in the technique of the unaffected, we have seen it transformed into spurious disquisitions on "poesy" and the artful poses of projectivism. If we believed that poetry was somehow "against this sea of stupidities"; "against this sea of vulgarities"; "against this sea of imbeciles" we have found that stupidities, imbecilities and vulgarities have become the stuff of poetry. Someone had made the wrong move back in 1952-1954. Souster and *Contact* magazine may have helped to make that first move. Souster and *Combustion* may have helped to make that move again in 1957-1960. *Tish* ended the game. And after that the little Millwins, and the turbulent and undisciplined host of poets. And the audience. No, not the few, not readers and lovers of perfection; not with knowledge or a fine sense, but the tolerant, confused, parasitic consumers of mass-cult. Poetry has married a truly ugly wife.

Now, where do we begin?[30]

The editorial also denounces the Vancouver movement and the "new wave" of poetry that had arisen in the 1960s, which was clearly influenced by the American Black Mountain poets. It is a reaffirmation of the social realism that had emerged out of the forties, and that continued as the mode in Montreal poetry of the sixties. But by 1969 the social-realist mode of writing had been eclipsed and a new fashion had been adopted by most of the young poets writing in Canada. The magazine sought to work poetry back towards a more productive vein. Unfortunately, the new *Yes* was to last for only three more issues.

The emergence of *Yes* in 1956 was followed by two personal little magazines in 1957: Raymond Souster's *Combustion* and, later in the year, Louis Dudek's *Delta*. Both of these magazines reflected the personalities and tastes of their editors — like *Northern Review* in the Sutherland-dominated years, each represented the programs of a single man. But neither *Combustion* nor *Delta* was reactionary. The two magazines broke new ground rather than follow outmoded poetic traditions. Both editors made a concerted effort to find young poets who would provide Canadian poetry with its next forward development. Like Contact Press, the magazines provided publication for those who had no access to commercial publishers.

The precedent for an international poetry magazine had been set in 1952 when Raymond Souster started *Contact*, a publication designed to counter the reactionary nationalism prevalent at the time. When *Contact* folded in 1954, *CIV/n* continued to maintain the traditions *Contact* had initiated; *CIV/n*, however, only outlasted *Contact* by two issues. By 1957 a general atmosphere of dullness had once again fallen upon poetry in Canada. In the United States the *Origin*/Black Mountain group was writing innovative verse; north of the border Dudek, Souster, and Layton were also writing. The impetus for poetry was not lacking; rather, the general atmosphere, which the writers saw as increasingly "academic," was stifling and unproductive. Souster's *Combustion*, first printed in January of 1957, was an attempt to counteract the doldrums.

Combustion, which was mimeographed, was sent to a select mailing list (a procedure that was adopted by *Tish* and *GrOnk* in the 1960s and several magazines in the 1970s). Like *Contact*, *Combustion* was launched with a direct and straightforward editorial, in which Souster expressed his opposition to the academic tendency in verse. In the tradition of Lawrence and Henry Miller, he was rooting for writing that is vital and deals directly with human experience.

One can see the pulls that had been exercised upon *Contact* magazine: Corman trying to influence Souster to forget about Canadian content and lobbying for a true international content; Dudek reminding Souster that the first purpose of the magazine was to help foster a viable and vital Canadian poetry. In *Combustion* the Corman influence won out. *Combustion* is a Canadian magazine by virtue of the fact that it was printed in Toronto and edited by a Canadian. On the basis of contents it might just as well be considered an American little magazine. The list of poets included in *Combustion* anticipates those who were to be included in Donald Allen's anthology, *The New American Poetry* (1945-1960). American poets Jonathan Williams, Cid Corman, Charles Olson, Allen Ginsberg, Jack Kerouac, Gregory Corso, Michael McClure, Ron Loewinsohn, Denise Levertov, Theodore Enslin, Larry Eigner, Gary Snyder, Fielding Dawson, Robert Duncan, Philip Whalen, Louis Zukofsky, and Leroi Jones all appeared in the magazine's pages. To a great extent *Combustion* points in the direction of the American influence that was to be so marked in Canada with the young poets of the sixties. Many of these American poets would be looked upon as the mentors of the next generation of Canadian poets. *Combustion* also printed the work of Canadian poets, but one is impressed by the vast amount of work by this group of Americans and by European poets in translation. Many of the translations were provided by Cid Corman; in fact, Corman may be said to have "edited" the foreign material in *Combustion*, just as Ezra Pound "edited" the London poetry in Harriet Monroe's *Poetry* in 1912 and 1913. Nevertheless, in *Combustion* Souster was opening up the poetic horizon for Canada; in its internationalism, *Combustion* stands as the antithesis of Sutherland's *Northern Review*, since it presented translations of Japanese, German, Chinese, French, Finnish, Italian, and Latin American poets. Canadian poets were constantly juxtaposed to foreign poets in the pages of the magazine.

Combustion was run in a fashion similar to *Contact*. Apart from some commentary, Souster's own work never appeared in the magazine. There are few editorial statements; the emphasis is on the poetry itself. No arguments are made for a specific approach to Canadian poetry; rather, an international atmosphere is taken for granted, and Canadian poetry is judged by international criteria, rather than in local or parochial terms. Poets who would be important to the development of Canadian poetry in the 1960s appeared in *Combustion*'s pages, among them Alden Nowlan, Al Purdy, Milton Acorn, Margaret Avison, and John Robert Colombo. The energy and interest generated in *Combustion* would continue through the 1960s.

Dudek's *Delta* was the last significant magazine to begin publication in the 1950s. The first issue of *Delta* appeared in October 1957. Like Souster's *Combustion*, *Delta* was a personal magazine, run under the editorship of one man and serving as an extension of the editor's intellectual concerns and literary tastes. Again like *Combustion*, *Delta* emerged in response to the needs of Canadian poetry in 1957. But *Delta* differed vastly from *Combustion* in that Dudek's sense of situation was entirely different from Souster's. A primary difference is that *Delta* was "a local affair," a magazine concerned with Canadian poetry rather than with broad internationalism. *Delta* differs from *Yes* in discriminating between what is relevant and important to contemporary writing and what is not. In many respects, *Delta* is the first avant-garde magazine intent upon rooting itself firmly in Canadian poetry. The main body of writing that appeared in *Delta* was Canadian in origin and sensibility; at the same time, Dudek tried to be aware of developments in writing outside of Canada. Because of *Delta*'s dedication to native writing, and its refusal to relapse into isolationism, it is more historically important than *Yes* or *Combustion*.

With *Delta*, Dudek wanted to inject some vitality into the Canadian literary scene, to try to redirect the course of Canadian poetry, through pertinent articles and criticism (often by Dudek himself); to foster energy and promote new movements among the young poets. *Delta* published a significant number of younger poets as well as those who had begun writing in the 1940s and early 1950s. Young poets such as Daryl Hine, George Ellenbogen, Michael Gnarowski, Al Purdy, Milton Acorn, John Lachs, Alden Nowlan, Gerry Gilbert, Joan Finnigan, Sylvia Barnard, Malcolm Miller, Michael Malus, Marquita Crevier, John Robert Colombo, Lionel Kearns, David Solway, George Bowering, Anne Szumigalski, Margaret Atwood, Frank Davey, Gwendolyn MacEwen, James Reid, Red Lane, John Newlove, Alan Pearson, Raymond Fraser, Pierre Coupey, Harry Howith, Tom Marshall, Steve Smith, Victor Coleman, and Seymour Mayne all appeared in the pages of *Delta* during its nine-year, twenty-six-issue run. Dudek's policy was to publish new young writers; this policy was evident in his small-press activity as well. Young writers were published in the McGill Poetry Series and later by Delta Canada Press. When a new movement appeared in Vancouver, with the publication of *Tish* in 1961, Dudek was quick to devote an issue to the new Vancouver poetry. (The editor of *Tish*, Frank Davey, selected the contents of issue number nineteen, October 1962, *New Vancouver Poetry*.) Although *Delta* was very much a magazine edited by one individual, it was open to new contributors. Though Dudek was by conviction a social realist, he was willing to publish those who did not belong to the same branch of poetry. In the first issue of *Delta*, he reviewed F. R. Scott's *The Eye of the Needle* and Jay Macpherson's *The*

Boatman; in the review he attempted to challenge current critical opinion on these books by pointing out the inherent value of Scott's experimental and realist poetry, then somewhat disparaged, and the defects of Jay Macpherson's formal mythopoeic work, which had been highly lauded. Yet, despite the criticism of Miss Macpherson, a healthy sampling of her work appeared in the next issue.

Although Dudek was capable of considerable liberality in his selection of material for *Delta*, he was not publishing an eclectic magazine. In numerous editorials and articles he defined a very clear position on the current state of the arts. In several articles ("Julian Huxley, Robert Graves, and the Mythologies," number four; "Frye Again [But Don't Miss Souster]," number five; "Northrop Frye's Untenable Position," number twenty-two), he disputed the mythopoeic doctrine of Northrop Frye. Frye contended that literature exists as a self-enclosed medium, a frame in which it is continually relating to itself, and that it bears no relation to life. Dudek, ever the rationalist, consistently argued in favour of a rationalistic approach to poetry, as against a mythopoeic approach, such as Frye's or that of the Canadian poets influenced by Frye (James Reaney, Jay Macpherson, and Eli Mandel). He also argued for the experimental development of free-verse form in poetry against the reactionary return to metrics that was evident in the 1950s in all North American universities. He also continued to investigate the relationship between literature and the commercial press. He fought a constant battle for freedom, honesty, and integrity in poetry as an art; he opposed what he saw as commercial degradation or the theoretical elaboration of the academies.

Delta printed its last issue in October 1966. By then, the general atmosphere of Canadian poetry had changed significantly. Many of the young writers Dudek had included in *Delta* had begun to develop their own individual voices and had begun to define a new age in Canadian poetry. *Delta* played an important part in the new poetic developments by providing a bridge from the developments of the fifties into the sixties. The sixties would present new schools of poetry within the context of new little magazines. This generation would draw their inspiration from a wide variety of sources, but an indigenous tradition of poetic development and a Modernist foundation would already have been laid down for them by preceding groups and little magazines.

5

New Wave Canada

Struggling to keep Modernism alive in the 1950s, Louis Dudek, Raymond Souster, and the other magazine editors would have had no idea of the vast literary proliferation that was to follow them in the sixties and seventies. In the sixties the course of Canadian poetry changed radically. Great pains had been taken to establish poetry as a valuable and vital minority interest, and suddenly there was poetry everywhere; indeed, Canada, at times, seemed as if it had become a country of poets. In addition to producing a vast quantity of poetry — there were ten times as many books and magazines published — the sixties saw radical shifts in aesthetics: the ways in which poetry could be written increased considerably. The different elements that had been evident in early Modernism began, at long last, to appear in full force and to combine with the innovations of later poets and poetries.

There are many unusual aspects to the sudden poetry explosion in the sixties. Economic, sociological, educational, statistical, and technological developments affected the evolution of Canadian poetry. Without going too far into the sociology of literature I would like to note briefly some of the more important changes.

In the sixties, the post-war "baby-boom" generation began to come of age. There was a sudden population bulge that began to reflect itself in all aspects of society. Gradually, more people were available in all occupations and areas of interest. One would be able to predict, on this ground alone, that there would be more young people involved in poetry. Yet the number of poets writing in Canada at this time seems to increase out of all proportion to the population rise, indicating that there were other factors at work.

The sixties were years of significant social change in North America. In the United States, the civil-rights movement and the peace movement held the spotlight in the political arena, while rock music — and a whole style of life that seemed to derive from it, or to accompany it — affected a changing morality; this new morality embodied changes in sexual mores, in physical appearance, in attitudes towards work and the job market, and in the use of drugs. An

76

American generation that grew up in affluence seemed to reject that affluence, as well as the morality and the exploitive economic system that had produced such wealth. Much of the dissatisfaction with the social system was directed at the educational institutions, since these, it was argued, engaged in war research and moulded students to serve the corporate society's aims. Indeed, universities felt the force of the new social upheaval more than did the business interests that actually dominated the war economy.

In the universities, many students turned their backs on the business interests of their parents' generation and concentrated on the arts and humanities. More emphasis was placed upon individual creativity, and there was an increase in creative-writing classes and classes in all aspects of the fine arts. University people of the sixties were never very far away from the act of creation, and so the number of young poets, artists, and artisans multiplied.

Changes in the United States were felt in Canada. Canadian students demonstrated against the war in Vietnam and held sit-ins at universities, and changes in behaviour among youth became evident in Canada as well as in the United States.

For the young artist, economic conditions in Canada were also changing significantly. In 1953, after a two-year study, the Massey Commission recommended that a governmental body be formed to foster and promote the study and enjoyment of the arts. This recommendation resulted in the formation of the Canada Council, which began its operations in 1957. Although at first it offered assistance mainly to large performing institutions, it gradually began to offer aid in the form of grants to writers and publishers of books and periodicals. Thus, the young writer and magazine editor in the sixties had a new financial resource available to him.

There was also a revolution in printing in the early sixties. A new process, photo-offset, became available to those who could buy the printing equipment or hire printers. This technological advance provided a much faster and cheaper method of printing than letterpress; in fact, it has made possible instant-print facilities for little-magazine publication. The photo-offset revolution followed quickly on the heels of a mimeograph revolution of the fifties. A broad range of new printing facilities was made available to the burgeoning young poet.

What we find, then, in the generation of the sixties, is a body of young people who, in detective-story parlance, had opportunity, motive, and weapon. All signs indicated that the time and the country were ripe for poetry.

The little magazines in Canada from the twenties to the fifties have been fairly easy to chronicle and assess. The magazines of the sixties and seventies, though, are a bibliographer's dream of the flood, and they call for selective evaluation. An entire volume could be devoted to an indexing of the magazines of the period, another to critical evaluation. I propose instead to plot a course through the labyrinth of little-magazine publication of the last score of years mainly to emphasize the on-going Modernist development in the magazines, and to concentrate on the few important magazines relevant to that development. Specifically, I am concerned with following the Modernist line of succession. Yet, before proceeding with this task, some light can be thrown on the little-magazine movement as a whole.

The proliferation of little magazines in the sixties and seventies was a sudden burgeoning of Canadian literary life. The writing of poetry is no longer concentrated in major cities; it extends across the country and into the territories. Every little magazine that appears is useful to the poets whose work it promotes and to the community in which it appears. Hundreds of magazines have appeared during this period. A short list, limited to those that have registered some impact:

Island, Moment, Cataract, Evidence, Alphabet, Blew Ointment, Ganglia, GrOnk, Tish, Imago, Open Letter, Intercourse, Blackfish, Vigilante, Repository, Grain, Applegarth's Follies, Copperfield, It needs to be said, Northern Journey, The Golden Dog, CrossCountry, B.C. Monthly, Anthol, Air, White Pelican, CV/II, Ingluvin, Booster & Blaster, The Poem Company, 3¢ Pulp, Square Deal, Edge, Weed, Mountain, Hyphid, Is, Kontakte, Versus, Porcepic, Ellipse, Salt, Black Moss, Stuffed Crocodile, Mouse Eggs, Hh, Boreal, Matrix, and *The Front*

There have been, of course, a good many others, each of them serving some local or particular constituency. There have been coterie magazines *(Tish, Open Letter, Cataract)*; eclectic magazines *(Grain, Evidence, The Poem Company)*; regional magazines *(Salt, Copperfield, B.C. Monthly)*; magazines printing concrete poetry *(GrOnk, what is, Spanish Fleye)*; magazines emphasizing bilingualism *(Ellipse, The Golden Dog, Boreal)*; magazines that focus on the relation between poetry and politics *(Alive, It needs to be said)*; antinationalistic magazines *(CrossCountry)*; magazines filled with "serendipidity" *(Applegarth's Follies, Is)*; and even magazines that try to develop serious Canadian criticism *(CV/II)*. Add to this the many university magazines, and we have a very broad panorama of literary activity. If some of the magazines drift into conformity or cultivate conventional literary stuffiness rather than stand out as "true fighting little magazines," they at least all share a common commitment to literature.

The mags of the sixties and seventies we are interested in are all avant-garde periodicals; they continue to pioneer, to argue and debate the ground rules of poetry and the validity of specific aesthetic programmes. Much magazine activity falls outside this range; the majority of magazines that appear today operate on eclectic principles. Though interesting, they lack the bite of the magazine that promotes a shared aesthetic or a specific point of view, a conscious orientation.

A few specific magazines helped to create the atmosphere of the sixties. Though they do not represent the full dynamics of the era, they are significant magazines. The first of these is *Teangadoir*, which originated in Toronto in 1953, and was edited by Padraig O Broin and Hazel Yake. For the first four volumes of its existence it was a small Celtic literary journal. With the beginning of the fifth volume, in July 1961, the magazine began to publish Canadian work. (This was due, in part, to an extensive reading series then taking place at the Bohemian Embassy in Toronto, a café that had become a literary centre.)

The magazine was a modest pamphlet with a wrapping-paper cover. Throughout 1961 it published work by O Broin, Gwendolyn MacEwen, Luella Booth, Fred Cogswell, G. C. Miller, Al Purdy, Alden Nowlan, George Bowering, Milton Acorn, Joan Finnigan, and Gregory Cook. The March 1962 issue carried a review of the recently published anthology *Poetry 62*, which featured work by some of the more accomplished members of the new generation.

Another magazine, *Evidence*, began as a rather lacklustre quarterly publication. Also from Toronto, it was edited by Kenneth Craig. The first issue appeared in November 1960. Then the magazine changed editors and it became, under the editorship of Allan Bevan, one of the more important little magazines of the early sixties. Eclectic from the start, *Evidence* published a variety of work of different kinds. Slick and professional-looking, it served as an interesting meeting place for the different literary movements of the time. Poets from the *Tish*, *Moment*, and *Cataract* groups all appeared within its pages. For many of these poets, *Evidence* provided a first opportunity to see their work in "real" print, as opposed to Gestetner or mimeographed form.

Issues five and six are good examples of its eclecticism. In issue number five we find a story by George Bowering, poems by Eugene McNamara, Al Purdy, and Bryan McCarthy, and an essay, by Milton Acorn, entitled "I Was A Communist For My Own Damn Satisfaction." Issue number six featured poems by K. V. Hertz, Purdy, James Reaney, Acorn, Alan Pearson, Layton, David McFadden, and George Bowering as well as a section by Lionel Kearns called "Stacked Verse...a definition and four poems." Interestingly, some of the most accomplished essays written during this period by the *Tish* poets appeared in *Evidence*. Beginning with issue six, the magazine featured a lively review section. Issue number seven contained "Poems by the Ladies," work by Phyllis Gottlieb, Margaret Avison, Elizabeth Brewster, Jay Macpherson, Margaret Atwood, Denise Levertov, Miriam Waddington, and Gwendolyn MacEwen.

Evidence ceased publication in 1967.

One of its shorter-lived contemporaries was *Mountain*, edited by David McFadden out of Hamilton, Ontario. The first issue appeared in May of 1962. Like *Evidence, Mountain* was extremely eclectic. The first issue included poems by Acorn, O Broin, Frank Davey, MacEwen, Fred Wah, Hertz, Raymond Fraser, John Robert Colombo, David Cull, and Seymour Mayne. The second issue presented forty-four poems by K. V. Hertz, as well as poems by Bowering, Purdy, Fraser, John Newlove, David Dawson, and editor McFadden. In issue number three we find a large selection of McFadden's early work, accompanied by work from Purdy, MacEwen, Bowering, and others.

The final issue of *Mountain*, number four, appeared in October 1963. It is a slimmer issue than the other three and contains a note calling for contributions. Most of the poems are by McFadden. On the whole, *Mountain* was a lively magazine that reflected its editor's searching eclecticism and his commitment to individual poets and poems of an independent sort.

Talon began on the west coast in 1963 as an independent non-profit magazine owned and published by students with the purpose of providing them "with a medium for free expression."[1] For the first two years of its existence the magazine devoted itself to student writing. In May 1964 David Robinson joined the *Talon* staff; beginning in the fall of 1965, relatively established young writers, such as Seymour Mayne and John Newlove, began to appear in the magazine.

With the magazine's fourth volume in 1966 we notice other changes. Now edited by Jim Brown, *Talon* published work by Patrick Lane, Barry McKinnon, Helene Rosenthal, Seymour Mayne, Tom Marshall, bpNichol, Raymond Fraser, and David Philips. Robinson returned as editor in the second issue of volume four; that issue included poems by bill bissett, Fred Candelaria, J. Michael Yates, and Ken Belford. *Talon* was beginning to open itself to the wider contexts of west-coast poetry.

In the third issue of volume four, 1967, a book series is launched:[2]

THE EDITORS WOULD LIKE TO ANNOUNCE TALONBOOKS
a new series of books published
jointly by TALON and VERY
STONE HOUSE

This notice signals the beginning of one of Canada's most important literary presses. The change in editorial direction brought about by Brown and Robinson carried the magazine into the midst of British Columbia writing; out of that came the desire and machinery for a small press that could produce book-length volumes of poetry. *Talon* is a typical example of the literary magazine that serves as the stepping stone to a book-publishing press.

These four magazines — *Teangadoir, Evidence, Mountain, Talon* — share an eclectic policy and a commitment to the needs of a literary community, whether local or national. But other magazines have radically enlarged the range of Modernist techniques in Canadian poetry. Magazines like *Alphabet, Tish, Open Letter, GrOnk* and *Blew Ointment* present new aesthetic orientations. Radical transformations are wrought in Montreal — where the modern movement started in Canada — in the sixties and seventies. The little magazines have been the crucible in which Modernism reached its culmination: what Raymond Souster, in his landmark anthology called *New Wave Canada*, announced as a renaissance is a distinct phase of modern literature in its full flowering.

6

The Iconography of the Imagination:
Alphabet

The first thirty years of Modernism in Canadian poetry reflect a predominantly metaphysical or a social-realist bias. The McGill metaphysicals of the twenties (Smith, Scott, Klein, Kennedy) found much of their early influence in the satiric poetry of Eliot and the lyrical precision of Yeats and the Imagists; their early political commitment also cannot be overlooked. In spite of Yeats's influence upon Smith — a full retinue of classical allusions can be found in his work — and despite the infusion of Frazer's *The Golden Bough*, by way of Eliot, in Leo Kennedy's *The Shrouding*, the tendency towards symbolism and myth did not take root in early Modernist Canadian poetry. On the whole, the group strived for a dry, austere, critical poetry that would reflect the age in which they lived. The commitment to social and political realities that was to come to full flower in the social realism of the forties was already in evidence in the early Modernist efforts from the mid-twenties on.

The social-realist movement of the forties intensified the determination to write about the realities of modern life. The effort to bring poetry out of the ivory tower and down into the street, which had begun with the McGill group, was realized in the forties. In the poetry of the *Preview* group, particularly in the work of Patrick Anderson, the associations of high culture and erudition were still in evidence, but in the work of poets such as Dudek, Layton, and Souster the language of common speech, in all of its vigour and even in its vulgarity, makes its appearance. These poets hammered home their desire for a direct poetry of first-hand experience. Their prime motivation seemed to be to break down the barriers between life and art, to let life be fully represented in art. They also fought for freedom of form and content; this fight went on into the fifties, when a new tide of academic conservatism was washing across North America. Thus for a time they joined hands with the American Black Mountain group and shared Ezra Pound and William Carlos Williams as primary liberating influences.

In the work of the metaphysicals and the social realists, we can see a variation on several elements that had been present in the literary Modernism of the early twentieth century: satire, imagistic precision, a throwing down of the icons of "high art," a revolutionary attitude in both politics and poetry, a commitment to "make it new" and to adopt a principle of concreteness: "No ideas but in things." These elements, however, were not a complete account of the dynamics of Modernism's evolution, and in Canada in the sixties other Modernist tendencies began to assert themselves. Some of these were aspects taken from early English Modernists. In the imagism of H. D. and Richard Aldington, for instance, we can see a considerable interest in myth. The mythic backdrop that appears in the poetry of Eliot and Yeats and in the prose of Joyce reflects the modern temper as much as Eliot's ironic tone, Yeats's passionate contemporary speech, Joyce's compacted prose style. With hindsight one can easily appreciate that the mythological element in Modernism was bound to influence Canadian poetry. With the dissipation of leftist political fervour after World War Two and a return to more normal conditions, and with an increasing academic return to seriousness in the period of entrenchment and conservatism during the fifties, a symbolic and mythic poetry arrived in Canada under the aegis of Toronto critic and scholar Northrop Frye.

The stature of Northrop Frye as a theorist of literature is well-founded. His central work, *Anatomy of Criticism*, won international recognition as a theory with profound critical implications. He has also had an impact on twentieth-century Canadian poetry. Frye was one of the most comprehensive critics of Canadian poetry during the fifties (see his "Letters in Canada" reviews in *University of Toronto Quarterly* from 1950 to 1959, collected in *The Bush Garden*). But it is Frye's "theory of literature," as set down in the *Anatomy*, that has most influenced the aesthetic concerns of many Canadian poets.

In *From There To Here*, Frank Davey presents a tidy breakdown of the contents of *Anatomy of Criticism*:

> The *Anatomy* is divided into four essays, "Historical Criticism: Theory of Modes," "Ethical Criticism: Theory of Symbols," "Archetypal Criticism: Theory of Myths," and "Rhetorical Criticism: Theory of Genres." The first essay proposes a classification of literature into myth, romance, high mimesis, low mimesis, and irony according to the relationship between the hero and both his fellow man and environment. The second proposes the classification of writing as literal, descriptive, formal, mythical, and anagogic and argues that "literature" comes into being as writing moves from the "discursive" or "literal" phase toward the anagogic and thus becomes increasingly indirect in its signification. The third essay suggests the continuing presence of myths and archetypes in literature of all modes and genres

83

through the process of "displacement," and the consequent presence of Classical and Biblical myth within all western literature. The fourth essay attempts to distinguish between literary forms largely on the basis of rhythm; the rhythm of epos is recurrent, of prose-fiction continuous, of drama decorous, of lyric associative, and of non-literary prose logical.[1]

All of Frye's theories about literature spring from his desire to develop criticism as a science, or field of endeavour. Frye provides a theoretical basis for criticism; he finds past criticism inadequate for the task of addressing itself to a theory of literature. He contends, for example, that too often the critic must adopt a historical or philosophical point of view to analyze a literary work. Frye also finds too much distance between a critic's rôles: "scholar" and "public critic." The scholar is one who "studies" literature; the public critic passes judgement upon it. Although he finds some worth inherent in the "new critics," he sees their orientation as only a starting point:

> It is right that the first effort of critical apprehension should take the form of a rhetorical or structured analysis of a work of art. But a purely structural approach has the same limitation in criticism as it has in biology. In itself it is simply a discrete series of analyses based on the mere existence of the literary structure, without developing any explanation of how the structure came to be what it was and what its nearest relatives are.[2]

In his attempt to stake out a claim for criticism as a science in its own right, Frye insists upon the separation of art from the systematic study of it, which is criticism. He maintains that one cannot teach literature, but only the study of it.[3] He believes that "the critic [of literature] should be able to construct and dwell in a conceptual universe of his own."[4] A "theory of criticism whose principles apply to the whole of literature and account for every valid type of critical procedure is what I think Aristotle meant by poetics,"[5] Frye says, and continues:

> It occurs to me that literary criticism is now in such a state of naïve induction as we find in a primitive science. Its materials, the master-pieces of literature, are not yet regarded as phenomena to be explained in terms of a conceptual framework which criticism alone possesses. They are still regarded as somehow constituting the frame-work or structure of criticism as well. I suggest that it is time for criticism to leap to a new ground from which it can discover what the

organizing or containing forms of its conceptual framework are. Criticism seems badly in need of a coordinating principle, a central hypothesis which, like the theory of evolution in biology, will see the phenomena it deals with as parts of a whole.[6]

Frye frequently uses this analogy between criticism and science; he makes the comparison when he says that the "first postulate" in attempting to organize criticism "is the same as that of any science: the assumption of total coherence."[7]

Frye's attempt to locate the central hypothesis for criticism takes him into a consideration of poetic image:

> We say that every poet has his own peculiar formation of images. But when so many poets use so many of the same images, surely there are bigger critical problems involved than biographical ones. As Mr. Auden's brilliant essay *The Enchafed Flood* shows, an important symbol like the sea cannot remain within the poetry of Shelley or Keats or Coleridge: it is bound to expand over many poets into an archetypal symbol of literature.[8]

Frye defines "symbol" as "any literary structure that can be isolated for critical attention"[9] and "archetype" as "a symbol which connects one poem with another and thereby helps to unify and integrate our literary experience."[10] He sees archetypal criticism as an attempt "to fit poems into the body of poetry as a whole,"[11] and archetypes as an essential part of the coordinating principle upon which to base criticism:

> It is clear that criticism cannot be systematic unless there is a quality in literature which enables it to be so, an order of words corresponding to the order of nature in the natural sciences. An archetype should be not only a unifying category of criticism, but itself a part of a total form, and it leads at once to the question of what sort of total form criticism can see in literature.... Total literary history moves from the primitive to the sophisticated, and here we glimpse the possibility of seeing literature as a complication of a relatively restricted and simple group of formulas that can be studied in primitive culture. If so, then the search for archetypes is a kind of literary anthropology, concerned with the way that literature is informed by pre-literary categories such as ritual, myth and folk-tale. We next realize that the relation between these categories and literature is by no means purely one of descent, as we find them reappearing in the greatest classics—in fact there

seems to be a general tendency on the part of great classics to revert to them. This coincides with a feeling that we have all had: that the study of mediocre works of art, however energetic, obstinately remains a random and peripheral form of critical experience, whereas the profound masterpiece seems to draw us to a point at which we can see an enormous number of converging patterns of significance. Here we begin to wonder if we cannot see literature, not only as complicating itself in time, but as spread out in conceptual space from some unseen center.[12]

What serves as the "unseen center," according to Frye, is a central informing myth:

In the solar cycle of the day, the seasonal cycle of the year, and the organic cycle of human life, there is a single pattern of significance, out of which myth constructs a central narrative around a figure who is partly the sun, partly vegetative fertility and partly a god or archetypal human being.[13]

According to Frye, it "is part of the critic's business to show how all literary genres are derived from the quest myth."[14] For Frye, the quest is a specific one: the return to the lost garden.

Frye makes several statements about the nature of art. These statements tend to divorce art from life; they also represent literature as a kind of snake that is eternally swallowing its own tail. Concerning the presence of the "real" in literary art, Frye notes:

Art deals not with the real but with the conceivable; and criticism, though it will eventually have to have some theory of conceivability, can never be justified in trying to develop, much less assume, any theory of actuality.[15]

Frye sees works of literature as being enclosed in a world of literary art in which they are nourished by other works of literature:

Just as a new scientific discovery manifests something that was already latent in the order of nature, and at the same time logically related to the total structure of the existing science, so the new poem manifests something that was already latent in the order of words. Literature may have life, reality, experience, nature, imaginative truth, social conditions, or what you will for its *content*; but literature itself is not made out of these things. Poetry can only be made out of other poems; novels out of other novels.[16]

In seeing poems as being made out of other poems we are far from the premises of social realism: we have entered a world of artifice. Much of the political power of the poetry of social realism tends to be relegated to a minor place in Frye's criticism; and the poet's desire for social justice represents, to Frye, a mythic desire for a return to the lost garden where human life is perfect. But the social-realist poet's version of this return is too literal and simplistic for Frye's purpose.

Frye's influence upon poets such as James Reaney and Jay Macpherson, the main representatives of the mythopoeic shift in Canadian poetry, is debated. Reaney's *A Suit of Nettles* (1957) and Macpherson's *The Boatman* (1957) were the first books of poetry in Canada in which Frye's theories could be seen as an influence. Frank Davey has been quite critical of the ways in which poets such as Reaney and Macpherson have incorporated Frye's hypothesis about litera-ture into their work:

> [A] misconception about Frye is that his theories of poetry require a conscious effort by the contemporary poet to incorporate mythology into his writing. This idea had led to the so-called "mythopoeic" or "Frygian" school of Canadian poetry and to such ill-conceived works as Reaney's *A Suit of Nettles* and Macpherson's *The Boatman*. Rather than being Frygian, this school constitutes a betrayal of Frye's ideas. To Frye the significance of the mythological patterns evident in literature resides in their having arisen spontaneously and unself-consciously from human life and in their thus reflecting desires and urges completely innate within man.[17]

Margaret Atwood disagrees with Davey. She stresses Reaney's independence from Frye and commends him for the individuality of his work:

> Because Reaney cheerfully acknowledged an interest in Frye, hasty codifiers stuck him in a Myth School of their own creation and accused him of the sin of "being influenced," without pausing to consider that for an artist as original as Reaney, "influence" is taking what you need because it corresponds to something already within you.[18]

The poets considered to be "mythopoeic" have put forward no manifesto or programme, although a mythopoeic point of view is developed in Frye's critical writings. The "mythic" poets are a group simply by comparison with those poets who chose to not work with myth at all. The magazine *Alphabet* proposed to present "An Iconography Of The Imagination," thus moving in a direction that had previously never been explored in Canadian little magazines. As Margaret Atwood has pointed out, *Alphabet*'s editorial decisions were based upon a particular set of premises about literature.[19]

Reaney presents several interesting premises in the editorial of the first issue. What Reaney finds most exciting about writing in this century "is the number of poems that cannot be understood unless the reader quite reorganizes his way of looking at things."[20] This may be the most significant touchstone in Modernism: a demand for a total revolution in human consciousness. Although one could point to the clarity and precision of the Imagists as a refutation of Reaney's premise that much of the work of twentieth-century poets is oblique and obscure, the fact remains that all of the "isms" that have come to constitute Modernism — Cubism, Imagism, Vorticism, Futurism, Expressionism, Dadaism, Surrealism — have forced their audiences to "change their minds," that is, reorganize their modes of perception and patterns of imagination. Reaney, however, takes things one step further than this: he believes that many works cannot be apprehended unless one comes to understand "their secret alphabet or iconography or language of symbols and myths."[21] Rather than seeing Modernist poetry as a revolution in consciousness and techniques that bring poetry into the twentieth century, as the McGill movement and the social realists saw it, Reaney envisions a kind of "Order of the Golden Dawn of Literature," in which there are secret rites and codes of knowledge. Modernism does contain this tendency, in the more elaborate symbolic poems of Yeats, in Joyce's *Ulysses* and *Finnegans Wake,* in the copious references of T.S. Eliot's *The Waste Land,* with their rich lode of quest and fertility myths. Contemporary image and mythical symbol are present and active in Modernist writing. Reaney, following Frye, has simply chosen to emphasize the myth and the symbol.

At the same time Reaney does not seek to exclude elements of reality from poetry; rather he seeks to intertwine the real with the mythical, for that's "how poetry works: it weaves street scenes and twines around swans in legendary pools."[22] Reaney envisions a poetry with "documentary on one side and myth on the other."[23] He also sees a magnetic attraction between them that draws them together. It is Reaney's belief that a grasping of the truths of the "secret alphabet" and of the correspondences between life and art lead to "a more powerful inner life."[24]

By emphasizing myth and symbol, Reaney sees man as being able to escape "the final clutch of the so-called scientific world."[25] He sees metaphor as having as much validity (if not more) as scientific fact. This, again, represents a significant departure from the social realists' emphasis upon the hard-core reality of the experiences of life.

A close knowledge of Frye is evident in Reaney's initial editorial. He sees discussions of myth and symbol adding to Canadian cultural life; hence a journal devoted to iconography is, in his view, a wonderful opportunity to serve a good cause. Indeed, a whole new set of influences entered into the picture, thus radically changing the atmosphere of Canadian poetry in the sixties and seventies.

The first issue of *Alphabet* set the tone and pattern for the magazine's eleven-year run of nineteen issues. Subtitled "A Semiannual Devoted to the Iconography of the Imagination," the first issue, printed in London, Ontario, made its appearance in September 1960. Each issue would centre around a unifying myth; the first issue concerned Narcissus. The essential structure of the magazine was also established from the beginning. There were six sections: "Editorial," "Juxtaposition: Myth and Documentary," "Articles," "Poetry," "Short Stories," and "Reviews." (In later issues, visual images would also become a feature of *Alphabet*.) The first issue was eighty-six pages — remarkably large, considering that editor Reaney handset and printed the first ten issues by letter-press.

The first issue contains an interesting mixture. The opening article, "To Harpooneers," by Richard Stingle, affirms the value and validity of myth.

When the new high priests of science tell us of their latest miracles we respond with a touching faith in their validity. Why do we trust science so much when most of us know so little about it, and mistrust poetic truth or myth? It is not because we have no knowledge of mythic truth; in fact, we know far more about it than we do about scientific truth. Everyone dreams, and in his dreams, he often expresses truth in just the way that myth does. However, we have been conditioned, by Freud, to regard dreams as irrational, and by our whole materialist civilization to give the greatest respect to empirical truth. Throughout man's history, truth has been revealed in dreams and visions, when men have been, in sleep, released from the monsters of time, space and social conditioning. And those visions have come clearest to poets.[26]

Glimmers of those visions are then presented in the poetry, by Colleen Thibaudeau, Daryl Hine, Jay Macpherson, Reaney, M. Morris, and Norman Newton. Hine's two poems had specific reference to the theme of Narcissus;

under the heading "Two Lovers" are two poems, "Narcissus" and "Echo," both formal in style. Jay Macpherson's poems, too, have a formal structure, reminiscent of Shakespeare's songs and the lyrics of the seventeenth century:

> We'll wander to the woods no more,
> Nor beat about the juniper tree.
> My tears run down, my heart is sore,
> And none shall make a game of me.
>
> But come, my love, another day,
> I'll give you cherries with no stones,
> And silver bells, and nuts in May
> — But make no bones.[27]

The subject matter of the poems included in the first issue of *Alphabet* is striking. The poems speak of Eternity, the Labours of Hercules, queens, Homer and Euripides, dancers, Heaven, Hell, Artegall, Adonis, Azazel, Abel and Adam, Ophelia, mermaids, Penelope, and Death-Angels. Consciously mythic, they are also consciously constructed in traditional forms. They represent a counter-movement to what had essentially been a reality-oriented and open-structured Modernist poetry in Canada.

Also included in the first issue were short stories by Edward Kleiman and Colleen Thibaudeau, a commentary on the Fool in the Tarot pack, a review of Layton's *A Red Carpet For The Sun*, and the section entitled "Juxtaposition: Myth and Documentary." Hope Lee's account of being a twin was juxtaposed with Jay Macpherson's myth-studying essay "Narcissus: Some Uncertain Reflections." Macpherson discusses the myth of Narcissus as it appears in Renaissance and Post-Renaissance English poetry: Milton's *Paradise Lost*, Blake's *The Four Zoas*, Coleridge's "Kubla Khan," and the poetry of Gray, Goldsmith, Macpherson, Byron, and Shelley. The essay is replete with Frygian terminology.

Although it has a strong central orientation, the magazine is not strictly prescriptive: it is programmatic. Margaret Atwood has explained the magazine's programme:

> To those unfamiliar with *Alphabet*'s actual methods, the terms "iconography" and "myth" may suggest rigidity and a tendency to collect and categorize. But the editor's faith in the correspondence between every-day reality (life, or what *Alphabet* calls "documentary") and man-made symbolic patterns (art, or what *Alphabet* calls "myth") was so strong that in practice he [Reaney] left interpretation and

pattern-finding to the reader. He merely gathered pieces of writing, both "literary" and "non-literary," and other subjects... and let the echoes speak for themselves; coincidences were there, he insisted, not because he put them there but because they occur.[28]

Atwood's explanation suggests a more random selection than Reaney actually shows; it is, after all, Reaney, as editor, who has juxtaposed the materials or put them between two covers, even if he has "let the echoes" speak for themselves. There was, in fact, a strong controlling editorial consciousness guiding *Alphabet*, bringing materials into close proximity with each other so that patterns could become perceivable. Although the magazine, with time, became more loosely organized, the first few issues reflect a definite critical selection.

There was a marked scholarly bent — some might say a pedantic touch — in *Alphabet* from the very beginning. In addition to Frye's influence, *Alphabet* had a researched intensity that appeared particularly in the literary essays; these essays, more often than not, were the work of scholarly critics in the graduate-school milieu, rather than of working poets. Also, in accord with the view of poetry as artifice, there was always the possibility of poetry lapsing into "literary sensibility," that is, a poetry derived from other poems. From the Frygian point of view that is no danger; nevertheless, in *Alphabet*, some of the poems seem too consciously controlled and deliberately constructed after a conventional pattern.

In the editorial to the second issue (July 1961; myth: Dionysus) Reaney rather cleverly describes the role of the issue's central organizing myth. Insisting that many of the thematic echoes in the first two issues were purely coincidental (and he is prepared to swear to this "on a heap of mandalas"), Reaney describes how each myth serves only as a kind of key:

> Actually the same thing happens if you take the face cards out of a card deck; then put a circular piece of cardboard near them. Curves and circles appear even in the Queen of Diamonds and the Knave of Spades. But place a triangular shape close by and the eye picks up corners and angularities in even the Queen of Clubs. What every issue of *Alphabet* involves, then, is the placing of a definite geometric shape near some face cards. Just as playing about with cubes and spheres can teach an artist and a critic a better sense of composition, *Alphabet*'s procedure can have the same result with iconography and symbolism.[29]

The issue contains poems by Richard Outram and Alden Nowlan and an extensive parody of T. S. Eliot by R. K. Webb. Reaney's principles of selection were general; there was room for Nowlan's Maritime realism and Webb's cutting humour. The issue is, of course, heavily laden with myth-oriented articles. Daryl Hine contributed "The Childhood of Dionysus: A Bacchic Dialogue"; Jay Macpherson submitted the second installment of "Narcissus: Some Uncertain Reflections"; and Norman Newton wrote "The Lyric Poetry of Ancient Mexico (Anahuac)."

The third issue (December 1961) concerned the Prometheus myth and continued the mythy articles. It also included poems by two young women who would come to represent most fully a mythic orientation in the poets of the sixties generation: Margaret Atwood (who signed her work "M. E. Atwood") and Gwendolyn MacEwen.

The myth in *Alphabet* number four (June 1962) was Icarus. In an editorial, Reaney turns his attention to the status of the indigenous Canadian artist, particularly the playwright. He explains why we need a "native drama": "I don't believe you can really be worldly, or unprovincial or whatever until you've sunk your claws into a locally coloured tree trunk and scratched your way through to universality."[30] *Alphabet's* pages testify to a concern for the Canadian arts. In issue four, for instance, drawings by Harold Town accompany fables by M. Morris. (Reaney's interest in a native drama began to manifest itself in the writing of plays dealing with specific Canadian locales and situations.)

The fourth issue marked the appearance of another poet interested in the mythic possibilities of poetry, Eli Mandel, who had been a student of Frye. Mandel was published by Contact Press and publications of the Montreal school, but even his early work, *Trio* (1954) and *Fuseli Poems* (1960), was located more in a world of myth and literature than in the world of actuality. *Alphabet's* Icarus issue contains an essay by Mandel, "Lapwing You Are. Lapwing He — A Note on Icarus in Myth and Poetry," as well as a review in which he gives favourable critical notices to *Double Persephone* and *The Drunken Clock*, two myth-oriented first books by Margaret Atwood and Gwendolyn MacEwen.

In the same issue is a review by Reaney of several books, among them *D-Day & After*, a first book by Frank Davey, editor of the Vancouver poetry newsletter *Tish*. Davey's book and the others reviewed by Reaney represent a very different orientation to poetry from Reaney's mythopoeic concerns; they are in the Canadian documentary tradition, if anything. As a result, Reaney has few kind words for Davey's work or for the creative impetus behind it.

In succeeding editorials, Reaney discussed the question of Canadian culture. In issue number six (June 1963) he defended Canadian intellectual life against charges that it lacked boldness and vigour, citing Frye's *The Educated*

Imagination and McLuhan's *Gutenberg Galaxy*, which to him represented important and exciting critical thinking. In the next issue he discusses a Canadian cultural identity; this question of Canadian identity recurs in the editorial in number eight, which marked the death of E. J. Pratt, whom Reaney calls "our great poet."[31] After paying tribute to Pratt, Reaney laments Canada's "stale" tradition, and says that "What our poets should be doing is to show us how to *identify* our society out of this depressing situation."[32] Reaney sees a Canadian self-identification taking place in the poetry of Pratt; he also sees this as the task of *Alphabet*.

Issues five to eight contained drawings by Harold Town, Jack Chambers, and Greg Curnoe; essays by Frye on Haliburton and by Richard Stingle on the Donnellys; and poems by Tom Marshall, Colleen Thibaudeau, Margaret Atwood, and others. There were also academic literary essays: "James Joyce and the Primitive Celtic Church" by Edward Duncan, "W. B. Yeats and the 'Electric Motor Vision'" by Edward Yeomans, and "Altarwise By Owl-Light" by Peter Revell. Issue number eight also contained an item titled "Jonah: A Cantata Text," commissioned verse by Jay Macpherson set to music by John Beckwith; and "Mary Midnight: An Oratory" by Eli Mandel, a verse play. Obviously *Alphabet*, like Sutherland's *Northern Review*, was ranging beyond poetry into "culture." Film reviews, articles on drama, criticisms of earlier twentieth-century writers, visual arts, calligraphy, and music all were included in the magazine. The tenth and eleventh issues signalled a greater expansion of the poetic concept, featuring calligraphic poems by bill bissett and "ideo-pomes" by bpNichol. Both bissett and Nichol, working in their own forms of radical iconography, continued to contribute to *Alphabet*.

Interestingly, as time passed, Reaney saw much of what *Alphabet* had stood for becoming the subject matter of popular culture. In an editorial in issue fourteen, he cited pop lyrics (the Fugs, the Beatles, the Doors), films, and movies that incorporated aspects of mythology. But if popular culture was being inundated by mythology, poetry was also beginning to be influenced by popular culture, as Reaney notes in a later editorial: "Our collage of letters from poets is also noteworthy in that it shows so many different situations; also how much interests have changed since the *CV & Northern Review* decades. You never used to get poets interested in film, sound or building a special truck to stage their poetry-cum-light, show with."[33] This interest in popular culture became evident in *Alphabet*; despite his antipathy towards Frank Davey's early work, Reaney published Davey's essay "Leonard Cohen and Bob Dylan: Poetry and the Popular Song" in *Alphabet* number seventeen.

The poetry that appeared in issues eleven through seventeen was quite diverse, and drew upon a variety of modes and schools. Never much in favour of poets inclined towards social realism, Reaney nevertheless began to publish a broad cross-section of varied younger poets: Pat Lowther, George Bowering, David Helwig, bill bissett, bpNichol, Gwendolyn MacEwen, Peter Stevens, Joy Kogawa, Robert Kroetsch, Lloyd Abbey, Anne Szumigalski, Patrick Lane, Jay Macpherson, Michael Ondaatje, Robert Gibbs, Elizabeth Brewster, and Catherine Buckaway all appeared in *Alphabet* between December 1965 and December 1969.

Although Reaney proposed, in the editorial of issue fifteen, to publish twenty-six issues of the magazine, *Alphabet* completed its run with a double issue in 1971. Issue eighteen-nineteen encompassed two myths: "Hieroglyph" and "Horoscope." The Hieroglyph section marked a significant interest in concrete poetry. The issue opens with Eugene Eoyang's article "Concrete Poetry and the 'Concretism' of Chinese"; it is followed by a calligraphic concrete poem by P. K. Page, a typewriter concrete poem, "Pig's Blood," by David W. Harris, four poems by bill bissett, an interview with bpNichol conducted by George Bowering, "Paleo Poems" by "Child Roland" (alias "Peter Noel Meilleur"), nine poem-drawings by Judith Copithorne, which are visual configurations of the written word, and Jane Shen's poems based on Chinese characters. This concern with concrete poetry was related to myth by seeing the hieroglyph as a sign with mythic power, but it also shows Reaney relaxing the program of the magazine to publish whatever he found interesting at the time.

Margaret Atwood has said that *Alphabet* was "Canadian in *form*, in how the magazine was put together."[34] (In presenting his central hypothesis for literature, Frye had suggested that behind all literary content there is the *form* of the myth.) Atwood seems to be saying that there is a structure of thought that is Canadian in character:

> What follows is hypothetical generalization, but it is of such that
> national identities are composed. Saying that *Alphabet* is Canadian
> in form leads one also to say that there seem to be important differen-
> ces between the way Canadians think — about literature, or anything
> — and the way Englishmen or Americans do. The English habit of
> mind, with its preoccupation with precedent and the system, might be
> called empirical; reality is the social hierarchy and its dominant
> literary forms are evaluative criticism and the social novel. It values
> "taste." The American habit of mind, with its background of intricate
> Puritan theologizing, French Enlightenment political theory and
> German scholarship and its foreground of technology, is abstract and
> analytical; it values "technique," and for it reality is how things work.
> The dominant mode of criticism for some years has been "New
> Criticism," picking works of art apart into component wheels and

springs; its "novel" is quite different from the English novel, which leans heavily towards comedy of manners and a dwindled George Eliot realism; the American novel, closer to the Romance, plays to a greater extent with symbolic characters and allegorical patterns. The Canadian habit of mind, for whatever reason — perhaps a history and a social geography which both seem to lack coherent shape — is synthetic. "Taste" and "technique" are both of less concern to it than is the ever-failing, but ever-renewed attempt to pull all the pieces together, to discover the whole of which one can only trust one is a part. The most central Canadian literary products, then, tend to be the large-scope works like *The Anatomy of Criticism* and *The Gutenberg Galaxy* which propose all-embracing systems within which any particular bit of data may be placed. Give the same poem to a model American, a model English and a model Canadian critic: the American will say "This is how it works"; the Englishman, "How good, how true to Life" (or, "How boring, tasteless and trite"); the Canadian will say "This is where it fits into the entire universe." It is in its love for synthesis that *Alphabet* shows itself peculiarly Canadian.[35]

Atwood's thesis is both interesting and original: perhaps it is true that Canadian thinkers are inclined to "pull all the pieces together," or again perhaps they're more single-minded than people in other English cultures. Atwood is astute in pointing out that this is an "ever-failing, but ever-renewed attempt," doomed to fail because the individual theories are never satisfying to everyone, and always attempted anew because of the human desire to know and to integrate.

Of course, whether *Alphabet* is Canadian in form is debatable; I would argue that the assertion is tenuous at best. But the magazine was important: it brought a new orientation to bear on Canadian poetry. Although it took much of its general outlook from Frye, the pure mythic basis of the early issues widened out, as the magazine developed, to include other possibilities, such as regionalism, experimental concrete poetry, and the attempt to foster a broad Canadian culture. In spite of its insistence upon a central informing myth, *Alphabet* served as a haven for Canadian intellectual and cultural life rather than merely as a militant literary periodical. Once its intention had been defined, its policy was relaxed, with few polemical arguments directed at the opposition. In later issues, work by west-coast theorists (*Tish* poets, bill bissett, bpNichol) were incorporated into the magazine, and reviews of books by Montreal poets (Layton, Siebrasse, Mayne, Scott, Steve Smith) were evaluative but generally unargumentative. In *Alphabet* Reaney chose to embody rather than assert a mythic orientation; as editor he operated according to a flexible policy that aimed at retaining his original objectives while welcoming new writers and changing interests as time went on.

7

The Black Mountain Influence:
Tish and Beyond

Tish, "a poetry newsletter—Vancouver," is perhaps the most famous and controversial of the Canadian little magazines; it is certainly the best documented. The first nineteen issues have been reprinted and two book-length studies have been written, *The Writing Life* and *Poetry and the Colonized Mind: Tish*. The magazine appeared at a crucial time in the evolution of Canadian Modernism, and it represented a well-defined theory and belief as to how poetry should be written. The readings of what *Tish* meant, however, have been various.

Louis Dudek fought long and hard for a developing Modernist poetry in Canada; in *Tish* and its poets he saw "the main line of continuing modern development" and the continuation of "the authentic modern tradition in Canada."[1] West-coast critic Warren Tallman sees in the *Tish* group not so much a continuation of the modern tradition as a rejection of the humanist approach evident in earlier Canadian poetry (including that of Dudek and his colleagues Layton and Souster) and the beginnings of Post-Modernism in Canadian poetry. Robin Mathews sees *Tish* as a betrayal of the native tradition in Canadian poetry and as a stage in the "[United States] invasion and colonization of a part of the poetic culture of Canada."[2] In the *Tish* poets, and in their orientation towards poetry, we find controversy—and possibly something central to the great question of Modernism.

Mathews's view of *Tish* is hostile. He sees *Tish* as a "bête noire," the most extreme example of the invasion of the Canadian poetic tradition by American influence. The effect of the American Black Mountain poets on the *Tish* group is seen as a betrayal of Canadian aesthetic and political identity— although not the first such betrayal.

> The invasion has not been confined to the Pacific Province of Canada. It began, elsewhere, a half century ago, at least. It has, however, gone virtually unrecorded because US "influences" and "cosmopolitanism" have often been offered as desirable. Canadians have been

97

told that they must accept the leadership of foreign poets and styles if they are to be serious, contemporary and good. The foreign poets are usually US poets or poets who, for some reason, support the poetics US poets claim are central in our time.[3]

In his essay "Poetics: the Struggle for Voice in Canada," Mathews describes the betrayal of the Canadian tradition in greater detail. He notes that the "battle about poetics has been a battle with an ideological basis, a basis in political reality, political power, and political influence."[4] Then he recounts some of the prime determinants of the struggle:

> One of the fundamental determinants of the struggle about Canadian poetics and a Canadian voice in more recent decades might be called the rejection of the Canadian tradition, or — for those who want a less partisan phrasing — the misunderstanding of Canadian poetry written before 1920. That rejection or misunderstanding is visible... especially from the McGill Movement onwards.... Since the McGill Movement the hallmark of general misunderstanding has been the tendency to lump good and bad poetry into "the maple leaf school," dismissing the whole without examining the parts.... [As] part of the rejection of the Canadian tradition a number of Canadian poets and critics... have gone outside Canada as a fundamental policy, in search of major leadership, models, and theories of poetic imagination.[5]

The spurned Canadian tradition is replaced by elements of the United States poetic tradition, and the initial "betrayal" by the McGill Movement led to a constant string of "betrayals" that bring us up to the present day:

> [T]he McGill Movement eventuated in Sousterian colonial-mindedness, and it, in turn, was followed by the Black Mountain Imitation School, theories of "North American" poetic sensibility and publications like *Boundary 2* and *CrossCountry*, both of which serve to "continentalize" poetic imagination. The result is not to bring two poetic imaginations into fruitful dialogue. It is to assimilate Canadian poetic production into the US tradition.[6]

Mathews's strident argument and his view of Canadian poetry are essentially anti-Modernist. (For Mathews, the Confederation poets started a Canadian tradition. He allows that tradition to be influenced by English Romantic models but denounces American influences.) He criticizes the Modernist movement in Canada because he does not care for the movement's aesthetics or inherent politics. His misreading of the sources in Scott and Smith is a particular distortion; he sees them as derived from American rather than English traditions. *Tish*, for Mathews, is only the latest in a long line of innovations of which he disapproves. But Mathews provides no alternative to the poetry of the Modernists. He argues that we should ignore fifty years of Canadian poetry, but does not point to a continuation of the "genuine" Canadian tradition. In attempting to reroute American poetry around Allan Tate and John Crowe Ransom, the Black Mountain poets could note a continuation of Pound's and Williams's Modernism in Objectivists like Oppen, Reznikoff, Rakosi, and Zukofsky, who served as a bridge between the early Imagists of 1910 and the Black Mountain and Beat poets of the 1950s. Mathews is incapable of bridging the gap in this way because there is no intelligent continuation after the Confederation poets. Mathews does not accept that the Modernist tradition is incorporated into Canadian poetry, and has been the most vital force in Canadian poetry in the past fifty years.

Louis Dudek views the Vancouver *Tish* movement as an extension or continuation of the Modernist movement. (See his essay "Lunchtime Reflections on Frank Davey's Defence of the Black Mountain Fort," *Tamarack Review*, Summer 1965.) Dudek's essay was a response to an essay in the previous issue, "Black Days on Black Mountain," in which Davey tried to defend the presence of the Black Mountain influence in Canadian poetry by detailing its basic premises and insisting upon its widespread influence. Dudek argues that the common source for all Modernist poets is Imagism and the poetry of Pound and Williams. Dudek rightly sees the new school of poets — the Black Mountain and *Tish* poets — as a "hopeful continuation or would-be theoretical fulfillment"[7] of what the early Modernist fathers had proposed.

Irving Layton, Raymond Souster, and Louis Dudek were contemporaries of Charles Olson, Robert Creeley, and other Black Mountain poets. The Canadians and Americans formed a kind of continuing beachhead of Modernism in the conservative and retrenching fifties. Olson and Dudek drew upon Pound and Williams for inspiration; Layton tried to steer his own idiosyncratic course, though paradoxically he was the Canadian most readily embraced by the Black Mountain poets. Souster fell most under the sway of Williams, and then of Olson, via the "Projective Verse" essay. Yet these Canadian poets of the fifties — especially Dudek and Layton — were unwilling to be drawn into too tight an association with their compatriots to the south (although Souster's *Contact* and *Combustion* at times look like versions of *Origin/Black Mountain Review* in Canada).

The poetry of the American and the Canadian groups derived from common sources, but developed quite differently. Warren Tallman places the

Canadian group within a humanist tradition and the Black Mountain group in the central-Modern tradition. Tallman includes the poets associated with *Tish* in the central-Modern group. Black Mountain poetry is a specific derivation from Pound's and Williams's Modernism, and it differs clearly from the Modernism practiced by the *Cerberus* trio. When the Black Mountain influence hit the shores of Vancouver it brought into Canadian poetry developments that were new and different from those practiced by the older East-coast poets. To understand just how the *Tish* poets continued the progress of Modernism in Canadian poetry, and also to understand how their poetry differs from what preceded it, a quick look at Black Mountain poetics may be useful.

In Canada the term "Black Mountain" has often been used too loosely to refer to the influence of American poets of the fifties and sixties. Critics have included members of the New York School and the Beats under the general category "Black Mountain." All the poets included in Donald Allen's seminal anthology *The New American Poetry* have been seen as having a monolithic influence upon the West-coast *Tish* poets. After the Vancouver poetry conference of 1963, a more general American influence was felt in Vancouver, but the first editorial period of *Tish* (1961 to 1963) reveals a very specific strain of Black Mountain-poetic thinking in that magazine. The words "Black Mountain" actually refer to a highly individualized group of poets; it was not an inclusive Pan-American phenomenon. In his anthology, Donald Allen was careful to point out that the ten poets he grouped under the heading "Black Mountain" all appeared in the little magazines *Origin* and *Black Mountain Review*; some of them, though not all, had some association with Black Mountain College. The ten poets Allen included were Charles Olson, Robert Duncan, Denise Levertov, Paul Blackburn, Robert Creeley, Paul Carroll, Larry Eigner, Edward Dorn, Jonathan Williams, and Joel Oppenheimer: a precise working list of the Black Mountain poets.

And yet, as with all literary movements, the placing of ten poets under a single banner is probably more convenient than it is exact. The group shared a certain aesthetic sympathy, not a manifesto, although one could argue that Olson's essay "Projective Verse" did much to embody a set of common assumptions. More than anything, these poets shared a time and an outlook. But if we turn to the work of individual writers, we notice at once each poet's individuality.

The beginnings of the Black Mountain group can be traced to the spring of 1951, when Cid Corman started a magazine called *Origin* that served as a meeting place for many of the writers who later appeared in *Black Mountain Review*. As Duberman writes in his book on Black Mountain:

[T]hese writers, in rebellion against the modalities then dominant in poetry and criticism, had few other outlets — among them, *Golden Goose*, *Merlin* and Rainer Maria Gerhardt's *Fragments*. Toward late 1953-early 1954 certain haphazardly related circumstances conspired to add one more, and probably the most significant: *The Black Mountain Review*.

Origin, having done its pioneer work, seemed to be faltering: "It's not tired," Creeley said, "but it's really been carrying a lot of weight for some time." There seemed to be room — even demand — for a publication that would admit some further possibilities. Creeley and Olson, for example, wanted "an active, ranging" section for critical writing that would be "prospective" — "would break down habits of 'subject' and gain a new experience of context generally."[8]

Charles Olson, at that time rector of Black Mountain College, served as prime mover for *The Black Mountain Review*.

The starting point was Olson's conviction that a magazine would help to promote the college, and that a reinvigorated college, in turn, would help to break the hold of the New Criticism and give needed support to literary expression with quite different concerns.[9]

The Black Mountain poets were unified in their rebellion against New Criticism and their discontent with the growing conservatism of the late forties and early fifties. They opposed the regression with an aesthetic that they saw as central to the fathers of Modernism: the aesthetic of Pound and Williams. They wanted to carry the innovations of Modernism to the next logical stage. Robert Creeley addressed himself to the question of the continuity of modern poetry:

I think that what's happened, at least in the context of the States, is that the poetry of the Twenties and Thirties... — let's say the poetry of Ransom and Tate and Bishop and...younger men such as Jarrell — this poetry, in effect, tended to block off...the actual tradition that was still operating in the poetry of say Zukofsky and Reznikoff and George Oppen, but I feel that the continuity is there, suffers no break, keeps going....[O]nce the social aspect of the Roaring Twenties died out in writing, people assumed that the actual work that had been initiated in the same period was done too, but we find that people actually worked continuously all during the time....[10]

The Black Mountain group took up the Modernist line begun by Pound and Williams, a tradition they saw continued by the Objectivists.

What do the Black Mountain poets share? Creeley attempts to supply some definition.

> [What joins] us all together [is] a very conscious concern with the manner of a poem, with the form of a poem, so that we are...freed from any solution unparticular or *not* particular to ourselves.
>
> I think of Paul Blackburn...Paul and I spent two and a half days and nights simply talking about *how do you write a poem?*...We all had to find the character of our own intelligence...and we did it by this preoccupation with *how is the poem to be put on the page*...how shall we actually speak to other people in this medium in a way that's not exclusively personal, but in a way that is our own determination.[11]

The preoccupation with how the poem is to be put on the page points out that Black Mountain poetics are essentially technique-oriented; the central issue is one of poetic notation. Another key premise is that "poetry is a vocal art" (described by George Bowering in his essay "How I Hear Howl."[12]) In seeking to free poetry from the trammels of end-rhyme and a metronomic regularity of metre, the Imagists had attempted to bring the language of poetry closer to the language of speech. Black Mountain poetry brings the language of poetry into the same realm as the speech of each individual. And it attempts to provide a notation that corresponds to real speech.

These concerns give Black Mountain a specific literary identity and provide as much definition to the group as the Imagists, with their three propositions, had in their time. The Imagists had Pound as their central figure; the Black Mountain poets had Charles Olson as theorizer and rallying point. Creeley describes their concerns:

> We did use Olson as a locus without question.... We weren't leaning, I think, on Olson's condition, but we were using a premise which he of course had made articulate in projective verse. We were trying to think of how a more active sense of poetry might be got, and that's I think the coincidence we share, or rather the coincident commitment... we each feel that writing is something we're given to do rather than choose to do; that the form an actual writing takes is very intimate to the circumstance and impulses of its literal time of writing ...that the modality conceived and the occasion conceived is a very similar one.[13]

The Black Mountain impulse shares much with the aim of the Canadian *Cerberus* group: to keep Modernism alive in the face of an encircling conservatism and formalism. The Black Mountain poets were particularly intent on finding their way to freedom in poetry through form, especially the open form that Olson described in his essay "Projective Verse." The essay is a central manifesto, invoked time and again by the Black Mountain and *Tish* poets.

Olson's "Projective Verse" extends and elaborates the early Imagist principles, and thus carries modern verse in the English language into a new phase, generally referred to as "Post-Modernist," a term originated by Olson himself. In many ways, Olson's theory makes free verse a more systematic poetic form.

The Black Mountain group acted in a kind of dynamic tension with and opposition to the traditionally based New Criticism poets. By the fifties, New Criticism had spawned a second generation of poets, a generation effectively anthologized in Donald Hall's and Robert Pack's *New Poets of England and America* (1962). If we contrast this anthology with Donald Allen's *The New American Poetry* (1960), we find two totally different lines of development. The poetic fathers of *New Poets of England and America* are John Crowe Ransom, Allan Tate, W. H. Auden, Stephen Spender, Carl Sandburg, Robert Frost, and Dylan Thomas, whereas the poets of the Allen anthology have drawn their influences from Walt Whitman, William Carlos Williams, Ezra Pound, and H. D. We can see here the contrast between an essentially traditional line of poetry and a radical Modernist line. When Olson wrote "Projective Verse," the traditional line was predominant, as it had been since the mid-1910s or 1920s. Olson went against the accepted standards of the day in his attempt to move Modernism ahead.

Olson contrasts "projective" or "open" verse with "non-projective" verse: "or what a French critic calls 'closed' verse, that verse which print bred and which is pretty much what we have had, in English & American, and have still got, despite the work of Pound & Williams."[14] Opposed to the closed poetry (or rhymed and metrical poetry) print bred, Olson proposes a forward-moving verse that includes "certain laws and possibilities of the breath, of the breathing of the man who writes as well as of his listenings." (p. 147) For Olson, this verse was preceded by the "revolution of the ear, 1910" (p. 147) (that is, the revolution of Imagism. Imagist poetry was to be composed in the sequence of the musical phrase, rather than to the beat of a metronome). Olson aimed at a free verse more precise than the abstract "musical phrase." He proposed to integrate poetry and the human voice.

"Projective Verse" is divided in two parts. In the first part Olson shows what his concept of projective verse is and how it is achieved; in the second part he suggests "a few ideas about what stance toward reality brings such verse into being, what that stance does, both to the poet and to his reader" (p. 148).

Olson defines "projective verse" as "open" verse and as "composition by field"; these are opposed to a poetry of "inherited line, stanza, over-all form, what is the 'old' base of the non-projective" (p. 148). Olson objects to an accepted or "inherited" form into which a poem is molded; in the "non-projective" poem, form precedes content or dictates the verse structure of content. As Olson defines it, the three primary concerns of the projective poem are "kinetics," "principle," and "process." Olson sees a poem as a way to transfer "energy" from the poet to the reader. The poem itself must "at all points, be a high energy-construct and, at all points, an energy-discharge" (p. 148). To maximize the efficiency with which energy is transferred, the composition of the poem must adhere to the essential principle of composition by field, defined in the formula, "Form is never more than an extension of content (p. 148). Finally, there is "the process of the thing, how the principle can be made so to shape the energies that the form is accomplished.... one perception must immediately and directly lead to a further perception" (p. 149).

The contrast between projective and non-projective verse is well marked. Projective verse strives to be kinetic rather than static; it is written in a form that projects or carries the kinetics of content, rather than molding them to a fixed pattern. Finally, the projective poem is a series of perceptions, always kinetic, always moving towards an undefined goal. It is a process rather than a formally developed single perception.

Olson stipulates that a poet "register both the acquisitions of his ear *and* the pressures of his breath" (p. 149). Having denounced the set line, stanza, and form, Olson posits poetry as an aural/oral record of speech. For Olson, the essential unit of speech is the syllable:

> It is the king and pin of versification, what rules and holds together the lines, the larger forms, of a poem.... It is by their syllables that words juxtapose in beauty, by these particles of sound as clearly as by the sense of the words which they compose. In any given instance, because there is a choice of words, the choice, if a man is in there, will be, spontaneously, the obedience of his ear to the syllables. The fineness, and the practice, lie here, at the minimum and source of speech. (p. 149)

The idea of composing in the sequence of the musical phrase, inherent in Imagism, lies behind Olson's assertion of the syllable as the "king and pin of versification." The syllable, a unit of sound, contains the essential qualities of the music of language. To this Olson adds the sense of phrasing that results from the pressure of the breath:

> But the syllable is only the first child of the incest of verse.... The other child is the LINE. And together, these two, the syllable *and* the line, they make a poem...the line comes...from the breath, from the breathing of the man who writes, at the moment that he writes...only he, the man who writes, can declare, at every moment, the line its metric and its ending—where its breathing, shall come to, termination. (pp. 150-51)

The written poem is a transcription of how the poem would be spoken aloud. The aesthetic base of the projective poem confirms Eliot's assertion that free verse is not free. For Olson, the principle of measure for this verse form is the breath-line.

> It is now only a matter of the recognition of the conventions of composition by field for us to bring into being an open verse as formal as the closed, with all its traditional advantages. (p. 154)

Projective verse has its own formal principles.

After defining projective verse, Olson comments upon "rhetorical devices which have now to be brought under a new bead" (p. 151). Simile is to be avoided; description should be limited, because its easiness can often drain the energy from a poem. All slackness, which disperses energy, must be avoided. Observation, which he likens to argument in prose, Olson considers to be "properly previous to the act of the poem" (p. 152). If it is to be contained in a poem at all it must be "juxtaposed, apposed, set in" (p. 152) so that it does not enter between the poem's content and its form as an extraneous element. Olson also explains that "the conventions which logic has forced on syntax must be broken open as quietly as must the too set feet of the old line" (p. 153). In fact, Olson considers all the old poetic devices interferences that disperse the intensity and authenticity of the poem.

Olson's final point in the first part of "Projective Verse" is that the typewriter is a great writing tool that provides clarity and exactness in notation. This precision in notation enhances the relationship between poem-as-written-medium and poem-as-auditory-experience:

> [W]hat I want to emphasize here, by this emphasis on the typewriter as the personal and instantaneous recorder of the poet's work, is the

already projective nature of the verse as the sons of Pound and Williams are practicing it. Already they are composing as though verse was to have the reading its writing involved, as though not the eye but the ear was to be its measurer, as though the intervals of its composition could be so carefully put down as to be precisely the intervals of its registration. For the ear, which once had the burden of memory to quicken it (rime & regular cadence were its aids and have merely lived on in print after the oral necessities were ended) can now again, that the poet has his means, be the threshold of projective verse. (p. 155)

After five hundred years of print poetry, Olson is attempting to align modern poetry with the oral tradition.

In the second part of "Projective Verse," Olson explains that the projective purpose in verse involves a new stance towards reality (as well as a new poetic stance). We must realize that the beginning and end of the poem is "voice in its largest sense." This realization will change the conception and material of verse. Olson proposes "objectism" as the prime aesthetic for projective verse:

Objectism is the getting rid of the lyrical interferences of the individual as ego, of the "subject" and his soul, that peculiar presumption by which western man has interposed himself between what he is as a creature of nature (with certain instructions to carry out) and those other creatures of nature which we may, with no derogation, call objects. For a man is himself an object, whatever he may take to be his advantages, the more likely to recognize himself as such the greater his advantages, particularly at that moment that he achieves an *humilitas* sufficient to make him of use.

It comes to this: the use of a man, by himself and thus by others, lies in how he conceives his relation to nature, that force to which he owes his somewhat small existence. If he sprawl, he shall find little to sing but himself, and shall sing, nature has such paradoxical ways, by way of artificial forms outside himself. But if he stays inside himself, if he is contained within his nature as he is participant in the larger force, he will be able to listen, and his hearing through himself will give him secrets objects share. And by an inverse law his shapes will make their own way. (pp. 155–56)

Olson's approach to reality incorporates man into an object-object (as opposed to a subject-object) relation with the world of nature. He is not looking for a revelation of the emotional intensity an individual experiences and then expresses in verse; instead, he seeks the "secrets objects share" that are revealed in the medium of poetry. Olson believes that the poet should be present in the poem not as an ego, but as a creature of nature that has the power to articulate. Warren Tallman uses the word "proprioceptive" to describe the focus of the Black Mountain poets; in other words, they concentrated on stimuli that were internal, inside the poet.

> Modernist writing has shifted emphasis from the perceptive view in which attention focuses on the surrounding world to a proprioceptive view in which *self*, having subjected itself to its surroundings, becomes the *subject* of a new writing which it is easiest to define as a *life* sentence. Self is the subject, writing is verb and the object is life, to be as fully alive as one can manage by way of sight, hearing, thinking, feeling, speaking—that is, writing.[15]

Tallman bases his argument on Olson's dictum that the poet should stay "inside himself." The revelation of life takes place when the poet is a "participant in the larger force," as Olson states it, instead of only a perceiving consciousness.

The *Tish* poets were proprioceptive; thus they are part of the Post-Modern stream. They do not see a poem as something shaped by human intelligence that imposes its order upon language. Instead, the *Tish* poets follow Olson and see poetry as a participation in a greater force. That force is language. The poet does not relate to language as artisan or craftsman, but as disciple or priest.

George Bowering discussed the rôle of the poet during the *Tish* years:

> The *Tish* poets have striven for accuracy and clarity, and have turned their attention upon the factual things that make up the world, men included among them. The young romantics...scoop a lot of slush into the space between themselves and natural phenomena. They think they have to *put* poetry into things; they don't have the sense and determination to find the poetry that is already there.[16]

The insistence upon accuracy, clarity, and the factual derives from Imagism, with its precise reckoning of the actual. Taking their cue from the Black Mountain poets, the *Tish* group shared basic premises about the writing of poetry. They formed an almost communal identity. Black Mountain poetics are concerned with technique and with freedom from the impositions of abstract intelligence; *Tish* poetics are concerned with prosody rather than theme. As well, the *Tish* poets developed a commitment to place, or "locus," which led them to emphasize the particularities of their *own* place: Vancouver,

British Columbia. (In the past twenty years, west-coast poets have been intensely aware that they *are* west-coast poets—as opposed to Canadian poets.) The *Tish* poets were committed to language and to place.

Frank Davey explains:

> It is the sense of *belonging* that is projected by *Tish* magazine, and by Vancouver poetry since *Tish*, that has been the most incomprehensible, even unacceptable, to writers and critics in other provinces: the sense of belonging to a specific geography, of belonging to the political and social life of that geography, of belonging to both a local community of writers and an international community of writers, of belonging to (rather than possessing and *using*) language, of being *at home* in place, community, and language....
>
> No one will ever fully understand *Tish* magazine or BC writing since *Tish* who does not understand this concept of community. This concept assumes that man must find his place in the cosmos, in the physical geography of his place, in the social fabric of his human settlement, in the rhythmic and syntactic patterns of his language, that these patterns are liberating and sustaining rather than imprisoning.... The act of writing becomes a "poetics of dwelling."[17]

Tish had its true beginning in February 1961, when Robert Duncan appeared at the Festival of Contemporary Arts in Vancouver and read his poetry and talked to a capacity audience. Among those present were George Bowering, David Dawson, Lionel Kearns, Jamie Reid, Frank Davey, and Fred Wah. In the late spring of 1961, these six young poets formed a study group and discussed the work Duncan had introduced to them. The primary text for their readings and discussions was Donald Allen's *The New American Poetry*.

Warren Tallman explains what happened next:

> With that kind of good sense that goes with direct eyes and open responses, they did a typically absurd but intelligent thing. The group of six expanded their numbers to 20, so there were both poets and interested friends of poets, subscribed $5 each and offered Duncan the $100 to appear in Vancouver and lecture at length on Pound, the Imagists, Olson and the *Maximus Poems*, his own "Structure of Rime" poems in *The Opening of the Field*, and, as it turned out, Creeley, Levertov, Ginsberg and early days with Jack Spicer and Robin Blaser during the Romantic "Berkeley Renaissance" of the mid-1940s.[18]

The Vancouver poets had not read any east-coast Modernist Canadian poetry. (Bowering and Kearns had some awareness of the Contact Press books, but they knew nothing about A.J.M. Smith or F.R. Scott.) Duncan brought Modernism to Vancouver.

> Duncan, a walking and talking university of verse lore, filled the air with his most influential predecessors (Ezra Pound, William Carlos Williams, H.D.) and his closest contemporaries (Charles Olson, Robert Creeley, Larry Eigner, Denise Levertov). The gain for Davey and the others was not simply in the names but in the keys, clues and comments on the art of articulation. Tone leading, rhyme, sound resemblances and disresemblances, the musical phrase, composition by field and correspondence, as well as linguistic, musical, dramatic, and choreographic analogies to writing—all these began to buzz about like bees.[19]

The young poets were schooled in Black Mountain poetics by Duncan: he taught them as much as they could absorb. In earlier days, poets derived their influences through the medium of print; the Vancouver poets had first-hand instruction from the poets themselves. Robert Duncan, Charles Olson, Robert Creeley, Denise Levertov, Allen Ginsberg, Jack Spicer, Robin Blaser, Michael McClure, Jackson MacLow, and Philip Whalen all appeared in Vancouver between the years 1961 and 1966, to instruct young Vancouver poets in the elements of their poetry.

Tish grew directly out of three lectures by Duncan in July 1961. The young writers had been thinking about publishing a magazine, and Duncan played a large part in bringing the magazine into being:

> [T]he main push towards a magazine was Duncan's. His accounts of the histories of little mags such as *Origin, Black Mountain Review,* and *The Floating Bear* began to promise freedom from received standards and establishment bias should we venture to create a similar publication. By the Saturday following his final lecture the question was shifting from "should we" to "how."[20]

On a Sunday in August 1961, the last day of Duncan's stay in Vancouver, the six poets decided to start *Tish*. Lionel Kearns was not an editor, but was constantly involved in the magazine's operations. Nineteen issues were cranked out between September 1961 and April 1963, when Bowering, Davey, and Kearns finished their MA exams at the University of British Columbia.

The title of the magazine, suggested by Duncan himself, is a phonemic inversion of a common four-letter word. It was never the desire of the editors to produce a highly polished literary periodical.

> Rather *Tish* was to be a record of on-going literary activity, a record that preserved every roughness, insight, and stupidity that this activity enclosed. The immediate models were two US underground magazines, Cid Corman's *Origin* and LeRoy Jones' and Diane Di Prima's *The Floating Bear*. A more distant model was Louis Dudek's *Delta*, although to us even this magazine had a professional veneer which concealed whatever human contexts the writings had occurred in. Had we encountered copies of *Contact* or *Combustion* instead of *Delta*, they would have undoubtedly been more useful.[21]

The new editors had to consider internal politics. Frank Davey explains:

> [T]he politics of the magazine began with the need to select an editor and devise an editorial structure. None of us five wanted a strong "editor-in-chief" (not one of us, in fact, trusted the literary judgement of all of his colleagues). Having an editor with veto power seemed of little advantage over submitting our work to alien quarterlies. My election that night was, I am told, due to my appearing the least doctrinaire of the older editors (Bowering, Wah, and myself) and being thus least threatening to all. From the beginning, a majority vote among the editors was held necessary to admit material — including material by the editors. In practice, we usually attempted to dissuade fellow editors from publishing work we suspected, and, if failing to move him, accepted his judgement....
>
> Outside poets caused more controversy. Wah and I were originally in favor of excluding all except those of the Vancouver scene. Bowering disagreed, being anxious to publish well-known writers (Eigner, Blackburn, McClure) as a way of increasing both circulation and credibility. Our policy soon became to publish up to two pages of "outsiders" per issue as a means of defining our "tastes"....
>
> [W]e gradually located *Tish*'s appropriate form and manner. By issue #4, the subtitle had become "a poetry newsletter-Vancouver" instead of the original "a magazine of Vancouver poetry." *Tish* was obviously a newsletter — a record of work-in-progress — rather than a magazine.[22]

Tallman has a different theory:

[I]n a deeper sense it was neither magazine nor newsletter but a meeting place for their lives.... Poems written one week went the rounds the next, were argued and selected or rejected the next, and printed, folded, addressed, stamped and mailed the next. Not waiting for subscribers the editors compiled their own mailing list, paid postage from their own almost empty pockets, and distribution was free. Poems and letters received were responded to within the day, the week. Everything that was feeding into their lives was being fed directly into a flood of poems: the city, their day-to-day activities, their love affairs, quarrels over poetics, their differences with Layton, Purdy, Acorn, Gwen MacEwen — one another.[23]

Tish was a little magazine that operated at peak efficiency. The editors developed their poetics by a continual integration of poetic theory into poetry, a constant process of probing and discovering. At meetings the editors discussed each other's poems; some of them, after group discussion, rewrote their work. The editors did not solicit subscribers — they chose their own audience, and mailed the newsletter to the people they wanted to read it. *Tish* abounded with an almost missionary zeal. The magazine published an interesting blend of aesthetic hits and misses, but its vital energy and its influence cannot be questioned.

The first issue of *Tish* appeared in September 1961. The masthead shows Frank Davey as editor; James Reid, George Bowering, Fred Wah, and David Dawson are contributing editors. The editorial is by Davey. More playful than militant, the editorial notes that *Tish* "is a moving and vocal mag," that it does not exist just to publish the work of its editors but is "proof of a movement which we, the editors, feel is shared by other people as well as ourselves." Davey states:

> *Tish* is articulate. Its poets are always obsessed with the possibilities of sound, and anxious to explore it meaningfully in relation to their position in the world: their stance in "circumstance." They also like puns.
>
> *Tish* will publish any poem, short story, or essay which its editors feel shows a direct relationship to *Tish*'s siring movement.[24]

The first issue contains statements of poetics and poems by the five *Tish* editors. The Black Mountain theories are much in evidence. James Reid, in an article about poetry, declares: "so a poem is a definition a graph a mind a map to define to locate the poet and to define the temporary momentary boundaries of the awareness, each succeeding poem is a realignment of the boundaries."[25]

Inherent in these statements is a belief in Olson's theory of composition by field. George Bowering speaks of the poetic process:

> The poet has a responsibility to the whole poetic experience, and it lies in responding to his assumed capacity to re-enact the experience. For while the written poem is only one exposure of the PE, it, like a single neuron, is the most reliable clue to the nature of the greater structure. That is why the smaller parts in the written poem are *things* pertaining to the PE, and not judgements emanating from the interpreting mind of the participant artist. The things themselves participate in the PE. Teachers of freshman English will stride in here and say you're talking about good ole selection. But these are the people who also talk about "giving birth" (to a poem), a process that obviates selectivity. The poet is neither a grader nor a mother. His job is to participate.[26]

Bowering's article does not break new ground: he restates, in his own terms, the essential propositions of Black Mountain theory. Olson recommended getting rid of "lyrical interferences," and said that the poet should record his participation in the process of life. Creeley sought a more active sense of poetry; he believed that poetry is something one is given to do, rather than something one must do. Bowering, in emphasizing "The things themselves" and their participation in the poetic experience, is echoing Williams' and Olson's notion of "objectism."

Frank Davey also contributed a statement to the first issue:

> I write poetry because I am alive — a mass of living sensations — and human — intelligently perceptive of sensation. Poetry is sensation. There is no such thing as an isolated image; poetry being sensation, image is omnipresent in a poem. A successful poem is one into which the poet has put the most possible of his body. Not just used his intelligence, not just his sense of rhythm, not just his occular powers, but used a combination of the maximum of his faculties.[27]

Like Bowering, Davey is echoing the Black Mountain poets. His statement echoes Olson's emphasis upon the kinetics, principle, and process of the poem.

Fred Wah's statement also echoes Olson:

> The origin of the poem is an action (interaction, reaction) between the poet and the actual living forces in our environment (objects, human behaviour, facts and events). There is that percussive and reverberat-

ing energy released from a cathexis of the poet on contemporary reality—a merging of himself with his natural surroundings, aiming at establishing a connection between language and reality. And this alliance, this new equilibrium set up, is the energy of musical release which is the poem, be it good or bad.

[T]he poem...must preserve the instants of the poet's own dance with his environment—the melodies, rhythms, and structures found in unique contact with environment and response....[28]

Olson viewed the poet as a participant in a force greater than himself; Wah views the poet merging himself with his natural surroundings. Like Bowering and Davey, Wah indicates the general source of his poetic theory: Black Mountain poetics.

The last poetic statement in the first issue of *Tish* comes from David Dawson:

a poem is an expanding structure of thought; a necessity; a freedom.

from the initial thrust (the impetus), the poem takes the
INSTANT response, and uses this initial energy expanding into
total structure.
my poems depend heavily on free association of idea perception
action...the freest minds pass lightly/in the patterns of
the step...
great freedom is allowed the unconscious mind, not only in
associations, but equally important, in rhythm and rime
...feet gaily cross the shadow-lines and/memorize the beat...

a poem is both a measurement of circumstance and a definition of stance.

writing by ear/by breath/by freedom, I follow my mind in the
poem, and DISCOVER what I have MEASURED.[29]

Dawson presents a composite of Black Mountain theory: the poet's concern with how a thing sounds, with energy, with how form is an extension of content. Note Dawson's idiosyncratic style; his use of the shillingstroke (/) echoes Olson's (which was derived from Pound's). The *Tish* poets absorbed the Black Mountain influence, then began to use it on their own terms.

How did these poetic theories operate in practice? The poetry itself is the test of a particular poetic. Perhaps the most accomplished poem in the first issue of *Tish* is George Bowering's "Radio Jazz":

Sucked into the horn of the jazz
on lonely midnight Salt Lake City radio
over to me alone in a big house
hundreds of miles in the mountains
fantastic piano then
key to me right hand left hand on silent radio sound
on a million radio America waves in the dark

Folks all gone folks
gone to the Coast leaving me and
the shelf radio in a hot night kitchen
old friends gone home three empty cups on the table here

Gerry Mulligan meets Stan Getz
in the next one in the last one
on the radio award bandstand
down away on the truck coming road
sound radio bound Salt Lake City comes on.[30]

Bowering recreates the music he hears over the air waves and the words create a sense of musical colour that is quite "jazzy." This poem brings the beat atmosphere of jazz, and an almost Kerouacian measure, into Canadian poetry.
    A poem entitled "Watch," by Frank Davey, was also in the first issue:

Watch that horse, Jack
he shouted
as the mare slipped out of her
riding breeches

but too late to stop
the runaway[31]

The first issue also included "A Tale," by Fred Wah:

The smoothness
of her thighs is
one thing.

The memory
of a cedar bough's
softness is
the same thing.

These two things
in one I could
be master of.

And am.
The sheets
are also
cool.[32]

Looking at these poems it might be worthwhile to consider for a moment the
kind of poems *Alphabet* was publishing at the same time. There a formal, set,
traditional line, entirely different from the tightly controlled and shaped
variations of phrasing and breath in the *Tish* poems, was being employed by
Jay Macpherson. Another point of real contrast is the content; whereas the
Alphabet poems were loaded with myth, the orientation in these *Tish* poems is
towards reality, even towards what can be considered the commonplace. The
aestheticism of Imagism has been loosened in *Tish* to contain almost any
day-to-day experience as content for poetry. A comparison of the writings in
Alphabet and *Tish* reveals the extremes of poetry that represented the sixties,
the former adhering to established, traditional form, the latter exploring a
poetry of kinetics, novelty in form, content, and effect. The conscious artistry
and artificiality of much of the *Alphabet* poetry stands opposed to this new
poetry which aims at nothing more than the expression of the actuality of life
and seeks a fluid form that corresponds to that actuality. In its realistic
orientation we can say that *Tish* is a further development of the Imagist line of
Modernism, while *Alphabet*, in some ways, harks back to the Symbolist
aesthetic. Seymour Mayne, then editor of the rival Montreal little magazine
Cataract, argued in a letter to *Tish* that, of the poems in the second issue of
Tish, almost "all were take-offs on poets in Don Allen's *The New American
Poetry 1945-60.*"[33] "Take-offs" may be an inappropriate term; Vancouver
poets were attempting to work out, for themselves and in their own environment, the implications of what they considered to be an important poetic. The
concreteness in the poems in *Tish* shows the poets' honest attempt to find their
own articulation and to define their own sense of place.

In editorials and articles, *Tish* stressed that poetry is a vocal art. "POEMS IN
TISH ARE INTENDED FOR READING ALOUD," a banner headline reads in *Tish*
number four,[34] and in the editorial of that issue Jamie Reid advises the reader
to "Listen to the sound of it. Pay attention to the automobiles and trains and
people and jazzbands and Beethoven. Listen to the strange music of your own
voice in the poem."[35] In an essay in *Tish* number three called "When A New
Music Is Heard The Walls Of The City Tremble," Warren Tallman contrasts
the "music of thought" and "a music at the heart of things":

115

Writing is a rhythmic art, but it is also an intellectual and a vocal one in which words on the page send out at least two sorts of signals, those the mind receives as the articulations of thought and those the ear receives as the articulations of voice. Because the words serve both an intellectual and a vocal master it seems impossible to separate the sense from the sound, and one easy solution is to assume that they are the same. Which they are. But it is even truer that emphasis makes for difference, it being a long way from the mind to the mouth, from writing that owes first allegiance to intellect and that which owes it to the voice. In our time the difference has become distinct as poetry has renewed an old affinity with song, fiction with the tale, and between the singing and the telling voice has regained recognition as the instrument that provides the actual path between the writer's reality and the reader's. "Taste my mouth in your ear," says Allen Ginsberg as he tongues a groovey bridge between.... [T]o say a music of thought is to insist that the music must precede and give rise to the thoughts. That is, the *reality* which surrounds the writer, determining what Lionel Kearns calls his "stance in circumstance," must precede and give rise to his thoughts. In the beginning there is what Duncan names "a music at the heart of things," and it is just the marvel of the voice instrument that it can transform this otherwise silent music from the breath that breathes it forth into the sounds that give it substance, and that these sounds can then search out a corresponding music in the language. When thought modulates itself to that music it is itself musical; a direct *projection* of the inner reality. But when the writing is worked the other way around, with intellect in control, the voice instrument is muted as the writing rhythms are *extended* at an even, patterned pace and the words form into the kind of bridges thought can easily move across. Pope "lisped the numbers," and the iambs came, pentameter to his mind — thousands of iambs in even-pacing flocks of five.[36]

Tallman is essentially arguing that, through breath and voice, an articulation of the music at the heart of things can be achieved, whereas when intellect is given precedence the voice as instrument is muted and the poem is expressed in even-measured rhythmical units, that is, as variations in a pre-established rhythm. The subordination of voice to intellect Tallman sees as creating a shift to what "intellect in fact does, which is to catch up these things that seem wrong in regions of experience by putting them right in realms of thought";[37] this divorces poetry from life and sends the poet off "in search for softer music on some farther shore."[38] This intellectual search for Eldorado that Tallman sees as predominating in so much of English poetry he also argues was losing intellectual momentum in the Romantic poets of the nineteenth century.

> From Keats' day to our own few such poems are even attempted in England, and this gradual decline of intellectual confidence (and a corresponding decline of confidence in the myths, symbols and ideas intellect has created) gives rise to the new and different confidence in voice. It was Walt Whitman's lean, lewd, hankering barbarian whose songs of self and earth brought voice back in with a yawp. What comes in with Whitman is an attempt to naturalize and humanize all those aspects of experience which earlier poets had attempted to intellectualize. He moves from myth on back to music, and his "I have an intelligence of earth," William Carlos Williams' "No ideas but in things," and Charles Olson's clincher, "Man and external reality are so involved with one another that, for man's purposes, they had better be taken as one," are some ABCs of the naturalizing process. These directives turn attention back to earth herself as the great rhythmic mother of all human activity, breathing out and breathing in.[39]

It is through voice and an emphasis upon the natural music at the heart of things that the poet as man finds his re-integration, so that he revitalizes poetry in the face of its increasing intellectual impoverishment. The emphasis here is upon voice, earth, things, and the unification of man and his external reality; it is out of these, Tallman maintains, that the vital poem springs.

Tish also presented the seeds of literary feuds that spread into Canadian literary history. In *Tish* number four, George Bowering wrote a damaging review of Milton Acorn's *Against A League of Liars*. (In the next *Tish* there was a long, argumentative letter from Al Purdy in defense of Acorn. This might be the origin of a literary quarrel that has continued through the years, culminating in 1970, when Bowering received the Governor-General's Award for Poetry and Acorn's *I've Tasted My Blood* did not. At a much-publicized dinner in Toronto, Acorn was awarded a cash prize and given the People's Poet Award by a group of poets, among them Margaret Atwood, Irving Layton, and Eli Mandel.) Other issues of *Tish* express a growing antagonism between the *Tish* poets and the young Montreal poets (Seymour Mayne, K. V. Hertz, Henry Moscovitch) who grouped around Layton in the sixties. Much of this early contention has hardened into hostility. (One example is Keith Richardson's *Poetry and the Colonized Mind: Tish*, a book critical of the *Tish* movement, which was published in 1976 through a press owned by Seymour Mayne.) Perhaps because any little magazine is a testing ground for challenging poetic theories, it is also the source of much continuing literary controversy.

David Dawson's editorial in *Tish* number five signals a sharpening of the magazine's policies:

> After four issues we now know what we want to do. We have reached the stage where we can say NO; we can reject a good poem if it does not interest us. The fact that it may be good does not alter the fact that it may not work the way we feel a poem should work. We print poems which conform to our taste, poems which move somewhat in the same direction as our own. This is true, not only of poems submitted by the readers, but of the poems submitted by the various co-editors as well. The desired result is a selection of poetry which indicates our poetic stance, which defines our scene.[40]

Although most of the poems in *Tish* were written by the editors, other poets were included: David Cull, Lionel Kearns, K. V. Hertz, Kelly Lane, Seymour Mayne, Larry Eigner, Padraig O Broin, David McFadden, Samuel Perry, bill bissett, Robert F. Grady, Bob Hogg, Ann O'Loughlin, Red Lane, Avo Erisalu, Brian Finn, Gwendolyn MacEwen, Daphne Buckle, Patricia Smith, Michael McClure, David Bromige, and John Newlove appeared in the first year. Poets like Cull, Kearns, Eigner, McFadden, bissett, Hogg, Buckle (Marlatt), McClure, and Bromige are all firmly rooted in the American or Canadian avant garde.

The editorial in *Tish* number eight is unsigned, and should probably be viewed as a general policy statement.

> Almost every month *Tish* is pestered by people who assert that "Canadian" poets such as Souster, Klein, Scott, Layton, Dudek, Birney, Cohen (to give one writer's list) are "equal" (usually "superior") to their contemporary American and English poets. We do not question here the merits of these so-called "Canadians"; what we do object to is their classification by their country.
>
> Poetry is not an international competition. Moreover, poets do not write as patriots, but as men. Their country is merely incidental. Canada does not exist except as a political arrangement for the convenience of individuals accidentally happening to live within its arbitrary area. . . .
>
> Let's have no more superficial jingoism in poetry. If a man/poet ever comes to represent his homeland or his home town, he will do so inevitably, not intentionally. As for comparisons, the community of poetry is a universal thing, as is man, and political divisions can never apply.[41]

This is a cosmopolitan, political statement, and later Davey would be able to assert that the *Tish* poets were "culturally historical... rather than nationalistic."[42] It also provides fuel for Robin Mathews, who asserted that Davey and other *Tish* poets place "against the sense of evolution and organic relation in Canadian history the anarchic individualism of US history."[43] The argument presented in the editorial is anti-nationalistic and pro-individual (though one could debate how much commitment to anarchy such a case contains). Recent work by Bowering and Davey would suggest that time has tempered their views, but in the atmosphere of the sixties the *Tish* poets presented a strong internationalist position.

The conflict continues in issue eleven. Milton Acorn, Al Purdy, and Gwendolyn MacEwen were then editing a little magazine, *Moment*, in Toronto. In a *Tish* editorial, Davey chastises MacEwen for inventing the "olson-jones school"; he calls her description "a glib bit of would-be jargon designed to make the unwary believe that Charles Olson's and LeRoi Jones' stances and techniques were virtually identical... and that they both flirted as capriciously with lower case letters as does E. E. Cummings."[44] Davey instructs MacEwen in the value of Charles Olson's work, then savages a recent editorial in *Moment*. The *Tish* poets were, in principle, antagonistic to the poets in *Alphabet*, *Moment*, and *Cataract*, who in turn responded with hostility to *Tish*. We see here the poetic and political rivalries that arise between little magazines, each believing it alone has the answer to the needs of poetry. Three of these magazines, *Alphabet*, *Moment*, and *Tish*, contributed some permanent lines of development for Canadian poetry; *Cataract* had less effect, and represented a group of young poets whose work has failed to have lasting significance.

Frank Davey continued to develop an aesthetic in the pages of *Tish*. In issue ten he writes:

> Robert Duncan has said that the age of the masterwork is dead — that ours is the age of testimony. Which, if I read it right, takes the emphasis away from the "work of art" and places it back on the creator and his concerns. Back on the creator as man rather than "artist."[45]

Davey is committed to a poetry that is content-oriented, and is expressly designed to communicate. We must also be aware of the man behind the poem — or rather, of the man in the poem whose testimony we hear. Davey sees the construction poet-as-formalist-craftsman as inappropriate, a betrayal of honest witnessing.

The first anniversary issue of *Tish*, number thirteen, appeared 14

September, 1962 and contained assessments of the magazine by two of the leading mentors of the *Tish* poets, Robert Creeley and Robert Duncan. Creeley's assessment is called "Why Bother?"[46] In it, Creeley defines what a little magazine can and should be; his definition fits in quite specifically with what *Tish*, in its time and place, already was. Creeley argues that a little magazine can define a new possibility for poetry by providing "the place where it can be formulated." By and large, the little magazine is a forum in which things are not merely proposed, but worked out. Certainly we can see *Tish* as the accumulated work-sheets of a group of young poets attempting to formulate new poetic possibilities in the place they live in.

Creeley also points out that poetry is learned by example. All poetry must derive from some source or influence; this, he says, does not have anything to do with the basic originality of a specific work. There is a distinction between influence and derivativeness. Once a literary style is adopted by larger magazines, Creeley argues, the act of definition has ceased and the reign of taste has begun. The pioneering little magazine that attempts to define a new local art is opposed to any principle of fame operating at that time. The fact that pioneering work is being done limits the possibility of readership and recognition. Those attempting to define new possibilities for poetry must be aware that their definition may prove to have only momentary import; yet this risk must be undertaken if new ground is to be broken. Creeley places his ultimate belief in magazines of this kind. They may "find the next step all must take if only because they are forced to take each such step with their own feet." The process of having to work out aesthetic problems for oneself facilitates the likelihood of working out future problems, including some that are more essential or more exploratory.

There is a similar recognition of *Tish* in Duncan's essay, "For the Novices of Vancouver." In the poetry in *Tish* Duncan sees "a breakthru to a tutelary daimon of an *other* Vancouver... a bridge in consciousness," and he notes that the "shores are shores of Vancouver, of an actual place that is also a spiritual beach-head."[47] (Duncan here is referring to David Dawson's "Tentative Coastlines," in issue twelve, but his comments reflect on all the *Tish* poets.) Duncan says that the young *Tish* poets have truly set "a poetry in motion" and that, in the first twelve issues, "a language appears thruout, the issues of their magazine become issues of a work, of something happening."[48] A community has been created.

One can see Creeley's and Duncan's statements as a certificate of approval for "Black Mountain North," but in genuine critical response it is also a recognition of the serious work and intention that are reflected in the first twelve issues of *Tish*.

The thirteenth issue of *Tish* represents the peak of the magazine and completes the period of intense theorizing, criticizing, and competing with other literary periodicals. The magazine acquires a quieter polemical tone, a confidence, and a greater concentration on poetry. The last seven issues of the first editorial period of the magazine contain poems significant in the development of the poets as poets; in the last seven issues we find Red Lane's "Margins" and the continuation of Dawson's "Tentative Coastlines" (issue thirteen), Davey's "Bridge Force" poems (issues thirteen and fifteen), and "Morte D'Arthur" (issue fourteen). This last is the beginning of an interest in Arthurian legend that will appear in the later Davey books *Arcana* and *King of Swords*. Also in these seven numbers we have Bowering's much anthologized "Grandfather" and "Circus Maximus," as well as "Points On the Grid," and Lionel Kearn's experiments in "stacked verse."

The first editorial period of *Tish* ended with issue nineteen on 14 March, 1963. Most of the editors had completed study at the University of British Columbia and were dispersing. As George Bowering noted in "The Most Remarkable Thing About Tish" in issue twenty:

> Frank Davey is moving to Victoria. Fred Wah is moving to New Mexico. James Reid promises to leave the continent. Lionel Kearns is going to lock himself in his writing room for a year. I'm moving to Calgary. That leaves Dave Dawson as the new editor of *Tish*.[49]

Along with Bowering's retrospective appeared Frank Davey's; he looked back at the role and achievement of the first nineteen issues of *Tish*:

> The intent of many a little magazine is altruism, but this could never be said of *Tish*. Writer conceived and directed, *Tish* was from the beginning selfish and pretentious. To the reader it could easily have appeared as a monthly exhibition, but it was never so to the editors.
>
> For them *Tish* became the nagging and insistent mother of almost all their writing. The more whimsical of them, myself especially, were glad of the controlled demand it placed on their energies, although the mechanical and editorial burdens were always somewhat discouraging.
>
> The increase in writing output was something the editors had anticipated when founding the magazine, but other dividends were entirely unanticipated. For instance, the improvement in writing skills which came to each of the editors with regular exposure to a critical audience. And, equally important, the friendship and advice of other writers, both beginning and established — and contact with book publishers and magazine editors.[50]

For the first group of editors *Tish* had served as a productive home-base; it gave them a forum for their writing and a place to work out their poetic and critical theories. It also provided them with a jumping-off point to other magazines and to book publication.

Tish did not terminate with the dissolution of the first editorial board, but carried on for another six years. In *Poetry and the Colonized Mind: Tish*, Keith Richardson has detailed four different editorial periods. The first lasted from September 1961 until March 1963, under the founding editors, who produced nineteen issues. The second editorial period began in August 1963 and ended in May 1964, with David Dawson, Daphne Buckle, David Cull, Gladys Hindmarch, Peter Auxier, and Dan McLeod as editors. The third period produced issues twenty-five to forty, from June 1964 until March 1967. Richardson describes this period:

> The principal editor during the third period was Dan McLeod; he was designated as the general editor of *Tish* 25, June 1964, and continued as such until *Tish* 28, January 1965, at which point everyone was designated as an editor. McLeod was also the most consistent editor throughout the entire editorial period.[51]

The fourth and final period started in February 1968 and ended in mid-1969; issues forty-one to E (forty-five) were edited by Karen Tallman.

Despite the fact that the magazine continued for six years after the first editorial period and served well various factions of the Vancouver literary scene, the important work done by *Tish* is contained in the first nineteen numbers, when a new poetics and a new orientation were first being worked out. We see the Black Mountain influence appearing in projects the original *Tish* editors initiated elsewhere; we see it in contacts they made and in magazines they began after the *Tish* experience. What had begun in *Tish* would radiate beyond Vancouver as the *Tish* editors travelled to other parts of Canada and as writers in other parts of the country began to discover the possibilities suggested by the poets in the Allen anthology, particularly the Black Mountain poets.

After graduating from the University of British Columbia, George Bowering took up a teaching post at the University of Alberta, in Calgary, where he began publishing *Imago* in 1964. The magazine was devoted to the long poem and the long-poem sequence. Bowering produced twenty issues of the magazine in ten years, moving from Calgary to London, Ontario, to Montreal, and back to Vancouver. In an opening editorial, Bowering defined the magazine's orientation and explained its title:

To image is to make it all appear. To this reader that is a meaning, image as verb. IMAGO is an old word for imitation. It also is a word for what you have at the end of metamorphosis. Not a wing, not a thorax—the whole thing, changed, developed.

This *Imago*, the magazine, is interested in the poem...more than in poems. It is intended, more than can be seen in this no. 1, for the long poem, the series or set, the sequence, swatches from giant work in progress, long life pains eased into print.... A 42 page poem will use up the whole mag, be in fact an *Imago* book, or a book imago.[52]

Implied in the "imago" is the creation of a perfect metamorphosed form of being, in this case the poem. Bowering, at this time beginning to work in larger forms, suggests that the long poem or poem sequence holds more potential for poetic realization than the short lyric. Bowering's "long poem" is not the narrative of a poet like E. J. Pratt, but rather the exploratory-expressive poem, like *The Cantos* of Pound or Williams's *Paterson*. The form was also developed by the Black Mountain poets and by San Francisco poets Jack Spicer and Robin Blaser, and in Canada by Louis Dudek.

Imago published work by American, English, and Canadian avant-garde poets, including the American poets Anselm Hollo, Robert Duncan, Margaret Randall, Paul Blackburn, Charles Olson, Theodore Enslin, Carol Berge, John Sinclair, Diane Di Prima, Jerome Rothenberg, Joel Oppenheimer, Anne Waldman, Michael McClure, Larry Eigner, Robin Blaser, Michael Palmer, and Fielding Dawson; the British poets Ian Hamilton Finlay, David Bromige, and Tom Raworth; and Canadian poets John Newlove, George Bowering, Frank Davey, Lionel Kearns, Al Purdy, Victor Coleman, David McFadden, Daphne Buckle (Marlatt), bpNichol, Doug Fetherling, Roy Kiyooka, Artie Gold, Dwight Gardiner, Margaret Atwood, Barry McKinnon, Robert Hogg, David Rosenberg, Gladys Hindmarch, Brian Fawcett, Fred Wah, Greg Curnoe, and Gerry Gilbert. *Tish* alumni are visible, as are many Canadian poets associated with *New Wave Canada*.

Every third issue of *Imago* was a book-length collection by a Canadian poet. Despite the integration with American contemporaries, the Canadians ultimately held precedence: *Listen George* by Lionel Kearns (number three), *The Scarred Hull* by Frank Davey (number six), *The Saladmaker* by David McFadden (number nine), *Sitting in Mexico* by George Bowering (number twelve), *Back East* by Victor Coleman (number fifteen), and *Five Books Of A Northmanual* by Brian Fawcett (number eighteen).

The first nineteen issues of *Imago* had an identical, unpretentious format: the magazine sported coloured-paper covers, it was stapled, and it was reproduced on a Gestetner machine. The last issue (number twenty) was a perfect-bound volume of one hundred pages (the others had been forty or fifty pages) published by Vancouver's Talonbooks.

When *Imago* began in 1964, there was no forum for the long poem. By the time the last issue appeared, in 1974, publishers were publishing book-length poems as a matter of course. The publishing boom that occurred in the late sixties had picked up the slack in the area that Bowering had chosen as the special preserve of *Imago*.

The most interesting magazine produced by the *Tish* alumni is *Open Letter*, begun in 1965 and continuing to this day, and edited by Frank Davey, with a varying group of contributing editors or associate editors (initially George Bowering, David Dawson, and Fred Wah; currently George Bowering, Steve McCaffery, bpNichol, and Fred Wah). *Open Letter* is a review "of writing and sources," and provides a forum for critical theory and evaluation. It has become the most important avant-garde periodical in Canada; it has sought to bring together all the different strands of experimentation and to unify them in a single web against the mainstream of Canadian writing.

In fifteen years of existence, *Open Letter* has changed its format, but it maintains its purpose, which was explained in the first editorial: the magazine would be "an attempt to combine within the pages of a periodical the features of both a symposium and a debate."[53] Frank Davey wrote the first editorial:

> The subject will be poetry and its medium, language. The debaters will be the editors, myself, George Bowering, David Dawson, and Fred Wah....
>
> Fifteen hundred years finds the total magic of the English language still untapped, and so will fifteen million. The power of the written sign is always open, always unexplored. *The Open Letter* begins its explorations with letters from its editors to each other, letters that describe the points they have reached so far in their lives with language. It is from these points that *The Open Letter* will start to measure its progress.[54]

To anyone unfamiliar with current North American poetry, Davey notes, "the *Open Letter* will present an ostensibly private world of baffling values, problems, place-names, and personages."[55] The sense of a "private world" has always been inherent to *Open Letter*.

Each set of nine issues of *Open Letter* composes a "series." The first series contained actual open letters as well as poems. With the beginning of the second series energy was directed to producing critical articles and more fully developed theory.

In the first series, the former *Tish* editors began an internal debate on questions that must have been present during the early *Tish* years but that, in *Open Letter*, developed into open criticism of one another's aesthetics and work. *Tish* had seemed almost monolithic; *Open Letter* shows the young poets attempting to assert their individual styles and views of poetry. This process begins with George Bowering's "Open Letter" in the first issue:

> When I was associated with *Tish* I was criticized from inside that group for being too eclectic, and from outside that group for being too inbred. The critics of *Tish* are pretty easy to dismiss; they usually did not know what they were talking about. They usually said the *Tish* poets were engaged in intellectual navel-viewing, but they did not demonstrate such a thing with any reference to the poetry and ideas being announced in the newsletter....
>
> I am more interested in saying something about the sometime differences I have had with the former *Tish* editors & poets. I would be jumped on with questions such as: why are you paying attention to those Canadian poets who are not writing out of our traditions? Answer: because I am a poet before I am anyone's monkey, and I like good poetry and signs of good poetry. Good poetry is poetry that speaks with an intelligible voice, and of things that matter. Ruben Dario was one of the greatest poets of the last 2000 years.
>
> Question: why do you write those smart-aleck poems that sound like bad Ferlinghetti? Answer: because I am not satisfied that I can write good and better poetry by sticking with one process and trying to improve on it. I will retain and improve certain skills, such as those I have learnt from Olson and Duncan and Creeley, but I want to try other things, too, the ones that don't work and must be thrown away included....
>
> Question: why do you waste your time with baseball, comic books, pop novels, university, academic poets, etc? Answer: I am large, I contain multitudes. How do you know they don't play baseball in Heaven?
>
> I liked the idea of *Tish*, and I still do. I like the idea of *The Open Letter*, and would urge the former *Tish* people to keep their noses in this new mag. For one thing, I want to know what you are all doing, even if it isn't what I'm doing. And I would like to see you quit arguing so much about things that concern the ego. Let's talk about poetry, and remember that good poetry, whatever you think that is, crops up anywhere.[56]

Bowering emphasizes his individuality as a writer and his right to that individuality; to accept all the tenets of the Black Mountain poets would be to conform, which the *Tish* poets did. But groups of poets work together with a shared aesthetic for a short period of time; eventually they must assert their own identity. The group begins to dissolve.

In a letter in the first issue, Frank Davey talks of his current activity, of what he calls a search "for all the facts." He continues:

> Of late, as you may have guessed, I have been turning back to Pound. Warren Tallman first indicated back in 1962 that we should know Pound and his methods well before hoping to write well ourselves, and, after finally taking his advice, I can't see how any of us can ever write anything major without at least a year on Ezra. For his methods, with or without the ego (but preferably without), are still the only ones today with epic potentiality. And from where I see all our writing from *Tish* 1 and onward, the epic — certainly like no epic seen before this century — and at least epic size, epic vision, has been always our final goal. And thus the need for the spade work, the bibliographies, the facts: for if we ever are to bring Pound's ideal of the facts as their own spokesmen into any real and significant existence, we must be collectors of these facts as well as writers who can render them with truth.[57]

The work of several of the *Tish* poets — Bowering's *Imago*, *Rocky Mountain Foot*, *Curious*, and *Autobiology*, Davey's *Weeds* and *The Clallam* — support Davey's claim that the work begun in *Tish* points in the direction of the "epic."

Many of the assertions in the early issues of *Open Letter* suggest something like a poetic rumble on the way. There is a great deal of fighting among a group of writers who still share fundamental assumptions. In issue number two, Daphne Buckle objects to Davey's view that "the epic...has been always our final goal." Buckle argues that the "single point is the place."[58] She also is concerned with technique, which she believes Davey neglects in the first issue. Davey responds that his sense of epic is in "scope of vision...not in the monumental man or event, the 'heroic'.... Yes, the single point is the place. But surely the points must correlate. For if they don't, we have what Warren once called 'incidental poems' — poems of such diverse kinds that they suggest no single being behind them."[59]

In issue number two we also find Bowering levelling criticism at David Dawson:

> I got no quarrel with anything anyone said in OLI, tho I have to admit that I am getting pisst off with David Dawson's poetry still dancing

and sighing around old-previous neo-Duncanisms, arrived at so easily by putting "the" in front of something, notably "the word" and "the dance" and "the poem" and "the mystery".... Daphne Buckle does a similar thing. That's Duncan's — he arrived at it, and I think naturally. Quit echoing.[60]

Critics of the *Tish* poets had often disagreed with the group's "monotony" and "derivativeness." In the early issues of *Open Letter*, members of the group level the same criticism at each other.

Also in the second issue of *Open Letter* is Frank Davey's assault on concrete poetry. Noting that both bpNichol and David McFadden offered some visual poems to *Open Letter*, Davey writes:

McFadden and Nichol send visual poems — which mode I still find irrelevant to what I know as poetry. For me poetry is of language, and language is still of sound with rhythm in stress & pitch, and is not just visual shape....[61]

Davey's view is less open than it would later become; he accepts some aspects of avant-garde poetry, and refuses others.

The internal debates continued in issue number three. In an open letter to Bowering, Davey writes about the two different kinds of poems he sees in Bowering's recent book *The Man In The Yellow Boots*: ego-centred poetry (with Bowering as subject) and poems that tap into the central issue of poetry and language (the kind of poetry Davey is interested in).

In issue number four there is an exchange of letters between bpNichol and Davey on the subject of visual poetry. Davey does not acknowledge a visual relationship between words as a form of poetry; Nichol counters that if a visual rhythm can be recognized in painting, it can exist in the medium of language. If one accepts the validity of visual poetry, one expands what is knowable as poetry. Davey argues that one should separate the oral and visual components of language. He maintains that writing "is a resource of *drawing*, not a resource of language." He is willing to concede that visual poetry might constitute an art form, but he argues that it is not "a *language* art form, & seems to have no direct connection to poetry."[62] In issue number five Victor Coleman comments on the debate (and the magazine in general): "Everybody's shucking. There's no room in *The Open Letter* for poems."[63] Coleman's point was well taken. Essentially, Davey wanted a journal of theory and research.

Issue number seven consists entirely of a collection of poems by David Dawson, *Where The Orders Are*. The contentious criticism began to decline (perhaps the poets associated with *Open Letter* began to realize they had little to gain by levelling criticisms at one another). With the beginning of the second series, the personal letters and poems disappear. The magazine is printed and perfect-bound. Each issue is given a title or critical theme, and includes essays, statements, and book reviews. Themes in the second series include "Politics and Poetry," "Olson and others," "Reductive Aesthetics," "Refinding the Language," and "Kinetic Mythology." With issue number four in the second series bpNichol and Steve McCaffery become contributing editors, and their Toronto Research Group reports — investigations of translation and narrative — begin to appear.

Now in its fourth series, *Open Letter* continues to be a pioneer critical journal. In format and content, it has acquired the appearance of a university journal or quarterly. In its criticism, however, it works as a little magazine. The second, third, and fourth series have included provocative essays ("Political Poetry" by George Stanley, "Heidegger and Poetry" by Leslie Mundwiler, "A Predictive Essay on the Future of Publishing" by Fielding Dawson, "A Neurology of Inductive Verse" by Christopher Dewdney, "Politics of the Referent" collected by Steve McCaffery); critical articles (on Charles Olson, Gertrude Stein, Gwendolyn MacEwen, John Newlove, Phyllis Webb, Louis Zukofsky, Leonard Cohen, Daphne Marlatt, Audrey Thomas, Les Levine, Christopher Dewdney, David McFadden, Clark Blaise, Alice Munro, T. S. Eliot, Louis Dudek, John Bentley Mays, Victor Coleman, Robert Kroetsch, and bill bissett); and issues devoted to one writer (Warren Tallman, Sheila Watson, Louis Dudek, and Robert Kroetsch). *Open Letter* remains an important example of avant-garde Canadian theoretical and critical writing.

Another magazine that derived from the original *Tish* editors is *Sum*, edited by Fred Wah. *Sum* was, in effect, an American magazine edited by a Canadian. *Sum* was edited from Albuquerque, New Mexico, and then from Buffalo, New York as Wah continued his studies, from 1964 to 1965, for a total of seven issues. Wah's guest editors were American: issue four, for example, was guest-edited by John Keys and bore the subtitle "Writing out of New York." The issue features work by Ron Padgett, Frank O'Hara, Paul Blackburn, Fielding Dawson, Ted Berrigan, Leroi Jones, Gerard Malanga, Diane Wakosi, Gilbert Sorrentino, Jackson MacLow, and Ted Enslin. Issue number six was edited by Ron Loewinsohn, and presented writing from San Francisco. Although Wah's magazine did not serve as a forum for the *Tish* editors, it did carry the *Tish* poetics to New Mexico, and demonstrated the continentalism of at least one of the editors.

The Black Mountain poets influenced many Canadian poets. In the fifties, for example, the *Cerberus* group encountered Black Mountain poetics. Raymond

Souster took an interest in the American poets and published their work in *Contact* and *Combustion*. The eastern thread of Black Mountain influence is picked up from Souster by Victor Coleman in Toronto during the early sixties, and reveals itself in Coleman's little magazine *Island*, which published eight issues between September 1964 and May 1967.

In the connection between Souster and Coleman we see the passing of a body of ideas from a poet of an older generation to the poet of a younger one. Souster had a strong and continuing influence on *Island*; in fact, *Island* number six is also the long-awaited fifteenth number of *Combustion*, which was edited by Souster. With Coleman's help, Souster assembled *New Wave Canada*, an anthology of Coleman and his contemporaries. As well, the demise of Souster's Contact Press is closely followed by the creation of Coach House Press, where Coleman was an editor for seven years. Contact Press and Coach House, two leading literary presses in Canada, are related by this transition.

Unlike *Contact*, *Combustion*, and *Tish*, *Island* was attractively printed from the very first issue. Contributors to the first issue are both American and Canadian: Gilbert Sorrentino, Thomas Clark, Ron Loewinsohn, Gael Turnbull, John Newlove, Gwendolyn MacEwen, Red Lane, Victor Coleman, Frank Davey, and Raymond Souster. An old letter to Souster from William Carlos Williams was also reprinted. And on the back cover we find a poem by Souster in memory of Williams, who had recently died.

The letter from Williams is dated June 1952. In it he says:

> It is not the way that the man speaks that we wait for. A poet does not talk *about* what is in him, he talks a double language, it is the presence in him that speaks. For the moment he is lost in that identity. And each age is marked by the presences that possess it as its poets are seized by them also, in the flesh, and strut about as unknown. Poor powerless ghosts, their only life is that which they gain from the poets who lend them a life now and then.[64]

Williams's view comes close to Olson's position concerning the poet's stance towards reality. Beyond the surface mysticism of Williams's statement is an insistence upon letting the deeper levels have their say (instead of letting the conscious mind fashion rational, logical structures, with the craftsman ever in control). The rejection of the poet as conscious artisan is essential to Black Mountain poetics, and also to Williams.

In all eight issues of *Island* we have a mixture of American and Canadian voices, although, unlike *Combustion*, the magazine does not include international poetry and large quantities of poetry in translation. In the second issue, however, we find Anselm Hollo, Joel Oppenheimer, Theodore Enslin, and Robert Kelly, Americans, and George Bowering, Joe Rosenblatt, and Al Purdy. In *Island* number three we have the poems of Red Lane, Seymour Mayne, Victor Coleman, and David Cull, as well as work by three Buffalo poets (Andrew Crozier, Stephen Rodefer, and Bob Hogg), three Bard College poets (Richard Clarke, Harvey Bialy, and Jonathan Greene), and Paul Blackburn and Diane Wakosi. Number four is the first of a sequence of special issues; it is a book-length collection of Fred Wah's poems called *Lardeau*. Number five consists of a book-length collection, *The Knife*, by Buffalo poet Stephen Rodefer; and number six is *Combustion* number fifteen, edited by Raymond Souster. The last issue, seven-eight, appeared in May 1967, in an enlarged format, and featured the work of Robert Kelly, Paul Blackburn, Theodore Enslin, Victor Coleman, Gerry Gilbert, Phyllis Webb, Raymond Souster, Bob Hogg, bpNichol, Clayton Eshleman, Ron Loewinsohn, Lionel Kearns, and Stephen Rodefer. A short note is included: "ISLAND PRESS & THE COACH HOUSE PRESS would like to focus any further attentions offered on IS. The second number has already appeared, edited by Victor Coleman."[65]

Is began its run while *Island* was still publishing. The first issue announced that the magazine was "dedicated to the Occasional Poem" and would be "Published whenever."[66] *Is* began as a small stapled pamphlet, but printing and format improved as Coach House imprints in general improved. *Is* continued the work of *Island*, publishing vast quantities of the literary avant-garde without any apparent manifesto or polemics.

While *Is* was a veritable who's who of Canadian experimental writing, the magazine itself experimented with different formats. Issue number two was printed; issue four presented work on individual printed sheets or in little booklets, which were then placed in envelopes; number five was composed of sheets of various sizes tied together with string. *Is* number eight was a special "Prose Forms" issue, which began a string of theme issues. Number eleven was devoted to unpublished young writers, edited by John Oughton; then issue twelve featured west-coast writing, issue thirteen west-coast art, issue fourteen writing by women, edited by Penny Chalmers; number sixteen featured "Collaborations," edited by Coleman, and issue nineteen-twenty was a special "Erotics" issue. The magazine was more interesting than it was important for poetic development in Canada; it was notable for its serendipity or charming variety rather than for any attempt to define a poetic direction. It presented a variety of work from writers experimenting in different open forms, and thus tended to consolidate the Canadian avant-garde and serve as an interesting house publication for Coach House Press, whose catalogue of books represents a more important contribution to Canadian writing than does the idiosyncratic magazine.

With Coach House Press, this survey of the Black Mountain influence comes to an end. Black Mountain poetics have become widely absorbed into Canadian poetry: it is easier to think of poets who subscribe to, or at least acknowledge, the poetic theories of Charles Olson than to find those who do not. At the same time, however, the original Black Mountain influence has been somewhat diffused and has lost much of its inner force as it has been adopted by scores of young poets. The initial energies apparent in *Tish* and in *Island* have converged in Coach House Press, where much of the avant-garde writing of the sixties group of writers continues to be published. Little magazines yielded to small presses; the original impetus that propelled the magazines eventually ends in book publication, as Michael Gnarowski has pointed out, since a book appears to be more important and durable than a magazine could be. Coleman gave up *Island* and moved to Coach House, where he served in an editorial capacity for seven years. When disputes with printer-owner Stan Bevington began to trouble the operation, Coleman left Coach House, to be replaced by an editorial group, which now includes poets bpNichol, Michael Ondaatje, and Frank Davey. Today, Coach House represents the most significant outpost of the Canadian literary avant-garde. Still central to most members of this avant-garde group are the poetic theories of Charles Olson and the Black Mountain poets.

8

Other Modernist Innovations:
Canadian Concrete and Sound Poetry

In considering Modernist development in Canadian poetry, we have seen the continuity of a Modernist line that stems from the early fathers: Yeats, Pound, Williams, and Eliot. The Black Mountain writers are the poetic sons and grandsons of Pound and Williams; the myth poets who clustered around *Alphabet* and absorbed Northrop Frye's theories are the poetic heirs of Eliot; Frye himself is a link in the Eliot chain. But Modernism was an international movement, in many of its most vital phases more European than English or American; there were many "isms" or radical directions opened to art in the 1910s and 1920s apart from the Imagism of Pound or the Vorticism of Wyndham Lewis: Futurism (both Russian and Italian), German Expressionism, Dadaism and Surrealism, and Symbolism were all germinating. Even Gertrude Stein's brand of Modernism stands out; it has precious little to do with the work pioneered by the Imagists.

Succeeding generations of poets in England, the United States, and Canada fought for the innovations of two particular lines of Modernism. Pound often served as the central figure for the English Modernists; we see Williams to his left and Eliot to his right. Subsequent generations of writers moved to either side. John Crowe Ransom and Richard Wilbur gravitated towards Eliot; Zukofsky and Olson accepted Williams as their poetic father. The academic poets in general relate to Eliot, while the bohemians turn to Williams. Williams and Eliot represent two opposed literary directions that are combined in the work of Pound. This pattern continued into the fifties, when some poets began to become aware of other innovations and possibilities, never fully exploited, that had been present all along in Modernism.

In Canada it was really not until the early sixties that a few poets discovered, almost accidentally, other international orientations. In the work of bill bissett and bpNichol we find the beginnings of Canadian sound and concrete poetry; in their magazines *Blew Ointment*, *Ganglia*, and *GrOnk* we see the proliferation of this kind of writing into wider contexts. In the early sixties there was almost no evidence of work in these media, yet there are few poets in Canada now who do not have some awareness of the sound and visual components of language, even if they do not choose to exploit them. There are at least a dozen Canadian poets who make use of some element of sound, song, or chant in their public readings; and there are two sound-poetry ensembles, The Four Horsemen and Owen Sound, who experiment in "collective communication." Writer bpNichol says, "I think that formal possibilities for writing or the range of craft is much more enormous in the 1980s than it's ever been in the history of writing."[1]

One element is common to all the branches that compose Modernism: in each "ism," the prime concern of the avant-garde is an investigation of the medium.[2] Impressionist painters asked, "What are the possible relations of colours?" The Cubists investigated (and undermined) representation and perspective. In music, melody, rhythm, harmony, and tonality are called into question, producing a music that destroys the classical balance between these elements and that often emphasizes dissonance and atonality. Modern dance becomes an investigation of the elements of movement. In literary Modernism we are faced with diverging concerns. For the classically based Imagists, the image — rather than the word — served as the basic unit. Pound and his cohorts thought that the basic element of poetry was the poetic experience — that is, the picture, or more precisely the Image, that "intellectual and emotional complex in an instant of time."[3] This is a consistent aesthetic for a poet who would later comment that "only emotion endures." For Pound, the essence of poetry is the poetic charge, the experience conveyed in the language most adequate to embody it.

For other literary schools, however, language and the word became all important. Investigating the word itself, different writers began to extrapolate the sound and visual components of the language. When the word as signifier is separated from the object or concept that is signified, the word can be seen to exist as a picture, and also as an element of sound. Within these frameworks, one finds totally different contents than are usually communicated on the semantic level. Work of this kind proliferated between 1910 and 1920, and often we find the same writers working with both visual and sound elements.

Italian Futurist F. T. Marinetti wrote *Zang Tumb Tumb* in October 1912. Here we see both verbal and visual invention at work. In his *Technical Manifesto of Literature* (11 May 1912), Marinetti had declared that "After Free Verse...we have at last Free Words."[4] Marinetti believed that "Free Words" should be coupled with a typographic revolution, one that would "help to express different ideas simultaneously. Twenty different types and three or four different colours can be used on one page if need be, to express ideas of differing importance and the impressions of the different senses."[5] As Judy Rawson has noted:

This is the style of *Zang Tumb Tumb*... Words in a variety of types are splayed out over the pages, interspersed with mathematical signs, and sometimes arranged in graphic designs... The spelling too bears witness to the liberation advocated in the opening Manifesto... The "sssssssiii ssiissii ssiissssssiiiii" of the first page, describing a train journey to Sicily while correcting the proofs of a book, expresses both the positive hopes he has for Futurism and the whistling of the train.[6]

In the Russian Futurist movement we find a parallel to Marinetti's free words. The movement's manifesto (*The Word As Such* by Khlebnikov and Kruchonykh) was written in 1913; as well, the poems of a Russian Futurist, Vladimir Mayakovsky, were appearing in volumes "given inventive typography and layout, either by Mayakovsky himself (who was a considerable graphic artist) or by one of his colleagues,"[7] A. M. Hyde, in his article on Russian Futurism, writes:

> So, as with Marinetti, words acquire new functions as they disport themselves up and down the page, growing larger and dwindling away to nothing, or forming shapes and patterns that may endorse or alternatively violate their semantic content.[8]

In Dadaism, an essential aspect of performance was the use of elements of visuality and of sound. Lucy R. Lippard, in her book on Dada, writes: "The poets (and some of the artists, notably Schwitters and Hausmann) developed simultaneism, sound poetry, and the typographical literature of chance which became 'concrete poetry.'"[9] Add to this Apollinaire's *Calligrammes* (1918), or word-pictures, and there is evident a formidable front of visual and sound experimentation. Futurism and Dadaism were not purely literary movements, but incorporated the visual arts as well, so a visual aspect was added. Experimentation was an integral part of the aesthetics of these two movements.

The general point of view represented by these two approaches to language influenced Canadian poetry in the 1960s; to understand that influence some historical background is helpful.

Twentieth-century experimentation with the sounds that compose language can be seen to be a return to a more primitive understanding of language. Before there was written language there was language as an oral phenomenon, and before a set of verbal patterns had been established as signifiers there were only sounds accompanied by gestures, through which primitive man communicated. Verbal language can most easily be seen as the systematic ordering of sound; through commonly recognized patterning, that sound comes to mean something. Sound poetry brings language back in touch with its primitive roots. Sound is an element in the literary traditions of native peoples. As Steve McCaffery puts it,

> The first phase, perhaps better termed, the first area of sound poetry, is the vast, intractible area of archaic and primitive poetries, the many instances of chant structures and incantation, of nonsense syllabic mouthings and deliberate lexical distortions still alive among North American, African, Asian and Oceanic peoples.[10]

In the poetry of the Navajo Indians, for instance, we find the use of "vocables," meaningless as words but essential to the chant base of the poetry. The vocables provide a droning continuation that facilitates the flow of semantically recognizable language. The use of sound as sound has been a part of poetry for as long as poetry has existed.

Twentieth-century avant-garde artists returned to this phenomenon to enrich their literary art. The experiments of Italian Futurism included Marinetti's poetic technique of *"parole in liberta,"* or "free words." Of this technique, Canadian sound poet Steve McCaffery has observed:

> It was an attempt at syntactic explosion, at the liberation of the word from all linear bondage and the consequent conversion of page, from a neutral surface holding neutral graphic signs, into a dynamic field of typographic and sonographic forces. In performance Marinetti laid heavy stress upon onomatopoeic structures...one may think of Marinetti's work as an attempt to find a more basic connection between an object and its sign, a connection predicated upon the efficacy of the sonic as a direct, unmediated vector. Perhaps the most significant aspect of *parole in liberta* was its lasting effect upon the poem's visual notation. Marinetti's famous *Bombardamento di Adrianapoli*, for instance, is a stunning handwritten text of great visual excitement, employing different letter sizes, linear, diagonal and vertical presentations of non-gravitational text, all intended for vocal realization. It marks one of the earliest successful attempts to consciously structure a visual code for free, vocal interpretation.[11]

In attempting to "free" words, or to have words exist in freedom, Marinetti found it necessary to overthrow the normal syntactical conventions. The notation of the poem provided a visual representation of material that was dependent upon how the work was vocalized. Standard linearity was abandoned.

Velimir Khlebnikov's and Kruchonykh's Russian Futurist manifesto *The Word As Such* (1913) is an important experimental document that marks the beginning of new developments in sound poetry. The two poets emphasized oral and auditory effects; they drew upon folk poetry and on "the Scythian myth," a conception they define as "an extreme and mystical nationalism invoking the imminent triumph of primitivistic irrationalism, symbolized by the Scythians, over European rationalism."[12] The Russians also emphasized the shamanistic aspect of the poet. They maintained that the "language of poetry should be 'transrational'...freed from the rigid forms of logic...its expressive sonic powers should make their impact without an intermediate conceptualizing process, which dissipates energy."[13] This emphasis upon the transrational ("*zaum*") led Khlebnikov and Kruchonykh to compose a poetry that sacrificed meaning to language's phonic possibilities.

Sound poetry as a performance art gained its impetus in the nightly activities of the Zurich Dadaists at the Cabaret Voltaire; new sound-poetry forms were pioneered at the cabaret. A dip into Hugo Ball's diary reveals the activity and the theory of these poets. In an entry dated 30 March, 1916 Ball records:

> All the styles of the last twenty years came together yesterday. Huelsenbeck, Tzara and Janco took the floor with a "poème simultan." That is a contrapuntal recitative in which three or more voices speak, sing, whistle, etc., at the same time in such a way that the elegiac, humourous, or bizarre content of the piece is brought out by these combinations. In such a simultaneous poem, the willful quality of an organic work is given powerful expression, and so is its limitation by the accompaniment. Noises (an *rrrrr* drawn out for minutes, or crashes, or sirens, etc.) are superior to the human voice in energy.
>
> The "simultaneous poem" has to do with the value of the voice. The human organ represents the soul, the individuality in its wanderings with its demonic companions. The noises represent the background — the inarticulate, the disastrous, the decisive. The poem tries to elucidate the fact that man is swallowed up in the mechanistic process. In a typically compressed way it shows the conflict of the *vox humana* with a world that threatens, ensnares, and destroys it, a world whose rhythm and noise are ineluctable.[14]

A more detailed account of the Dadaists' language experimentation is set forward in an entry dated 18 June, 1916:

> We have now driven the plasticity of the work to the point where it can scarcely be equaled. We achieved this at the expense of the

rational, logical constructed sentence, and also by abandoning documentary work (which is possible only by means of a time-consuming grouping of sentences in logically ordered syntax). Some things assisted us in our efforts: first of all, the special circumstances of these times, which do not allow real talent either to rest or mature and so put its capabilities to the test. Then there was the emphatic energy of our group; one member was always trying to surpass the other by intensifying demands and stresses. You may laugh; language will one day reward us for our zeal, even if it does not achieve any directly visible results. We have loaded the work with strengths and energies that helped us to rediscover the evangelical concept of the "word" (logos) as a magical complex image.

With the sentence having given way to the word, the circle around Marinetti began resolutely with "parole in liberta." They took the word out of the sentence frame (the world image) that had been thoughtlessly and automatically assigned to it, nourished the emaciated big-city vocables with light and air, and gave them back their warmth, emotion, and their original untroubled freedom. We others went a step further. We tried to give the isolated vocables the fullness of an oath, the glow of a star. And curiously enough, the magically inspired vocables conceived and gave birth to a *new* sentence that was not limited and confined by any conventional meaning. Touching lightly on a hundred ideas at the same time without naming them, this sentence made it possible to hear the innately playful, but hidden, irrational character of the listener; it wakened and strengthened the lowest strata of memory. Our experiments touched on areas of philosophy and of life that our environment — so rational and so precocious — scarcely let us dream of.[15]

Ball's analysis synthesizes the theories of Marinetti with those of Khlebnikov and Kruchonykh. The shamanistic emphasis of the Russian Futurists is echoed in Ball's "evangelical concept" of the word as a "magical complex image"; the new sentence constructed out of freed words is the Russian's transrational "*zaum.*" Liberated in this transrationalism is all meaning; all things can be touched on in a totally freed language structure, and yet nothing is named or denoted. Primitive sense and sacred time are being reawakened.

Ball's diary contains an important entry dated 23 June, 1916:

I have invented a new genre of poems, *"Verse ohne Worte"* (poem without words) or Lautgedichte (sound poems), in which the balance of the vowels is weighed and distributed solely according to the values of the beginning sequence. I gave a reading of the first one of these poems this evening. I had made myself a special costume for it. My legs were in a cylinder of shiny blue cardboard, which came up to my hips so that I looked like an obelisk. Over it I wore a huge coat collar cut out of cardboard, scarlet inside and gold outside. It was fastened at the neck in such a way that I could give the impression of winglike movement by raising and lowering my elbows. I also wore a high, blue-and-white striped witch doctor's hat.

On all three sides of the stage I had set up music stands facing the audience, and I put my red-penciled manuscript on them; I officiated at one stand after another. Tzara knew about my preparations, so there was a real little première. Everyone was curious. I could not walk inside the cylinder so I was carried onto the stage in the dark and began slowly and solemnly:

gadji beri bimba
glandridi lauli lonni cadori
gadjama bim beri glassala
glandridi glassala tuffm i zimbrabim
blassa galassasa tuffm i zimbrabim…

The stresses became heavier, the emphasis was increased as the sound of the consonants became sharper. Soon I realized that, if I wanted to remain serious (and I wanted to be at all costs), my method of expression would not be equal to the pomp of my staging. I saw Brupbacher, Jelmoli, Laban, Mrs. Wigman in the audience. I feared a disgrace and pulled myself together. I had now completed *"Labada's Gesang an die Wolken"* (Labada's Song to the Clouds) at the music stand on the right and the *"Elefantenkarawane"* (Elephant Caravan) on the left and turned back to the middle one, flapping my wings energetically. The heavy vowel sequences and the plodding rhythm of the elephants had given me one last crescendo. But how was I to get to the end? Then I noticed that my voice had no choice but to take on the ancient cadence of priestly lamentation, that style of liturgical chanting that wails in all the Catholic churches of the East and West.

I do not know what gave me that idea of this music, but I began to chant my vowel sequences in a church style like a recitative, and tried not only to look serious but to force myself to be serious. For a moment it seemed as if there were a pale, bewildered face in my cubist mask, that half-frightened, half-curious face of a ten-year-old boy, trembling and hanging avidly on the priest's words in the requiem and high masses in his home parish. Then the lights went out, as I had ordered, and bathed in sweat, I was carried down off the stage like a magical bishop.[16]

With time, Ball was to give up all performance of sound poetry, fearing that he was being possessed by demons. In his performance at the Cabaret Voltaire, however, Ball had truly opened the floodgates to the new medium of sound poetry.

Other contributions to this new area of endeavour were made by Dadaists who incorporated phonic and chant elements into their work. McCaffery writes:

> Tristan Tzara is noteworthy for his development of a pseudo ethno-poetry realized most successfully in his "Poèmes Negres": loose and often pataphysical translations from the African which Tzara then used for sound texts.... Raoul Hausmann is perhaps the most significant of the Dada sonosophers and largely because of his instrumental advancements in the techniques of notation. Hausman in 1918 developed his "optophonetics" which used typographic variations in pitch and volume.... Perhaps the greatest scope is evidenced in the sound poems of Kurt Schwitters (1887–1948) whose phonetic experiments took him into large and small structures alike. His "Ur Sonata" ranks as one of the longest of all sound poems, whilst "W" (a single letter on a white card, and performed with the full gamut of pitch, tone, volume and emotional intensity) must be one of the shortest.[17]

More than any other of the early movements the Dadaists consolidated the different elements of sound experimentation and presented them with accomplishment and in high profile.

In the period between the end of World War One and the beginning of the second, sound experimentation went through a lull. In the 1940s the Paris Lettrists picked up the fallen gauntlet of sound poetry. McCaffery summarizes the period:

> Founded by Isadora Isou and Maurice Lemaitre in Paris, Lettrisme offered a full-scale lexical revolution. Their poetic strategy was to be based...upon an alphabetic renaissance, and the use of a totally new lexicon. This *Lexique des Lettres Nouvelles* drawn up by Isou and Lemaitre comprised over 130 entries to be employed as an alphabet of sound in vocal performance. Other members of the group (still flourishing) were Roland Sabatier, J.-B. Arkitu and Jean Paul Curtay.

Francois Dufrene, a former member, left the original movement to pursue his own "ultra-lettrism." Dufrene's work in many ways culminates the phase of second generation sound poetry; it is characterized by a vocal purity (Dufrene eschewed entirely the attraction and dangers of the tape recorder), an energetic intensity and — in his *cri-rhythmes* — an intensely somatic base in sub-phonemic units.[18]

All sound poetry up to and including the Lettrists was voice-oriented and presented sound as an extension of the human voice. Poets worked with freed words, transrational structures, simultaneous poems, vocables, and even letters of a newly constructed alphabet; the agent of presentation was the human voice. In the 1950s, however, French poet Henri Chopin began to use the tape recorder as a medium for sound poetry, and began to effect a separation of speech from voice:

> Henri Chopin (b. 1922) makes the decisive break from a phonetic basis to sound poetry and develops his self-styled "audiopoems." The audiopoem utilizes microphones of high amplification to capture vocal sounds on the threshold of audition. In this respect Chopin's work can be regarded in the tradition of lexical decomposition.... Chopin's early work (ca. 1955) comprised the decomposition and recomposition of vowels and consonants. Still connected to the word, these pieces can best be described as technological assaults upon the word. The word is slowed down, speeded up and superimposed up to fifty times, whilst additional vocalic texture is provided by a variety of respiratory and buccal effects. Later, Chopin discovered and used the "micro-particle" as the compositional unit of his work, abandoning the word entirely. This marks the birth of "poésie sonore," which Chopin distinguishes from "poésie phonetique."
>   Chopin's art is an art entirely dependent on the tape recorder. Chopin's vocal "micro-particulars" are only realizable through the agency of modern tape technology. It is an irrevocable marriage. His material comprises the full gamut of orally produced phenomena beyond and beneath the atomic limit of the phoneme.[19]

Chopin's work is, in the truest meaning of the word, "sound" poetry. With the tape recorder, Chopin totally transmutes human vocables into something that sounds nothing like the productions of the human voice.

The avenue of "poésie sonore," which Chopin opened in the 1950s, has been followed by European sound poets. Bernard Heidsiech (France); Lars-Gunner Bodin, Sten Hanson, Bengt Emil Johnson, Ilmar Laaban, Ake Hodell, and

Christer Hennix Lille (all of Sweden); Arrigo-Lora Totino (Italy); Herman Damen (Netherlands); and Gust Gils, Tera de Marez Oyens, and Greta Monach (Holland) subject their texts to electronic modification. Poets Bob Cobbing (England) and Ernst Jandl (Austria) work in phonetic modes; but "poésie sonore" has tended to be in vogue in Europe during the past twenty-five years.

Sound poetry has been primarily a European art form in the twentieth century. In North America, "poésie phonetique" has tended to dominate, and emphasis is on the capacities of the human voice rather than on the manipulations of technology. Jackson MacLow has worked with chance composition and multiple-voice overlays, often using the tape recorder in the service of voice. Jerome Rothenberg has done much exploration in the area of ethno-poetics, including some translations of Navajo horse songs. John Giorno uses repetitious syntactical structures, which he then subjects to verbal overlays. In Michael McClure's beast language, and in the work of most of the Canadian sound poets, voice also tends to be primary.

Sound poetry is a sub-branch or sub-division of poetry. It is an international community that generates festivals, publications, and recordings, which embody and document pioneering work. Canadian magazines that present sound poetry are also international in scope.

Concrete or visual poetry emphasizes the poem as picture and works with the potential of written language. John Sharkey has provided an evaluation of the parameters of concrete poetry:

> Concrete poetry "begins by being aware of graphic space as a structural agent," so that words or letters can be juxtaposed, not only in relation to each other but also to the page area as a whole.... The visual and semantic elements constituting the form as well as the content of a poem define its structure so that the poem can be a "reality in itself and not a poem about something or other."... In concrete poetry words can be presented in their totality. In practical terms this meant that the material was a valid source of inspiration and communication, a situation long accepted in other art forms.[20]

Concrete poetry works with the idea of "text," and utilizes the page as the ultimate organizing unit. The visual and graphic possibilities of language are emphasized; repetition is organized around a principle of visual onomatopoeia. It is a poetry of direct presentation, which uses the semantic, visual, and phonetic elements of language in the service of the word.

From the moment the Futurists and Dadaists tried to notate their sound poems they began to also do primitive work in the area of visual poetry. F. T. Marinetti's interest in typography, the scripting of trans-rational texts, Raoul Hausmann's "optophonetic" technique of notating sound poems, all were concerned with the visual elements of language. These poets had to use written equivalents to represent sounds; the written symbols became sound's pictorial counterpart. The typography employed by Marinetti and the Dadaists represented an interest in how the poem looked, but these poets did not develop the form they began.

Concrete poetry begins in the 1950s. Its history is one of simultaneous international development:

> Eugen Gomringer, a Bolivian-born Swiss, was the acknowledged father of Concrete poetry. He called his first poems in the new style, written in 1951, "constellations."... When Gomringer and the Noigrandres poets of São Paulo, Brazil, agreed upon the name "Concrete" to describe the new poetry in 1956, they were mutually unaware that Oyvind Fahlstrom... had published the first manifesto of Concrete poetry — *manifest for konkret poesi* — three years earlier in Stockholm. While Diter Rot, German-born and Swiss-bred, was publishing his "ideograms" in geographically remote Iceland, and Carlfriedrich Claus was experimenting with Klang-bilden and Phasan in politically remote East Germany, in Vienna concrete poetry was developing out of the collaborative efforts of a composer, Gerhard Ruhm, an architect, Friedrich Achleitner, a jazz musician, Oswald Wiener, and the poets H. C. Artmann and Konrad Bayer. In 1957, the year Haroldo de Campos of Brazil introduced Concrete poetry to Kitasano Kitue of Japan, a Romanian-born artist, Daniel Spoerri, leader of the "Darmstadt Circle" of Concrete poets (which included a German dramaturgist, Claus Bremer, and an American expatriate, Emmett Williams), published the first international anthology of Concrete poetry.[21]

Each poet brings to visual poetry a unique approach, and there are countless possibilities for visual presentation, allowed by method and materials. Concrete poems are hand-drawn, type-written, typeset, printed in Letraset, computer coded, created with cut-up techniques, straight visual presentation, found collage, or found visuals; poets can work with typography, semiotics, or even the comic-strip frame. Like sound poetry, concrete belongs to a European rather than to an English tradition, although in the past twenty years it has begun to be practiced in North America and Britain.

Interestingly enough, when bill bissett began writing in Vancouver in the early sixties, he was hardly aware of established modes of visual and sound poetry. Bissett started out as a painter. Then, in 1960 or 1961, he started to make drawings that began to resemble character writing. As the images he was employing became more and more like letters, he began writing visual poems. He was not working alone: he had formed a bond with two other young artists, Martina Clinton and Lance Farrell. Bissett describes those times:

> sitting up all nite laboring for brekthrus in what was handid down to
> us loving th words loving th space loving the sound finding th poem
> as sound/picture/breking up th words[22]

Working communally, the artists were making individual breakthroughs and beginning to discover their own specific areas of interest. For Clinton the poem became an exploration of space — visual space and the space between utterances. Farrell tended to work more in pictographical terms, using words as a method of illustration; the word or sentence, not the drawn line, was an element of the visual. Poet bissett employed minimal structures but used silence when reading his poems aloud. He was already using the dimension of the page as the primary organizing principle of his poetry.

According to bissett, Canadian poets had no aesthetic sympathy with the works of the radical European Modernists, and it was only in the late sixties that he realized a bond between his own work and that of the Dadaists and Surrealists:

> th surrealists wer nevr an influens on us or th dadaists gertrude stein
> we wer all reading discovring her in libraries as being th closest we cud
> find anywahr to wher we wer cumming from/going to... but dadaist
> texts for/with that i think what we wer all uv us finding was/is a
> confirmashun looking for that rathr than models say or thats how it
> was/is but th dadaists/surrealists cubists in breking up th tradishyu-
> nal elements veree important to anywhum looking at th lineage/li-
> near but we werent in fact dadaists or surrealist or cubist it isnt
> reallee a linear/lineage or why get up in th morning but theyr all veree
> important work what they ar dewing but from wher i was it was me
> martina n lance n judith n maxine n opning up to writing back n forth
> with barrie n d.a. levy nd d.r. wagner all our work was/is veree
> different from each othr nd we reechd out to all our selvs found
> support... so konkreet/sound/vizual thos wer names othrs gave to
> what we wer all dewing nd th thousands uv poets we didint get to

know but the whuns we did get to know the combustyun as being
spontaneous was/is intrnashunal[23]

Most important for bissett was a sense of community and of mutual support.
Upon this basis the magazine *Blew Ointment* was started, in 1963, by bissett
and Clinton. The group included two other young writers, Judith Copithorne
and Maxine Gadd. Bissett explains why *Blew Ointment* was started:

> we startid it... bcoz our writing nd that uv a lot ov the peopul we had
> most in common with aestheticallee... we cudint get printid any wher
> els bcoz our writing-vizual sound konkreet was lookd on as not realee
> the pome we wer into expanding th pome...we wer into a new
> notashun new as to what was around availabul to us at that time that
> wud include sound picture th whol sheet uv papr on wch th pome
> temporarilee apeers as space[24]

What bissett is citing certainly expresses a new aesthetic orientation in Canadian poetry, which, until then, had been concerned with the generation of a
linear text. For example, the *Tish* poets presented a new kind of notation,
taken from Olson, but their poetry was recognizable printed text. Olson's idea
of page as area for a notated oral text is taken further, with concrete poetry,
into a realm where the poet is a shaman or visionary. What appears on the
page is not the poem as artifact, but the poem as it "temporarilee apeers as
space." The concept of the poem and the rôle of the poet are undergoing a
change that is revolutionary. Speaking of the rôle of the poet, bissett says:

> we ar all instruments all being vessuls for what can flow thru/happn
> th desire for th langwage to be a precisyun/organik that is as close to
> what th pome is/seems to b as possibul that serch/xplorashun/hope-
> ful discoveree[25]

The poet is servant of life rather than master of language; the poem is seen as
organic process rather than perfected text. As well, bissett seems to be suggest-
ing that language must attempt to come close to what the poem *is*; the poem is
not really words, or even language, but rather experience or force, whatever it
is that flows through and happens. Poetry is something that partakes in and
celebrates life. For bissett, poetry and life are indivisible; poetry may enhance
life, but it is an intrinsic part of life and has little or no existence outside of or
beyond that context.
    From its very beginning in 1963, *Blew Ointment* reflected bissett's experi-
mental and organic poetics. It presented primarily work of the Vancouver

group that had gathered around bissett. Early issues are a mixture of visual poems, drawings, and fairly traditional language structures. The publication is sloppy and messy. Bissett's concrete work has been classed as "dirty" concrete, and this "dirtiness" was part of the magazine's format and presentation. Interestingly, as bissett became more involved with visual poetry, the contents of the magazine became more eclectic. The September 1964 issue (volume two, number four) serves primarily as a showplace for work by bissett and Judith Copithorne, for example, but the November 1965 issue (volume three, number one) features work by Milton Acorn, Margaret Avison, bill bissett, Judith Copithorne, David Cull, Maxine Gadd, Patrick Lane, Red Lane, Dorothy Livesay, Pat Lowther, John Newlove, bpNichol, and many others.

The July 1966 issue (volume four, number one) is filled with inserts and photo reproductions; many mixed materials are jumbled together. The contents of the magazine are predominantly visual; the reader is faced with an assault on the visual sense. We find restaurant mats, a picture of wine bottles and grapes, a picture of the Appian Way, ripped pieces of newspaper, drawings, small broadsheets printed on off-cuts of paper, typewriter concrete, stamp art, poems on unattached sheets, and anonymous works and photographs. The issue is marked by a wild, chaotic shapelessness that characterizes the printing. Some pages are quite unreadable. Bissett had a habit of slapping any old number on the front cover of a particular issue, so that the magazine follows no numbering system that respects sequence. (This is one more Dada element in the magazine.) One feels some sympathy with the harried librarian whose letter appeared on the inside back cover of an unnumbered issue in 1970:

> Dear Sir:
> We have a Press/Order release notice from you which quotes subscription rates as being $7.00 for five issues.
> What are these five issues of? Is this a numbered series, a periodical or something else with an identifying title?
> Any other information you could give us would be appreciated.
> May we add that we hope your priced publications are more legible than is this poorly prepared release.[26]

In publishing the letter, bissett thumbs his nose at rational order and declares his free and anarchic poetic principles. The aims of *Blew Ointment* were spontaneity, chaos, and freedom. The publication defied any attempt at coherent commentary. In many ways it served as an anthology of on-going avant-garde work, not restricted to the concrete-sound-visual context (although concrete-visual work is always highly in evidence).

In the 1970 issue, author credits are not presented on the pages with the poems; the work has a tendency to flow together, because it is not distinguished by immediate author identification. In the back of the issue there is an index, under the heading "FASCIST COURT," that lists the contributors and the pages on which their work appears. Perhaps bissett viewed the assigning of the names of authors to their works as a kind of tyranny.

From 1965 *Blew Ointment* tended to be anthological and eclectic, but only later does it actually call itself an anthology. Anthology (or "speshul") issues appeared about once a year. Some examples: *the blewointmentpress what isint tantrik speshul, the blewointmentpress occupashun issew, the blewointmentpress poverty issew, the fascist court, blewointmentpress Lady And Th Lion Issew, blewointmentpress oil slick speshul 71*, and *end of the* WORLD *speshul.* Their ordering and timing were chaotic. The issues contain broad cross-sections of work from many different Canadian poets writing in a very wide variety of styles; among them are F.R. Scott, P.K. Page, Tom Marshall, Margaret Atwood, Bertrand Lachance, Milton Acorn, Michael Ondaatje, Eli Mandel, Nelson Ball, Barry McKinnon, D.A. Levy, David UU, Dennis Lee, Earle Birney, Colleen Thibaudeau, Steve McCaffery, Al Purdy, Gerry Gilbert, George Bowering, John Robert Colombo, Raymond Souster, and Andrew Suknaski. The most traditional and the most experimental poets meet together in the pages of *Blew Ointment.*

Ultimately, *Blew Ointment* is a paradoxical magazine. Put out by one of Canada's leading experimental poets, it remains an interesting eclectic magazine. In its printing and format it shows the touch of a "messy" concrete poet; its messiness is its most liberating aspect. At the same time, it contains the first stirrings of visual and sound poetry in Canada; it validates work that, in the early sixties, was not readily acknowledged as poetry. In recent years the energies that went into producing the magazine have produced the books of Blew Ointment Press.

In 1966 bpNichol published one of bissett's early books, *We Sleep Inside Each Other All*, in the form of a single issue of his magazine, *Ganglia*. The book provides an extensive introduction to bissett's early work, and also includes an important article, "The Typogeography of Bill Bissett," written by bpNichol. Nichol presents a discussion of the visual aspects of bissett's poetry. He holds that the primary concern of bissett's writing is language, and that "Bissett is one of those who has tried to begin again, to take the language back to its pictorial roots & proceed from there."[27] In bissett's poetry there is a striving for a fresh articulation; bissett turns his back on tradition and convention, which he sees as language traps, and traps that can imprison the individual, as well. He attempts to start fresh, to remake the language; he attempts to strip language of all acquired association.

One of bissett's primary concerns, according to Nichol, is the atomization of words. Nichol observes that "Breaking up words &/or combining them is a way we gain new words & enrich our language."[28] When we break words up or combine them, we release a new range of content and a new range of meaning. Bissett employs run-on sentences and sentence combinations, which serve to undermine the conventions of language. Note, for example, bissett's highly individual spelling. Nichol claims that by using an individualized spelling, "What Bissett has done is to make the word distinctively his own."[29] His phonetical spellings also challenge concepts of illiteracy. All these variations in technique are attempts to establish a personal articulation. Bissett is a poet in revolution, determined to express himself in his own terms. He is preoccupied with overcoming the calcifications, the tyranny, and the rules of language, and in his work he attempts to restore and renovate language. As Nichol says:

> Bissett is reactionary in his attempt to bring the language back to its pictographic base. But Bissett's reactionary behaviour is the kind that brings renewal and gives rise to new possibilities.[30]

Bissett is a visionary poet. Although his satiric work is best known, much of his poetry is mystical and religious in its worship of and reverence for the organic principles of life. Central to his work is ecstatic imagery; many of his poems celebrate the joys of human existence, and tell of the powers of sex and dream. And bissett sings and chants much of his work: the poems are linked with joy and primal power. The aesthetic revolution evident in bissett's poetry is consonant with the aim of "living with th vishyun" his poems express.

Poet bpNichol began his career in the early sixties. An awareness of the possibilities of visual and sound poetry came a few years later to Nichol than to bissett. Born and raised in Vancouver, Nichol moved to Toronto in the early sixties and worked for a time in the library at the University of Toronto. His discovery of the visual medium happened in a specific way: it came through Kenneth Patchen, an American visionary who had often used drawings in his poetry. Nichol began to write some poems in the shapes of objects. Then, in 1965, he underwent a radical shift in his sense of the visual aesthetic. Talking of his writing during this period, Nichol has said:

> Then in '65... I just became aware that it didn't matter what I set down, what mood I was in, I was essentially churning out the same poem, and that I could become very proficient at *that* poem cause that's what it was, it was *a poem* and had this minor variation and that variation but had a complete lack of any technical facility. There was

147

a type of arrogance, I thought; that is to say I was coming to the occasion of the poem to force myself upon it. I was being arrogant rather than learning. So I sort of made a conscious choice to play.... Here I was, I was typing poems but I wasn't paying attention to the page. So I began to do it and I started with these things I called "ideopomes." They were very much that, very much based on type-writer things.... It's pretty early stuff, fairly *el primitivo*, but it sort of showed me the way in.[31]

Working in relative isolation, Nichol for a time found himself questioning the work he was doing. He looked, for support, to writers outside Canada:

[W]hen I started doing this stuff like there was *nobody*, and I mean but *nobody* who was doing it. I really felt sort of crazy; why was I doing it? Was it just because I was a failed writer or something, I really got churned up about it. There was really nobody at that time I could connect with about what I was doing. From 1965 to 1967 it was really vital that I have that European-South American connection because it was really the only place from which I got feedback/input that propelled me on.[32]

Nichol recalls his first awareness of the Dadaists:

I became aware of them through a friend of mine, Jim Alexander, probably around '63. I was into Patchen around '61 & 2 and the Dadaists around '63. I'll tell you what struck me about them; there were a number of things really. There were hardly any examples; I had nothing that I could actually look at. The whole problem with what is known as "avant-garde" literature in the 20th century...is that it's like we're dealing with amnesia; we've got this repressed tradition so that you end up...regurgitating a lot of what's already been done because you can't get your hands on the stuff. So you literally have to make your own way. In a way I made my own way...[S]ome reviewers have said, "Hey that was done in Berlin in 1921"; I look at it and say "Yeah, well I guess it was done in Berlin in 1921, but this was done in Canada in 1965 without knowing what was done in Berlin in 1921."... I was intrigued by the report of Schwitters's "W" poem, just that that was it and he read it, that blew my mind.... The Dadaists for me were more of a spiritual influence, that is to say, I knew *somebody* had done *something*, I wasn't quite sure what exactly they'd done, but the sense was that if some guys could get up there and kick out the jams why shouldn't I do it? That gave me encouragement. So it's one of those things, you start doing something and then you start to track down all the other writers you've heard rumours about who are doing it. So, in a sense, it gave me support.[33]

Nichol's attempts in the experimental media were a kind of groping in the dark; there were rumours of earlier experimental work, and some small sustaining support from experimental poets in Europe and South America.

Nichol's isolation was not total; bill bissett, Earle Birney in his more experimental moments, and Pierre Coupey were working in similar or related areas. Out of this sense of some potential community Nichol's magazine *Ganglia* was born in early 1965. It originated in Toronto and was edited by Nichol and David Aylward. The first issue was embellished with drawings by Aylward, bissett, Judith Copithorne, and Nichol. Nichol has said that the original impetus for *Ganglia* was a desire to publish, in Toronto, west-coast writers who were receiving little attention. The magazine reflects this purpose. The first issue featured work by Margaret Avison, bill bissett (in standard typography except for the calligraphic-visual poem "everlasting"), George Bowering, Copithorne, Nichol, and several lesser-known Vancouver poets. Only bissett's and Nichol's work can be called concrete; the bissett poem is a hand-drawn visual illustration, and Nichol's composition uses the graphic potential of the typewriter. In its eclecticism, *Ganglia* shares much with *Blew Ointment*. For experimental writers, bissett and Nichol are extremely tolerant and eclectic editors. In his own work, Nichol has attempted to combine practically every kind of writing that has arisen in the twentieth century. Eclecticism was a marked feature of *Ganglia*.

The magazine did not have a particularly long or energetic run, although it did present some interesting material. It lasted for only seven issues; the last one appeared in March 1967. Two of the issues were book-length collections of poems: number two (November 1965) contained *The 1962 Poems* by Red Lane; number four (June 1966) featured *We Sleep Inside Each Other All* by bill bissett. The regular issues contained works by poets of different aesthetic standpoints; these included Victor Coleman, Ian Hamilton Finlay, Pat Lane, D. A. Levy, Pat Lowther, Nelson Ball, Douglas Barbour, Wayne Clifford, John Furnival, John Riddell, and David Cull. As well, *Ganglia* published work by Margaret Avison, more traditional (though somewhat idiosyncratic) writing.

Ganglia lost impetus in 1966. The material Nichol collected for a concrete issue of *Ganglia* served as the point of origin for *GrOnk*. Nichol was becoming increasingly interested in concrete and visual poetry; but he was also becoming increasingly frustrated with the demands of the little magazine. The amount of energy involved in keeping accounts seemed hardly equal to the money that came in. Nichol decided to publish a monthly handout, a new magazine, called *GrOnk*. It would be sent free to subscribers and friends.

GrOnk was launched in January of 1967. The first issue was edited by Nichol with the assistance of David W. Harris and Rob Smith. David Aylward was added to the editorial staff in the fourth issue. Throughout its history, the magazine has added or dropped various editors, but Nichol himself has always been the guiding force, and *GrOnk* has been his magazine. Nichol projected that there would be sixty-four issues in all, to be issued in eight series of eight numbers each. The first series came out once a month; then David W. Harris moved to Vancouver and the magazine became rather occasional. The issues were compiled and sent out by Nichol in batches of five or six at a time. *GrOnk*, like *Blew Ointment*, has had a wayward numbering system and appeared erratically, but Nichol coordinated the issues so that the first run of *GrOnk* contained sixty-four issues, as predicted. The sixty-third issue was an index to the first sixty-four issues.

Nichol has maintained an active mailing list that contains between 180 and 250 names. The list represents an international community of avant-garde artists. After the first sixty-four issues, Nichol began an "intermediate" series of twenty-four issues, which contained work by individual authors; when this series is completed, he intends to continue the magazine for as long as his interest and means hold out.

Nichol's intention was to publish concrete poetry because no one else in Canada was publishing it. Nichol saw the magazine as a way of publishing *news*, informing not only writers in Canada but also writers in Europe and in South America. *GrOnk* was part of an international exchange.

The first issue of the magazine makes its poetic stance clear. An editorial notice on the front cover reads:

> manuscripts concerned with concrete sound kinetic and related bor-
> derblur poetry welcome   distributed by mailing list   limited number
> for public sale   published monthly[34]

In the first issue we find typewriter concrete by David W. Harris and Rob Smith; a mixed text by D. A. Levy using typewriter, handwritten sections, illustrative iconography, and smudge techniques; concrete by Nichol, which focuses on individual letters, random words, and phrases and non-language visual signs; a dense computer-structured piece by Pierre Garnier; minimalist verbal puns by Victor Coleman; a piece by D. R. Wagner called "Small Flag for Barb," which is a rectangle of type that works with the four words "hear," "tear," "barb," and "love"; and a calligraphic poem by bill bissett.

The first issue was eight pages long, and each page contained one or two poems. The format varied during the magazine's sixty-four-issue run. We find mimeographed covers, printed covers, printed inserts, different sizes, single-sheet issues, issues devoted to the work of an individual, books as part of a series, envelopes filled with various materials, mergings or co-publishing with other periodicals, small stapled pamphlets, and collections of printed cards. *GrOnk* was a changing, free-form magazine, constantly in flux, constantly in the process of pioneering new territory.

The second issue of the first series (February 1967) includes the ninth sequence of bpNichol's *Scraptures*; the eighth issue of the first series contains the eleventh sequence of *Scraptures*. In the ninth sequence of *Scraptures* Nichol uses cartoon, visual signs, letters, and words as visual signs, and language referents placed in thought balloons. Nichol discusses the work:

> *Scraptures* was my first attempt to bust out of simply being in one mold, that is simply being a poet who did visual things or being a poet who did sound things, or a poet who did traditional poems... *Scraptures* was the first one in which I cross-pollinated, in essence, where I started working between forms... The title came from the notion of scriptures, scraps of things, of pictures, of everything together, which became *Scraptures*. The very first one arose out of the opening of the Bible: "In the beginning was the Word and the Word was with God," redesigned on the pages visually. So it's a fairly classic and literal approach to visuality and then I began to bust out of that with the second and the third; I began to get into prose sections and I got into comic strip oriented sections, two of the sections are sound poems, though there are visual versions of those two as well, so it lends itself to a print text.[35]

Nichol had a motive for bringing together disparate and differing forms:

> [N]o one system is complete; it doesn't matter what system you create, it's simply one pair of glasses through which you view the world, you view reality. And because I believed that formal solutions released some contents and suppressed *other* contents, I was interested in greater hybrids, I was interested in creating alternative possibilities for myself... I believed... that if I could find a new form other contents would be released that I did not have a conscious awareness of at the time, that it was an issue of finding doorways. Form was a doorway through which you let certain contents emerge. Traditional form had its powers but alternative forms had different powers and released different contents and released new realities.[36]

Nichol was attempting a major reintegration of language elements.

Although *GrOnk* had a strong Canadian base, it also contained international work. Issue number three (March 1967) featured the work of D. A. Levy (United States); number six/seven (June/July 1967) presented work by Hansjorg Mayer (Germany), Brown Miller (United States), and Jiri Valoch (Czechoslovakia). Later issues featured the work of D. R. Wagner, Jiri Valoch, and French writer Julian Blaine. One issue was an anthology of Czech concrete poetry.

The second series, in issue number five, contains *The Captain Poetry Poems* by Nichol, part of a series that began in 1967 and was finally printed in 1970. The first issue of the third series contained a notice:

> series 3 of GrOnk will be mimeographed what have you type material
> and will be published simultaneously with series 4 a series of offset
> books & special productions[37]

On two occasions *GrOnk* merged with the publication *Comic World* to offer collections of comic strips.

GrOnk published book-length collections of work by young Canadian experimental writers. Books by Nichol and by John Riddell appeared; other issues comprised books by Gerry Gilbert, Nelson Ball, David UU, Hart Broudy, David Aylward, Judith Copithorne, Andrew Suknaski, Stephen Scobie, Steve McCaffery, Martina Clinton, and bill bissett. *GrOnk* provided first publication for many of these young writers, and served as the only organized available front for much experimental work.

One series of *GrOnk* is devoted to the work of Steve McCaffery, an experimental poet whose work has become increasingly interwoven with Nichol's. McCaffery and Nichol began writing collaborative work, and collaborative performances eventually led to the formation of the Four Horsemen, a sound-poetry ensemble. McCaffery and Nichol also work together to bring out the TRG reports that are a featured part of *Open Letter*. It is an interesting pairing: McCaffery's interests are theoretical, at times almost intellectually mechanistic, while Nichol tends to be more humanistically oriented. McCaffery, the author of *transitions to the beast*, theorizes:

> to the beast are for me transitional pieces moving towards a hand
> drawn set of visual conventions that have their roots both in semiotic
> poetry & in the comic strip. the semiotics or code poem (invented
> round about 1964 by the brazilians pignatori & pinto) uses a language
> of visual signs designed & constructed to suit the individual desires of

the poet & the needs that he as linguistic designer assures for the poem on that particular occasion of construction.

the striking impulse behind this type of poem is both alinear & nonlexical — the desire to expand language beyond the simple limited form of verbal expression.[38]

The work of Pignatori and Pinto is visual poetry that creates for itself its own lexical key; equations are made between recognized concepts and words and created shapes and symbols. These shapes and symbols come to represent a newly created language; in essence, poems can be written in a code language and translated into or out of that language. McCaffery is making such translations in *transitions to the beast*. He works with a poetry of visual design, and utilizes and departs from the geometric shapes of letters. In *Collborations* (series six, number five), McCaffery and Nichol work together in this field, incorporating Nichol's love of cartoon and its semiotic system with McCaffery's geometric-shape designs.

GrOnk's initial run ended with a bill bissett book, *Rush: what fucken theory, a study uv language*. Then Nichol undertook the *GrOnk* Intermediate Series, which consists of pamphlets or books by various experimental visual poets, among them McCaffery, Riddell, Gerry Gilbert, Shant Basmanjian, Paul Dutton, Jackson MacLow, P.C. Fencott, Bob Cobbing, R. Murray Schafer, and Opal L. Nations. Eighteen issues of the intended twenty-four issues of this series had been published by fall 1980. When that series is complete Nichol intends to begin the final series, so far undefined. Nichol continues to provide a forum for truly experimental work.

Bissett and Nichol are not the only poets who work with visual and sound poetry, but they have certainly been the most active and the most important. Their work presents a radical new aesthetic that did not exist in Canada before the early sixties. The lines between art and life tend to be erased in bissett's and Nichol's work; both revitalize language by exploring experimental avenues, and revitalize life itself by the use of language in organic processes of expression and psychic healing. If Nichol is correct in his assumption that working in new forms releases new contents for poetry, then new possibilities have been created, through bissett's and Nichol's branch of Modernism, for other writers.

9

The Poem as Vehic(u)le:
Montreal Poetry in the Sixties
and Seventies

Montreal has been an important cultural centre in the development of Modernism in Canadian poetry. Since the founding of the *McGill Fortnightly Review* in November of 1925 by F. R. Scott and A. J. M. Smith, the Montreal literary community has been an important shaping and directing force in Canadian poetic activity. One has only to remember the literary feud between *Preview* and *First Statement* in the 1940s, which sparked the fires of social realism, and the Montreal-based activities of Layton and Dudek in the 1950s, which combined to produce *CIV/n* magazine and Contact Press, to realize that, until the late 1950s, much of Canadian poetry was dominated by the Montreal poets. The poetic tradition established in Montreal was essentially a tradition of social realism.

During the fifties, and even more so in the sixties, the predominance of Montreal declined, the movement spread, and Canadian Modernism became a truly national phenomenon. But the "New Wave Canada" phenomenon that made its presence felt across the nation during the sixties did not appear in Montreal where a new generation, aware of the indigenous social-realist tradition, resisted the expansive Modernism of their American- and European-influenced contemporaries. With the succeeding generation, a group of young poets who gathered around the Vehicule Gallery in the early seventies, the next stage of Modernist development occurred in Montreal. This chapter will detail the crossroads of evolution represented by Montreal poetry of the sixties and seventies.

Three important poets emerged in Montreal in the fifties: Louis Dudek, Irving Layton, and Leonard Cohen. Without dismissing such important older poets as F. R. Scott or the ailing A. M. Klein, it was with these three poets that the new generation had to come to terms. Dudek was editing Contact Press with Raymond Souster and Peter Miller, running his own prestigious magazine, *Delta*, and publishing young poets in his own McGill Poetry Series. He was also teaching at McGill University, which has always been a valuable breeding ground for young writers. Just across town, Irving Layton was teaching at Sir George Williams University. He had been overlooked and underrated as a poet for more than ten years; but then, in 1959, his collection *A Red Carpet For The Sun* was published by McClelland and Stewart. A more public phase of his writing career had begun. In the wake of Layton's increased popularity, Dudek, long one of Layton's chief supporters, became one of his sharpest critics, and their long-standing friendship developed into an even longer-standing hostility. Leonard Cohen's first collection of poems, *Let Us Compare Mythologies*, was published by Dudek in the McGill Poetry Series. His second collection, *The Spice Box of Earth*, was published by McClelland and Stewart in 1961. With subsequent novels, films, and recordings, Cohen's reputation grew.

Montreal poets of the sixties moved between the pillars of Dudek's social realism and Layton and Cohen's celebratory poetry of personality. The new poets explored the urban realities a bit more extensively than their predecessors had; some followed in the footsteps of Layton, Cohen, and the older A. M. Klein in exploring the poetry of Jewish tradition; some followed Layton and Cohen and wrote a poetry of personality. When the Layton-Dudek verbal duels heated up in the early sixties, the editors of *Cataract* (Seymour Mayne, K. V. Hertz, and Leonard Angel) seemed to side with Layton by publishing some of his most vitriolic attacks on Dudek. The *Yes* editors, Michael Gnarowski and Glen Siebrasse, gravitated towards Dudek and shared his poetic orientation; finally the three joined together to found Delta Canada Press.

The magazines of this period were sporadic. Al Purdy and Milton Acorn published four issues of *Moment* in Montreal between 1959 and 1961, then moved the magazine to Toronto. *Cataract* was published from 1961 to 1962, then was superseded, for two issues, by *Catapult* in 1964. David Rosenfield edited one issue of *The Bloody Horse* in 1963; Stuart Gilman edited *The Page*, a series of broadsheets, in 1964; K. V. Hertz edited two issues of *Ingluvin* in the early seventies. Although *Yes* came out of Montreal for most of its fourteen years of existence (1956 to 1970), it was never a magazine that initiated a movement; rather it continued to reinforce the positions of the forties and fifties. It never took a fighting stand until its last few issues, when it opposed *Tish* and the new poetic innovations of the sixties (an attempt that came too late to stem the tide of New Wave Canada). Not surprisingly, *Yes* posited the poetry of social realism as the alternative to the New Wave. Late sixties magazines such as *Intercourse* and *Tide* were to experience longer runs than most magazines of the early 1960s; unfortunately they did not produce and publish a body of really significant work.

It was actually in Dudek's personal magazine, *Delta* (1957 to 1966), that the full panoply of young Montreal poets of the late fifties and early sixties appeared, though not as part of a militant movement. Young Montrealers such as Daryl Hine, Ian Clark, Michael Gnarowski, Milton Acorn, Al Purdy, John Lachs, Lionel Tiger, Sylvia Barnard, George Ellenbogen, Marquita Crevier, David Solway, Avi Boxer, Raymond Fraser, Seymour Mayne, Henry Moscovitch, and Steve Smith all appeared in the pages of *Delta*.

In an essay called "The Ego Has It Both Ways: Poets In Montreal," Al Purdy cites Irving Layton as an important influence in Purdy's poetic development and also as a central axis of his literary activity in the mid-fifties. Purdy moved to Montreal from Vancouver in 1956; in the summer of 1956 Purdy answered his doorbell and was greeted by a man who said, "Irving Layton sent me." The man was Milton Acorn, just arrived in Montreal from his home in Prince Edward Island. Purdy and Acorn quickly became friends. When Purdy moved back to Montreal in 1959 after a two-year stint in his own handmade A-frame house at Roblin Lake, Ontario, they also became literary collaborators; they began publishing the magazine *Moment* in the fall of 1959. Discussing the motivation behind the magazine, Purdy has said: "The reasons for *Moment* were both egotistic (we wanted to publish our own poems, tho I denied this to Milt) and altruistic (we wanted to publish good poems by other people.")[1] They presented their purpose in their initial editorial:

> *Moment*'s a way out type magazine which prints (pardon...mimeographs) poetry, opinion or fiction...especially good stuff that nobody else'll use. If you hate it write and tell us to stop cluttering up your mailbox. If you like it write and tell us so, maybe enclosing a buck or so. There's no charge and (curse it) no payment.[2]

When they started *Moment*, Acorn was thirty-six and Purdy forty-one. Both of them had come to poetry later in life than most poets, and they both started out with a rather formal, nineteenth-century approach to poetry, though this gradually gave way to a more modern technique. In the long, legal-sized pages of *Moment*, we see that development of modern voice, with a strong Canadian focus, tapping into the newly established Canadian tradition of Layton, Souster, and Dudek and carrying it on; Acorn and Purdy were concerned with promoting the new tradition. The first issue of *Moment* includes poems by Dudek, Purdy, Layton, Lowry, Acorn, and Cohen and also features a short essay-debate section called "Raymond Souster. Extempore Debate: Dudek and Acorn versus Purdy." Dudek and Acorn argue that Souster utilizes his own natural language, while Purdy argues that Souster doesn't work with the true structure of the English language or present it in its best light. The editors' purpose seems to be neither to re-evaluate nor to revolutionize Canadian poetry as it exists, but rather to become a part of it. Purdy and Acorn do not present a radically new aesthetic.

Issues two and three include poems by Phyllis Gottlieb, Alden Nowlan, Malcolm Lowry, Eldon Grier, Glen Siebrasse, Bryan McCarthy, Ralph Gustafson, F. R. Scott, John Robert Colombo, Irving Layton, and the editors.

Moment number four contains poems by Purdy, Nowlan, Larry Eigner, Alan Pearson, and Eldon Grier. It also includes an editorial of sorts, called "Open Letter To A Demi-Senior Poet," written by Milton Acorn and addressed to "Dylan." Acorn describes his personal view that "'Poetry' is only a convenient label for a kind of creativity with words,"[3] and maintains that poetry should be judged by whether it presents something. He offers an assessment of the Beats; a note at the beginning of the piece states, "In the letter below the whole new movement in The States, from Olson to Corso, is referred to as 'The Beats.'"[4] Acorn finds that the Beats lack intellectuality, but praises Olson as "an innovator in the science of poetics."[5] He notes the surety of the Creeley poetic touch, the strong dialectic evident in Corso's work, and Ferlinghetti's "marvellous sense of imagery."[6] Acorn then writes:

> I see bad and good in them, but don't allow anything to blind me to the fact that they are an important movement... Equally I don't allow their importance to blind me to the worth of Canadian poetry, which doesn't divide nearly as neatly into "schools," which progresses more evenly... but rarely losing sight of tradition. I think Canadians have much to learn from these Beats...[7]

Acorn's lumping of all the American poets in the Allen anthology as "Beats" was criticized by Frank Davey in the editorial of *Tish*, number eleven. But we find Acorn on the side of this new generation of American poets; this is remarkable, because later Acorn takes an anti-American, Canadian-nationalist position and condemns the west-coast *Tish* poets as colonials influenced by American literary imperialism. In later days, Acorn would emphasize the absolute importance of the Canadian tradition, like Robin Mathews; he did not think much could be learned from foreign, particularly American, models.

Moment number five announces that the magazine has moved to Toronto, and Acorn is named as the magazine's sole editor. The issue includes poems by Gael Turnbull, G. C. Miller, John Robert Colombo, and Acorn.

In issue number six things heat up considerably. Gwendolyn MacEwen (Acorn's newly-wed wife) is listed as an editor. In the editorial, Acorn notes:

> The more Milton Acorn gets to know poetry. The more he realizes that what he's writing is not poetry.... And the more he becomes opposed to poetry. This then is the sixth issue of Moment.... A magazine opposed to poetry.[8]

157

Despite Acorn's statement, the issue includes good poems by MacEwen, Padraig O Broin, Joe Rosenblatt, Acorn, and Purdy.

In issue number six, editor MacEwen states her opinion of the *Tish* poets. MacEwen's complaint is that, despite all the theoretical to-do in *Tish*, the poetry contained in it is at best a "carbon copy" of the American poets, and at worst devoid of original craft or importance. MacEwen notes that the work *Tish* publishes is "adolescent artiness" and "invalid poetry."[9] She defines her own poetic orientation: "[A]rt consists of concealing the craft of the artist, not elaborating tediously upon it."[10] She argues against the self-conscious element in *Tish* poetry, and says that the *Tish* poets are too much aware of themselves and their art. Acorn also wrote editorials criticizing the *Tish* poets and finding value in the Montreal line of poetry, which is socially engaged and well-crafted, committed to both art and life.

The polemics ran hot and heavy in the east-west debate. Yet, twenty years later, the poetry itself has paled into insignificance. Much of the poetry in *Tish* has faded, and so has the work championed by Acorn. The aesthetic debate, however, has not passed away. Acorn's and Purdy's poetry represents one pole of Canadian poetry; the *Tish* line represents the opposite pole on the national level. At times, aesthetic concerns transcend the limitations of a poet's or an entire group's early work. In its demand for engagement, for a poetry involved with the world, for a poetry conscious of craft, *Moment* foreshadows the mature work of Purdy, Acorn, and MacEwen, just as the early work in *Tish* foreshadows the later poetry of Davey, Bowering, and Wah.

Acorn discussed the Montreal poets from his home in Toronto. Meanwhile, the young Montreal poets themselves were setting to work. Seymour Mayne, Leonard Angel, and K. V. Hertz started a magazine called *Cataract* in the spring of 1962. Layton's influence on these three young poets was apparent.

Cataract began as a rather small, unpretentious pamphlet stapled across the middle. Issues two and three were larger, and stapled at the side. Its general focus was the younger poets of Montreal. Poems by Henry Moscovitch, Milton Acorn, Sidney Aster, K. V. Hertz, Leonard Angel, Charles Sise, Seymour Mayne, Avi Boxer, Stanley Nester, Malcolm Miller, Bryan McCarthy, Alan Pearson, and Irving Layton all appeared. The Layton manner is abundantly evident in the work of the younger poets; to cite an example, this section from Leonard Angel's "Winter Poem" will do for many others:

> Let illness stink in Heine's grave
> Where the poet's ghost now rots:
> — It's winter!
> Brilliant seed is icing miasmic air,

And the spit off a god's cursing tongue
Destroys the suspended dust of decaying bones.[11]

Layton poems are much in evidence, and in issue two there is also an article called "Open Letter to Louis Dudek." The feud that had developed between the two poets flares up in high rhetorical style. Layton accuses Dudek of being "a dying poet," "an over-timorous professor of English Literature," "a flunkey of the bourgeois," and "the Canadian babbitt,"[12] "a squid cleverly covering up movements by squirting ink all over the place and damning and praising the same people," and "an exhausted poet fallen among pedants, with all the fires gone out; a battered empty container whom the mocking gods have thrown on the slag heaps of literature."[13] He also accuses Dudek of becoming a member of the Establishment, of having sold out to comfort and a high standard of living. In publishing Layton's diatribe, one can only assume that the editors of *Cataract* endorsed Layton's view; at the very least, they were interested in controversy.

The editors of *Cataract* exercised their own voices, too. In their first editorial, they disputed the Governor-General's Award being given that year to poet Robert Finch:

> Reading over *Acis in Oxford* by Robert Finch...we challenge the selection committee to point out to us a single poem in it. As a matter of fact, we find it impossible to imagine why the book might have been chosen at all....[T]here happened to be a number of genuine books of poetry published in 1961...to which the award rightfully belonged: in particular, Leonard Cohen's *Spice-Box of Earth*. This collection has been widely praised and contains a solid core of exceptionally moving lyrics.[14]

The editors like poetry that is new and fresh with life; they demand recognition of vital poetry while it is still vital. And the editors are promoting a Montreal contemporary, a poet of their own locality.

Cataract endorsed Layton and Cohen but condemned Dudek and what they saw as the academic literary establishment. As well, they went after a distant *bête noire* — one of the *Tish* poets, Frank Davey. Henry Moscovitch reviewed Davey's book *D-Day and After*:

> [The] work is not poetry at all but dull drivel, lacking in significant experience, in passion, intensity and skillful language, originality of imagination, penetrating and complex self-awareness and above all, any precision or organic sense where each part contributes to the whole....[15]

Moscovitch deplores the tendency to present more theory than poetry and the fact that the theory, once decoded, proves to be either banal or absurd.

Moscovitch offers his view of what the poet should do:

> The true poet will…express fearlessly, and with all the power, intensity, and range he can muster the most varied emotions and experiential truths of man, taking tools from every discipline, by profound experience and imagination, and using to advantage every technical or other innovation….[16]

Moscovitch views the poet as the exceptional, superior man who is able to triumph over death and mortality. In contrast, the Black Mountain poets viewed the poet as medium. Moscovitch condemned the Black Mountain aesthetic, which Davey had taken upon himself and for which he was a Canadian spokesman.

Cataract made an effort to preserve and promote the principles behind the "Montreal Miracle," a poetry that is perceptive and engaged with the world and that places strong emphasis upon craft — the poet's ability to use language, to produce an individual voice through the use of poetic resources. The enemies, as seen by the editors of *Cataract*, are the impotent academic versifiers and the puffing, asthmatic *Tish* poets. Unfortunately, the work produced by the *Cataract* poets does not sustain the arguments of the magazine's editors. Hertz, Angel, and Moscovitch have all passed into relative obscurity; they made no poetic marks that lasted beyond the time of their youthful enthusiasm.

Cataract lasted for three issues, and in that time it made some waves. In 1964 it was superseded by *Catapult*, a magazine edited by Harvey Mayne and Seymour Mayne. *Catapult* was to last for two less controversial but fairly lively issues. *Catapult* published poems by Charles Sise, Stanley Nester, Milton Acorn, Malcolm Miller, Leonard Angel, Steve Smith, Avi Boxer, Alden Nowlan, John Glassco, Irving Layton, Ralph Gustafson, Earle Birney, and Leonard Cohen. In the second issue, *Catapult* handed out "literary awards," one to Layton for his book of poetry *Balls For A One Armed Juggler* and one to Cohen, the "Rookie prose award," for his novel *The Favorite Game*. Layton and Cohen were the shining lights for the *Catapult* editors, and for the poets who gathered around them. *Catapult* published no hard-edged editorials or reviews, and the magazine enjoyed a rather calm and peaceful existence.

The magazines of this period were rounded out by David Rosenfield's one-shot number, *The Bloody Horse*, and also by a series of single-sheet broadside poems that Stuart Gilman and Seymour Mayne brought out at McGill University under the periodical heading *The Page*. Most of these poems were by McGill students, although there was also a "faculty series," which ran for only two poems; one of these was by Louis Dudek. With time, the high-energy level of the early sixties waned. Purdy and Acorn both left Montreal in the early sixties; Seymour Mayne moved to Vancouver in the mid-sixties, where he helped Patrick Lane and bill bissett start Very Stone House Press; Moscovitch suffered a nervous breakdown; Steve Smith died an early tragic death; Hertz began to turn his attention to prose; and most of the others (Angel, Nester, Sise, Miller) simply stopped writing. In the mid-sixties Montreal went into a brief lull.

A new and somewhat reconstituted Montreal writing community did begin to reveal itself in the pages of Raymond Fraser's and LeRoy Johnson's *Intercourse*, a magazine that began publication in the spring of 1966. Subtitled "Contemporary Canadian Writing" and "Canada's literary eighthly," *Intercourse* began as a small pamphlet, then was printed in quarto size.

From the start, the magazine had an easy-going air of fun and casualness. The editorials in *Intercourse* speak of sexual encounters between women missing limbs, of men with incurable cases of acne, or of the art of collecting unemployment insurance or stocking a pantry. Though the humour tends sometimes to fall on the sickly side, the general atmosphere is one of happy irreverence and irrelevance. (With issue number eight, the editors began a pin-up section dedicated to "Miss Intercourse." The "pin-up" was a horrid-looking drawing of what was supposed to be a being of the female gender.) In the first issue we find parody poems that are signed "Buck Layton," "Charlie Souster," "Art Purdy," and "Jack Nowlan."

In many respects the poetry selection in *Intercourse* is eclectic. In the first issue we find poems by Seymour Mayne, Elizabeth Brewster, LeRoy Johnson, Fred Cogswell, George Bowering, Raymond Fraser, and others. The magazine also presented Leonard Cohen, Raymond Souster, Eugene McNamara, Al Pittman, Gregory Cook, Bob Flanagan, Len Gasparini, Barry McKinnon, Louis Cormier, C. H. Gervais, Joseph Sherman, Philip Desjardins, Marc Plourde, and Tim Inkster.

Raymond Fraser edited the first three issues of *Intercourse* in collaboration with LeRoy Johnson. Issues four and seven were edited by Al Pittman; Fraser edited the fifth and sixth issues. Issue eight was edited by Fraser and Pittman. The editorial notes:

> Comrades! *Intercourse* has now brought out a full year of issues — eight — although it took two and a half years to do it.[17]

Such is the fate of many little magazines: its editors start with the intention of bringing out a regular periodical, but, with the rush of time, with financial headaches, and with changes of editorship, the magazine appears irregularly.

Fraser edited issues nine to eleven, and he and Pittman edited issue twelve/thirteen together. Issue fourteen is edited by Louis Cormier, a young poet just come from the Maritimes. Cormier also edited the magazine's last issue, fifteen/sixteen (Spring/Summer 1971), which presented poems by C. H. Gervais, Ritchie Carson, David Fennario, Marc Plourde, Philip Desjardins, Brenda Fleet, Tim Inkster, Louis Cormier, and Tyndale Martin (then head of the Zen Meditation Center in Montreal). Much of the poetry contained in the issue is of an inspirational and devotional nature, with much haiku in evidence. The initial poetic (or other) intercourse has now transformed itself into religious intercourse. Eclectic and flippant through the thirteen issues of Fraser's influence, under Cormier's editorship, the magazine became sober and somewhat evangelical.

Intercourse was a center of activity during a dull period. It did not offer any new poetic perspectives. Yet there is something liberating in the tone and spirit in which the magazine was put forward, and in some ways *Intercourse* looks ahead to later magazine activity in Montreal.

Other magazines of the late sixties and early seventies tended to be ephemeral and ineffectual, and then vanished in a time of literary inactivity, perhaps for lack of clear definition or purpose. *Tide* was edited by Philip Desjardins and Normand Gagnon for seven issues, from October 1968 until 1971; Raymond Fraser, Louis Cormier, Al Pittman, Marc Plourde, Jack Hannan, and Philip Desjardins all appeared in its pages.

In June of 1971, the first issue of Leonard Russo's *Jaw Breaker* appeared. Russo intended the magazine to be eclectic. But the contents of *Jaw Breaker* were rather restrictive. The first issue contains poetry by Glen Siebrasse, a short story by editor Russo, and reviews of books by Eldon Grier, Stephen Scobie, and Douglas Barbour (all the books were published by the Montreal-based Delta Canada Press). In the second issue Russo presents the work of Daryl Hine and offers two poems by Marilyn Grace Julian; the third issue (February 1972) has a long article on black poetry by Russo, and three poems by Montrealer Sharon-Lee Smith. Though it showed some signs of taste, the magazine didn't have much vital energy, and it ceased publication after three issues.

In K. V. Hertz's and Seymour Mayne's *Ingluvin* (1971) we witness a brief renaissance of the early-sixties movement. *Ingluvin* produced only two issues. The first issue featured prose by K. V. Hertz and John Glassco, and poetry by Raymond Fraser, Harvey Mayne, Seymour Mayne, and Peter Huse. The second issue presented an interesting cross-section of work. There was an article on Canadian universities by Robin Mathews and a story by Leonard Cohen; the issue also included poems by Bryan McCarthy, John Glassco, Seymour Mayne, Sylvia Barnard, Irving Layton, Alan Pearson, Gail Fox, Marquita Crevier, and Tom Marshall. The early-sixties Montreal movement seemed to be showing some life again, after ten years. Unfortunately, with this issue, the magazine folded. The sixties movement in Montreal faded out of view.

The last two magazines of the period worth some mention are *Moongoose* and *the golden dog*. *Mongoose,* edited by Ralph Alfonso and Ron Morrissette, appeared in the early seventies. The editors described the purpose of the magazine:

> *Moongoose* is dedicated to Montreal and to printing the works of its poets, writers, and artists. *Moongoose* is dedicated to bringing our readers good reading and writing.[18]

In its dedication to the work of Montreal writers, *Moongoose* foreshadows the community-minded magazines that were then just starting to assert themselves. The editorial focus of *Moongoose* was never very strong; the magazine failed to produce much excitement or momentum. Like *Tide* and *Jaw Breaker*, *Moongoose* filled a void in a time of poetic recession.

Le chien d'or/the golden dog, edited by Carlo Fonda and Michael Gnarowski and subtitled "writing today," made its first appearance in January of 1972. The first issue featured poetry by Louis Dudek, an interview with Irving Layton, an article on the poetry of Leo Kennedy by Lorraine McMullen, and an essay, "Educating the Critics," by Louis Dudek. The magazine was essentially a journal of articles and criticism; it did little to foster new work or contribute to a developing poetry.

The Montreal poetry renaissance of the seventies began in 1967, when "New Wave Canada" made its first official entrance when George Bowering and Margaret Atwood took up teaching positions at Sir George Williams University. Before 1967, university students seeking to write poetry had the choice of Louis Dudek at McGill or Irving Layton at Sir George Williams as their teachers and mentors. Atwood taught Victorian literature and did a reading or two in Montreal before moving on; Bowering, on the other hand, began teaching creative-writing classes to fledgling poets. He awakened in his students the prospect of a literary community. The Montreal poets of the sixties tended to be highly individualistic, perhaps taking their cue from Layton and Cohen, who had managed to exploit their own individual voices. By the early seventies, Layton and Cohen had left the city and did not exercise as much influence through their work. It was while Bowering was present at Sir George Williams (1967 to 1971) that the English department there held its extensive reading series (originally instituted by Roy Kiyooka, Wynne Francis, Stan Hoffman, and Howard Fink, all faculty members). The series brought in many poets from across Canada and the United States, and exposed the young and aspiring Montreal poets to a wide diversity of poetic techniques. Poets in Montreal became aware of poetic developments taking place outside Montreal, and slowly the new Montreal poetry came to reflect recent international trends.

In many ways, the new generation of poets was starting from scratch. The preceding generation had all but faded away; there was no real establishment in Montreal for these poets to oppose. The first necessity, then, was to establish survival outlets. The magazines that began in the seventies tended to be open to writers with a different orientation from their own. Strong disagreements among Montreal poets did not disappear, but the formation of new outlets for Montreal poetry took precedence over jockeying for prestige and position.

In 1972, two Montreal little magazines made their appearance. *Booster & Blaster* lasted for two issues; *Anthol* published four issues. *Booster & Blaster* is something of an enigma as a little magazine. Although the quality of its poetry was, admittedly, generally not very good, it served as an important juncture in Montreal poetry. With time, it may be seen as an important link to the establishment of a literary community in Montreal of the seventies. The magazine was the brain-child of poet Bryan McCarthy, and from its first issue — in January 1972 — it was put out by a working committee consisting of McCarthy, Glen Siebrasse, Linda Jewel, Alan Pearson, Carol Leckner, Artie Gold, David Pinson, David Read, and Nancy Stegmayer. The people working on the magazine represent an interesting blend of older poets, who had weathered the sixties in Montreal, and younger poets, who were just beginning to write and take an interest in their contemporaries' work.

Booster & Blaster was totally democratic and designed to serve a literary community. Its aim was to bring poets out of their relative isolation and to make them visible to each other. It functioned, without an editor, in much the way that a print-cooperative workshop does. Each poet had to pay for the pages that contained his or her work. At the back of the magazine there was a section in which the contributing poets "boosted" or "blasted" each other's work; this section was designed to provide some perspective and view on what was being written and published. *Booster & Blaster* was an important magazine not because of the writing it contained, but because it attempted to draw together a fragmented and splintered poetic community.

The first issue of *Booster & Blaster* provides an interesting convergence of older writers and younger, untried poets. In the magazine we find the poems of

Avi Boxer, Phil Desjardins, Louis Dudek, Ron Everson, Raymond Fraser, Michael Gnarowski, Seymour Mayne, David Rosenfield, Renald Shoofler, and Glen Siebrasse, all familiar poets on the scene; there is also new poetry by Artie Gold, Carol Leckner, Marc Plourde, and Peter Van Toorn. In *Booster & Blaster*, the old met the young and passed on the torch.

Although the magazine was slated to appear six times a year, the second issue did not come out until December 1972 with a somewhat reconstituted editorial board: Raymond Gordy was managing editor, Glen Siebrasse handled production, Alan Pearson and Carol Leckner took care of publicity, and Artie Gold worked on circulation. We can already feel the new generation of poets flexing its muscles. The older poets of the sixties have all but vanished from the magazine. Contributors to this issue include Ian Burgess, Endre Farkas, Raymond Gordy, Artie Gold, Carol Leckner, Marc Plourde, Paddy Webb, and Richard Sommer, all members of the seventies renaissance. The quality of the poetry is uneven: "some good poetry, much indifferent, some very bad."[19]

The magazine disappeared after the second issue, though there had been plans for a third, to be edited by Glen Siebrasse. A mimeographed note from Siebrasse pasted to the inside front cover of the second issue notes:

> A change of policy will occur in the third issue. Manuscripts are invited, but poems will be selected by the editor. Please do not send money with submission. You need it more than me.[20]

Siebrasse desired a magazine of more discrimination and selection. The democratic spirit did not last long at *Booster & Blaster*, and it is perhaps just as well that an edited third issue never appeared. The two issues of the magazine testify to a brief period of literary democracy in action.

The other little magazine that began in 1972 was *Anthol*. It was intended to be an annual, and the first issue appeared in the spring of 1972. The first three issues were edited by Robert Morrison and Diane Keating; Gilbert Plaw was added to the masthead for issue number four. *Anthol* published only Montreal poets. Though editorial selections were made in *Anthol*, the magazine maintained a fairly open policy, accepting poetry of different orientations. Like *Booster & Blaster*, the magazine was dedicated to the idea of literary community;

> The editors wish... to help foster a poetic community in Montreal, and urge anyone with similar interests to contact them.... We have in mind the engendering of poetry readings, critical sessions, etc.[21]

In its own fairly quiet way, *Anthol* presented selections of new work by Montreal poets; the editors offered little or no editorial commentary. During its short run it published many of the younger Montreal poets on the scene. After issue number four the editors were hoping the magazine would take a national perspective but, as with *Booster & Blaster*, the change in the magazine's intention somehow resulted in its sudden demise. At any rate, for four years it served a useful community function.

The desire for poetry readings and other community activities expressed by the editors of *Anthol* was echoed by the slowly gathering Montreal poetry fraternity. By 1972 Sir George Williams University's rather extensive reading series was beginning to decline, though it would continue for another year or two. But the young poets just beginning to write in Montreal found that the university was not really interested in their efforts. They had no access to organizations that sponsored readings, and so were forced to fall back on their own resources. At this time the Canada-Council-sponsored parallel-art-gallery movement was just beginning to establish itself in Canada, and in Montreal the Vehicule Gallery opened at 61 St. Catherine Street West. Located in a part of town frequented by prostitutes and noted for pornographic movies, alcoholics, and ethnic markets, the gallery was meant to provide an alternative exhibition space for experimental artists. Through association with several of the Vehicule artists, a few poets established the gallery as their working location. Sunday afternoons were devoted to the poets, who began to hold readings there.

In the context of the reading series at Vehicule, the new community came into being. Claudia Lapp and Michael Harris organized the first reading series in the late fall of 1973. The series provided local poets with a place to be seen and heard. In 1974, Artie Gold and Endre Farkas brought Vehicule to the attention of all young poets by organizing a mammoth series of thirty-seven readings. Every local poet with anything worth hearing was given that hearing. The 1974 series created a centre of activity that reached out beyond the small circles of poets who already knew each other. From the fall of 1975 to the spring of 1976 Ian Burgess organized a series of thirty-four readings. Subsequent series were organized by Robert Galvin, John McAuley, and Stephen Morrissey from 1976 to 1977, and by Tom Konyves from 1977 to 1980.

The years 1974 to 1977 were the peak years at Vehicule Gallery, the years of community activity. Poets came to readings each week to hear what their peers were doing, to be stimulated, and to offer criticism. During this time many young Montreal poets published their first books, and the excitement level ran high: new poets were testing their fledgling wings. The early energy evident in *Booster & Blaster* and *Anthol* found its realization in convivial poetry readings. The new sense of community for poets had, at long last, arrived.

This sense of shared experience lasted for only a few years. Vehicule Press published an anthology called *Montreal English Poetry of the Seventies* in 1977, edited by Endre Farkas and Ken Norris; an era of controversy and minor factionalism began when the anthology was published. Shortly thereafter, most Montreal poets became involved in individual activities. There was little communal sharing.

Seven poets, who had met at Vehicule and done much of the organizational work there, were finding a sense of brotherhood: they discovered a small community in which they could share. The seven poets shared an aesthetic concern: they found most of the writing in Montreal too reactionary or conservative for their taste. As well, they shared an interest in Modernist and Post-Modernist art movements; they each had an experimental bent, evident in their books. Gradually, these poets — Endre Farkas, Artie Gold, Tom Konyves, Claudia Lapp, John McAuley, Stephen Morrissey, and Ken Norris — found themselves drawn into a tighter association with one another, until there evolved a sense of solidarity; this consciousness was heightened by the tendency of other poets within the community, and critics beyond, to refer to them as "the Vehicule poets." Eventually they would publish a group anthology, *The Vehicule Poets* (1979).

Much of the literary activity in Montreal during the seventies centred around the Vehicule poets. They ran the reading series at the Vehicule Gallery, edited books for Vehicule Press, put poetry on Montreal buses, put poetry and other art forms on cable television, created extensive mixed-media performances and collaborations with each other and with artists in other disciplines, and they ran a handful of little magazines. A sense of group cohesion was evident in all of these projects. In the seventies the seven poets published thirty-three volumes of poetry. A formidable movement was under way.

The work of the Vehicule poets ran the gamut from traditional poetry to concrete poetry, sound poetry, the use of collage techniques, and mixed-media performance; there were attempts to pioneer new media for poetry (as in Konyves's creation of video-poems). Imagism, Surrealism, Futurism, Dadaism, Absurdism, and the international concrete movement were all evident influences, as were also the Black Mountain and New York schools. The aesthetic orientations of the Vehicule poets are contained in the magazines they edited and published.

The first was Stephen Morrissey's concrete newsletter, *what is*, which published fourteen issues from 1973 to 1975. Morrissey had several motivations for starting *what is*. In 1973, there was no outlet in Montreal for experimental work. (Montrealers Artie Gold, Richard Sommer, John McAuley, and Endre Farkas all appeared in the pages of *what is*.) Morrissey also wanted to establish contacts with other writers who were interested in experimentation, who lived in other parts of Canada and in the United States. This communication was accomplished through a select mailing list of about sixty names and also by publishing experimental work from outside Montreal. The magazine had a visual bias, but textually experimental work sometimes appeared. Writers such as bpNichol, Gerry Gilbert, Richard Kostelanatz, and Edwin Varney were all contributors. For two years, *what is* served as the solitary outpost for avant-garde writing in Montreal.

When Ken Norris moved back to Montreal from New York in January 1975 he brought with him the magazine *CrossCountry*, which had just started publication. Subtitled "a magazine of Canadian-United States poetry," *CrossCountry* took a decidedly anti-nationalist stand, as we see in the magazine's initial editorial:

> In recent years poetry has evolved along national lines — this has led to a renaissance in North American poetry and the recognition of an individual poetic heritage in Canada. For the most part, this new Canadian-U.S. poetry has attracted only native readers. We feel it is time for a crossing of the borders. For too long schools of poetry have emphasized national differences and played down the similarities of our North American experience. With *CrossCountry* we hope to provide a forum for the cross-germination needed to stimulate this continent's poetic explorations and to bring them a common audience.[22]

The editors of *CrossCountry*, Robert Galvin, Jim Mele, and Ken Norris, wanted a magazine similar to *Contact* or *Combustion* or *what is*: one devoted to all the interesting developments in poetry in North America. The magazine would also try to overcome the kind of reader-prejudice that confined Canadian poetry to a Canadian audience. When it published Montreal poets, the magazine placed them within a larger continental context.

A magazine called *Mouse Eggs* served as the unofficial house organ of the Vehicle poets. Thirteen issues appeared between September 1975 and June 1977; a second series began in the fall of 1979. Endre Farkas usually did the production work. *Mouse Eggs* was the centre of eccentric in-group activity. Acknowledging that its readers were few, it was usually mimeographed in runs of fifty copies. The magazine had no regular editor and its list of contributors rarely ranged beyond the Vehicle poets. In spirit, it was like *Intercourse*; it didn't take itself too seriously and violated most of the functions of a little magazine. It did not present polemical editorials or take up serious positions. A close look at *Mouse Eggs* does not provide much grist for critical discussion; instead, we see a friendly group of poets trying out their work on one another.

The magazine abounded in satire, parody, poetic asides, the granting of false awards, criticism of poetic white-elephants, and poetic experiments. Because it appeared so frequently, it provided a place for writing that was scarcely days old. The material in the first series ranged from the terrific to the terrible, experiments that exploded and experiments that fizzled. The emphasis seemed to be on fun.

John McAuley's *Maker* was dedicated to concrete and experimental work. It was published from 1976 to 1978, and only three issues appeared. The first issue featured Montrealers (Artie Gold, Ken Norris, Stephen Morrissey, Endre Farkas, Richard Sommer, and John McAuley); the second issue included a wider diversity of work. Subtitled "a poetics newsletter (linear & concrete)," *Maker* presented work by Gerry Gilbert, Opal L. Nations, John Furnival, Richard Kostelanatz, Steve Smith, Penny Kemp, and Richard Truhlar. The quarto-format magazine was sent out to a select mailing list of four hundred working artists and writers in twenty-two countries. *Maker* attempted to present work as "news" rather than as aesthetically perfected art. Process was emphasized, rather than product. In 1978 McAuley started Maker Press, a small book press. Once again, the little magazine was a stepping stone to a small press.

Hh, edited by Tom Konyves, was "published minimally," as the cover of the second issue acknowledged. Two issues of the magazine appeared, one in 1976, the other in 1977. *Hh* concentrated on the surrealistic and Dadaistic side of contemporary Montreal poetry. The second issue included an editor's note:

> This is a Montreal (ltd.) magazine. We prefer the minimal. Two popular misconceptions: *Hh* is a formula. Poetry is of the spirit. The poem should have the function and appearance of a bicycle. We publish only what we see. The muse visits us on occasion, throws a couple of muse eggs, chats.[23]

The magazine published work by Montreal poets Artie Gold, Endre Farkas, and Steven Sky; there were also works of collage (done by Konyves) and collaborative works by Stephen Morrissey, Endre Farkas, Ken Norris, Opal L. Nations, John McAuley, and Tom Konyves. Editor Konyves rejected totally the conservative, genteel Canadian poetic tradition.

The *Montreal Journal of Poetics* contained the poetic theorizing of the Vehicule poets. Edited by Stephen Morrissey, the journal first appeared in the winter of 1978. Its title is somewhat deceptive: the magazine is much less impressive than a journal. It consisted of a number of sheets stapled together in the upper left-hand corner. Morrissey distributed it to a mailing list of about one hundred people. The first issue contained an editorial by Morrissey:

It has become fairly easy to get poems published in little magazines, but good criticism of younger poets is still not available. It is now essential that we, as poets, observe seriously what other poets are doing and evaluate it in the light of our own understanding of the creative process. We need intelligent non-academic criticism, the free discussion of poetics and reviews of books and readings. This magazine offers a forum where this discussion may occur.[24]

In the first issue of the *Montreal Journal of Poetics* we find an article on visual poetry by McAuley, an article by Morrissey called "The Purpose of Experimental Poetry," Norris's reviews of books by Richard Sommer and Tom Konyves, Farkas's "Confessions of a Collaborator," and the essay "Videopoetry" by Konyves. The concerns are diverse, but all the work pointed in an experimental direction.

Morrissey's essay reflects a tempered view of experimentation in poetry:

For anyone exposed to a lot of experimental poetry the question of its purpose and value is raised. It seems to me that the central reason for experimenting in poetry is that the forms one inherits have become obsolete: poets must discover and write in a form that corresponds to their time, times change and the vehicle for communicating that change is something alive, organic, and writers must be aware of this in their work. The second major reason is that experimental poetry is a form of lateral thinking, a way of getting "unblockt," a way of approaching poetry so that the poem needn't conform to preconceived ideas of how it should look and sound, but of allowing the poem to find its own form, its own way of being expressed.

What has happened is that the experiment has become an end in itself, so that we have a whole group of poets who can be categorized as "experimental." Perhaps their idea is that by "experimenting" they think they're being "experimental," unfortunately a new form doesn't necessarily provide a new content; in effect, the "experimental poet" often has nothing to say but is merely playing with form, and that "playing with form" soon becomes redundant.[25]

Konyves's "Videopoetry" describes a search for a new form for poetry. The search for a new form came out of a feeling that the printed word did not convey the full potential of language:

The printed work was looking more and more like a secret message sent from room to room, from the poet's den to the reader's bedchamber. In other words, a certain immediacy was lacking. Readings attempt to restore a missing link — the voice — while audio and video recordings wish to create a new immediacy, albeit an artificial one.[26]

Konyves hoped that poets would begin to work with new technologies. Konyves chose to make poems out of videotape:

> Writing for video should be easy enough. It is more malleable than print or audiotape. A good poem on tape will use all technology has to offer, repetition, dubbing, music mix, unexpected periods of silence, untranslatable sounds. "Special effects" will be the vocabulary of this new poem. . . .
>
> Whereas I consider a line the unit of poem-making, like bricklaying, in video we substitute visual lines for printed lines and proceed to "layer" a poem: spoken words (the poet-performer); words heard (taped, dubbed); and seen (signs, subtitles, printed, painted). Naturally, a poem written with these three forms of word-smithing is never "itself" until it is meshed with visual imagery (close-ups, cuts, dissolves, pans). If the end-product demonstrates a "judicious" mix of the two (even an interesting interplay) the poem will have a texture we will all admire.[27]

In Konyves's completed videopoems, we find theatrical elements or poetic elements dominating, but on the whole he has succeeded in judiciously mixing elements of performance, video art and poetry into "videopoetry."

One feature that defined the Vehicule poets was their ability to produce collaborative works. Norris and Konyves worked together on a book of aphorisms *(Proverbsi)* and a videopoem *(See/Saw)*; various groupings of the Vehicule poets took part in poetry performances and sound recordings; they assisted in the presentation of one another's work; Farkas directed a videotape presentation of Norris's poems, and assisted Konyves in the production of his videopoems. Farkas's "Confessions of a Collaborator," which appeared in the *Montreal Journal of Poetics*, testified to the collaborative, communal spirit of much of the Vehicule poets' work.

The second issue of the *Journal* (Spring–Summer 1979) is more eclectic than the first. Konyves continued his commentary on the videopoem; Louis Dudek contributed "A Brief Note on Writing Poetry;" Morrissey considered the rôle of "cosmic consciousness" in poetry; Artie Gold reviewed a book by Fraser Sutherland. Norris contributed two articles. One defended a "native" position in Canadian poetry ("The New World"); one defended certain experimental writers against Morrissey's criticisms, which had appeared in the first issue.

The third issue of the *Journal* was dedicated exclusively to the Vehicule poets. Each of them contributed at least one work that represented their poetic concerns. Claudia Lapp's "Some Aspects of Dream & Poetry" traced her interest in dream journals and her use of dreams as material for poems. Artie Gold contributed several short reviews of avant-garde poetry books. In "Norris & Cohen: The Limits of Self-Consciousness," Stephen Morrissey reviewed Ken Norris's *The Book of Fall* and Leonard Cohen's *Death of a Lady's Man*. Morrissey discussed the poet-as-subject theme in contemporary poetry, and the limitations self-consciousness imposes on the poet. "Poetry and the Fine Art of Deception" is a dialogue between John McAuley and Ken Norris, in which the poets discuss the use of deception and lying in poetry. Tom Konyves's "Poetika" is an obscure discussion of poetic craft and craftiness. In a critical piece called "Some Notes Towards A Definition of Phoney Formalism," Ken Norris discussed the "false formalism" dominant in Canadian writing.

The Vehicule poets attempted to explore new forms to release new contents. Although they were accused by many of their contemporaries of writing a poetry of pure content, they actually represented a new, aesthetically oriented theory of form. Their work also reflected a desire for a complete and organic sense of poetry's possibilities. As Tom Konyves observed: "There is a little bit of poetry in everything but by no means is there a little bit of everything in poetry."[28]

IO

The Little Magazine
in the Late Seventies

The literary atmosphere in Canada in the 1970s was vastly different from the atmosphere of the period 1925 to 1965. It seemed that, at long last, there was a modern Canadian literature: writers were writing it, the public was buying it, the Canada Council was funding it, and Canadian periodicals were reviewing it. Things had never been better. Yet some people argued that the complacency of the established Canadian publishers, editors, and writers was as pernicious as the views embraced by the Canadian Authors' Association in the early twenties, which Scott and Smith had argued against. The spirit of the little magazine was still at work as an agitator and as an alternative in the seventies, but this spirit had been somewhat transformed during the previous fifteen years.

From the twenties to the sixties, the battleground for Modernism in Canada was the periodical. There was no indigenous Canadian publishing industry; therefore the magazine was where poetry happened. For the poets of the McGill group, book publication came much later in life than for most poets. Only Leo Kennedy published an individual volume of poetry in the 1930s: *The Shrouding* (1933). Scott, Smith, and Klein all saw their first appearance in book form in the anthology *New Provinces* (1936) in which they appeared with Kennedy, E. J. Pratt, and Robert Finch. Klein's first separate book appeared in 1940 *(Hath Not a Jew)*, Smith's *News of the Phoenix* in 1943, Scott's *Overture* in 1945. A. M. Klein was thirty-one when his first book was published, A. J. M. Smith was forty-one, and F. R. Scott was forty-six. Klein had been published by Behrman House, Inc., in New York, which specialized in books by Jewish authors, the others had been published by Ryerson Press. *New Provinces* was published by Macmillan; the contributors themselves put up two hundred dollars towards the publication of the book.

In later generations, poets were more willing to take the publishing of their books into their own hands. First Statement Press emanated out of *First Statement*, the magazine; Contact Press came from *Contact* magazine; Delta Canada came from *Delta*; the short-lived Tishbooks came from *Tish*; Talon-

173

books emanated from *Talon*; and Blew Ointment Press evolved from *Blew Ointment*. Later generations had realized they could publish books as well as periodicals.

Since the mid-sixties, there has been a rise in the activity of the literary press. The little magazine has proliferated during this period as well, yet often the more dynamic energy has gone into book rather than periodical publishing. The McGill group arrived as authors by the standard method: there were no magazines sympathetic to the work they were writing, so they began their own periodicals. They then waited for established publishers to recognize their growing literary reputations. (F. R. Scott waited almost twenty years.) With Contact Press and its editors — Irving Layton, Raymond Souster, and Louis Dudek — a group of poets began to short-circuit the established method of arriving as a poet. They didn't wait for their work to be recognized by established literary magazines and then by literary presses; they brought their own work and that of others before the public. It is this spirit that fuels the current crop of literary presses, which derive at least some of their spirit from energy that originally went into the little magazine.

The publishing industry in Canada was centred mostly in Toronto, which meant that poets outside the city were without a local forum. During the seventies, a number of grass-roots regional presses were started, including Breakwater Books, Turnstone Press, Blackfish Press, Vehicle Press, Oolichan Books, Repository Press, Sesame Press, Hanaco Press, Caledonia Writing Series, Harbour Publishing, New Delta, Thistledown Press, Pulp Press, Intermedia Press, Black Moss Press, Aya Press, Guernica Editions, and many others. These small presses supported two ventures: local literary activity and continuing literary experimentation. Local writing was something commercial presses had no cognizance of; experimentation was something commercial houses steered clear of, because of its questionable marketability. In an earlier time, the publishers of these grass-roots presses might have been editing magazines dedicated to the work of new authors; the authors might have waited to be published by a commercial house.

Despite the increasing numbers of literary presses in the seventies, the activities of the little magazine went on. A number of the magazines produced in Canada were rooted in specific regions. Often they objected to being considered "regional," and were quick to point out that they cast a wide net, took in work from other parts of the country, and so on; in other words, they contended, they were national. Their defensiveness seemed to be prompted by the notion that "regional" means "parochial." But without these magazines, local writers would have had no outlets: the writers would have to send their work to publications in other parts of the country. Those far-away magazines would not be sensitive to any but their own local concerns.

One "regional" magazine, *Northern Light*, was edited by George Amabile and was published twice yearly by the University of Manitoba. Although the magazine was strongly rooted in Manitoba, it was open to submissions from anywhere in Canada; it was not, however, a totally eclectic magazine. In an early editorial, Amabile dismissed two schools of writing, which he designated as "the Black Mountaineers" and "the neo-Surrealists." In an editorial in the third issue of *Northern Light*, Amabile wrote:

> My impatience was inspired not by a distaste for experiment, but, on the contrary, by a severe case of boredom with the way these established and old-fashioned theories of verse have been compulsively paraded as "avant garde" when they are, in fact, the result of sheer poetic fragmentation and inertia. They are not new. They are old. And they are trivial points of departure because they are based on theories of poetry which specialize in one aspect of the verbal arts to the exclusion of all others. They are therefore inadequate, technological *cul de sacs*, and it is annoying to see how the genuine discoveries and contributions which Charles Olson and Andre Breton made so long ago to the art of poetry have hardened into something like political and religious doctrine.[1]

Amabile then puts forward his own view of what should be going on in poetry:

> The answer is quite simple. There are dozens of young (and not so young) poets in this country who have managed to stay clear of the stultifying and narrow-minded doctrines of the various poetic "schools," and the work they are doing is genuinely new because it is the expression of an individual aesthetic created out of the many poetic techniques available to us now in response to the wide spectrum of contemporary experience.... What's new in Canadian poetry, and in poetry in English generally, is this new confluence of older experimental gains into the work of individual poets.[2]

The poet should be aware of innovations in the craft, and blend his awareness of language's possibilities with his own individual experience. This is not a new insight, but it does hold down a middle ground between the Canadian avant-garde and the traditionalists.

A noteworthy magazine from Saskatchewan was *Salt*, in many ways the epitome of the regional magazine that strives to get things done. In eight years, Robert Currie edited sixteen issues of *Salt*, subtitled "A little magazine of Contemporary Writing." In its ninth year *Salt* was edited by Barbara Sapergia and Geoffrey Ursell. All of the issues feature a block of work by a writer who lived or was brought up on the Prairies. The poet contributed a selection of poems, and also a piece called "beginnings," which searched out the origins of the poet's creative impulse. The "beginnings" also included a bit of autobiography showing what it meant to grow up on the prairies. *Salt* contained an engaging and interesting approach to writing, one that went a long way towards validating the magazine's persistent aesthetic concern with roots and rootedness. *Salt* also contained reviews of significant books published in and around Saskatchewan. All in all, it was an admirable little magazine, a model for what can be done by a regional publication.

Even regional publications had a strong spirit of eclecticism. Indeed, most of the little magazines that appeared in Canada in the late seventies were eclectic in nature; the experimentation of the sixties, which came to be known as "New Wave Canada," had become the established norm. What had been vital and new was now becoming a new set of literary conventions. Many seventies poets were more articulate than their predecessors, but the seventies seemed to have little new to offer.

Many of the eclectic magazines were attached to Canadian universities, and were caught up in the trappings of academia. The universities provided the magazines with credibility, offices, and funds. The typical university magazine did not pioneer new territories, but echoed the accepted norms of the day. Most magazines coming out of the universities are of minor interest, not involved with the true revolutionary spirit of the fighting little magazine. A few of them, however, are noteworthy.

Waves was a tri-annual literary magazine issued from York University in Toronto. It was generally eclectic, and published "good" writing of whatever kind; the writing that appeared was occasionally uneven, but reflected a strong concern with craft. *Waves* published an interesting panorama of young writers, and many of the pieces that appeared were first publications or early strivings of poets who published a first or second book a short time later.

Matrix was published twice yearly by the English department of Champlain College in Lennoxville, Quebec. It, too, strived to publish "good" writing, although it presented no defined or preferred aesthetic. Early issues contain miscellaneous stories and poems of a conventional nature; then *Matrix* gradually evolved into a more engaged literary review. Many of its pages were filled with book reviews, sometimes written by the editors, that gave voice to a defined sense of poetry.

Perhaps the finest, certainly the most elegantly produced, periodical attached to a college community was *The Capilano Review*. It was published twice a year by Capilano College in North Vancouver. The publication was in no real sense a "little" magazine; it was expensively printed, impeccably designed, and had a surface slickness that outshone other university publications. *The Capilano Review* was involved in a very real engagement with the arts as they existed in and around Vancouver. The magazine occasionally published work by writers from other parts of Canada and from the United States; this work was usually presented in relation to the west-coast sensibility the magazine exemplified. *The Capilano Review* did not limit itself to the written arts, but published examples of visual art as well.

The most ambitious eclectic magazine of the late seventies was *CV/II*, published in Winnipeg. In the first editorial Dorothy Livesay defined the *raison d'être* of *CV/II:*

> We have our poetry, pushing up from every crack and cranny. What we now lack is sufficient outlets for serious criticism of it. You can only criticize such wide, large, and various production, we think, by taking samples; and CV/II proposes to do this.[3]

The name "CV/II" is an abbreviation for "Contemporary Verse Two." Dorothy Livesay had been closely associated with the original *Contemporary Verse*. Livesay's new magazine attempted to provide an eclectic forum for poetry criticism. And *CV/II* was a national review of poetry, which made it all the more important. It printed generous samplings of poetry from every part of the country, particularly poetry by younger poets; in addition, it contained a large body of criticism in the form of reviews. Its criticisms were not always judicious, but the magazine served as a lively forum.

Magazines that represented a specific group of poets and a strong purpose were few and far between in the late seventies. Again, this might be accounted for by the rise in literary-press activity, as many local poets involved themselves in book production. It is difficult to locate magazines that reflect a shared aesthetic. One magazine that did was *Kontakte*, edited by Richard Truhlar and John Riddell. *Kontakte* gave expression to the continuity of experimentation in concrete and sound poetry in and around Toronto. Particular attention was paid to work by the sound-poetry collective Owen Sound, of which the editors were members. *Kontakte* also published a special issue devoted to Hugo Ball, the twentieth century's first self-proclaimed sound poet. The issue included an intelligent introduction by Riddell, which gave the historical background of Ball and quoted some of Ball's important statements from his published diary, *Flight Out Of Time*. Riddell also explained Ball's relevance to poets working with sound. The issue included three of Ball's original sound poems, three translations of his surrealistic work, and tributes by poets such as Steve McCaffery, bpNichol, and Owen Sound.

The west-coast poetry newsletter *NMFG* was edited by Gordon Lockhead (alias "Brian Fawcett") in Vancouver. *NMFG* reflected the poetic politics of an individual editor rather than of a group. In the first issue, Fawcett announced that *NMFG* was "a newsletter of poetry published without much pretence for the information of writers, painters, musicians & kindred. It has the political and cosmical purpose of making the west coast & specifically Vancouver a better place to work & live."[4] The first eighteen issues appeared about once a month; then *NMFG*'s intention was somewhat amended: "Its energies derive from the idealism that poetic thought should be as clear about its origins & purpose as that of the nearest logician, & from an interest in working out the difficulty writers have making clear why they're doing what they're doing."[5] Like *Tish, NMFG* was sent out to a select mailing list and supported itself through contributions from its readers. ("NMFG" stood for "No Money From the Government.") The newsletter drew upon the writing of the British Columbia community more extensively than did *Tish*, with its tight circle of editors. As well, *NMFG* was a good deal less aesthetically minded than *Tish*, and continually addressed itself to the rôle of poetry in relation to society. In *NMFG* we see an attempt to work out a new, fully realized aesthetic that takes into account the political realities of every-day life.

The final magazine worthy of mention is *The Front*, which was edited by Jim Smith out of Kingston, Ontario. Produced in an unpretentious format, *The Front* provided readers with what Smith viewed as some of the more significant work produced by the literary avant garde. It reflected its editor's particular preferences; at the same time, it kept alive the creative aura of the understaffed, highly principled little magazine. In an editorial in the sixth issue, Smith announced his intention of reviewing books in future issues, but only those books published by what he deemed to be Canada's four avant-garde literary presses. He explained his decision as follows:

> [T]hese four poles encompass almost the entirety of the adventurous, exciting, & worthwhile small press publishing being done in Canada today. I attempt to read most literary magazines that come out these days & I have been continually disappointed by the lack of attention shown to the above-mentioned presses, while observing a virtual fixation on the staid, the ploddingly quotidian, and the banal. I have often wondered if EVERYBODY reviewing books in this country aspires to the same moribund level of myopic snobbishness. Or perhaps book reviews SHOULD only be another tool in the establishment of the reviewer in the chummy pecking-order of recognized Canadian letters. In my own experience, most recognized literati are more moved by the name (either of the writers or the publishing house) than by the work itself....

So beginning with the next issues, *The Front* will in its humble way try to fill a certain gap, providing reviews of work that is important for the boundaries it approaches.[6]

Smith's editorial takes us back to the original intentions and motivations of all little magazines. The ultimate aim of the little magazine is literary revolution, a call to a new order. If it succeeds, the old establishment is put aside and a new beginning is made; if nothing else, a few voices are heard saying something that was not said before. In its editorial intentions, *The Front* shares much with magazines that preceded it: the hope of forming "a front" against the accepted literary norms of the day.

That the little magazine is engaged in a literary ferment and literary transformation is a point I have tried to make clear. Beginning with Pound and his circle in England, we see the little magazine as a vital and necessary tool in the furthering of Modernist poetry. Indeed, because the inclinations of Modernism are anti-consumerist and non-commercial, Modernist writing must literally create a home for itself. That haven, first and foremost, is the little magazine, the testing-ground and proving-ground for subsequent generations of literary experimenters and innovators.

In Canada, literary Modernism has experienced a slow but steady growth and evolution in the pages of the little magazine. Each generation's renegades or trouble-makers have often come to be recognized as vital poets of the period. In plotting the course of Modernist development in Canada, it would be a misreading of the facts to suggest that, at all times, this development has progressed in a steady, linear fashion; as we have seen in *Alphabet*, *GrOnk*, and *Blew Ointment* in the sixties, there is always the possibility that poets will backtrack and develop elements of literary Modernism that earlier, more purely Imagist-oriented poets ignored. At all times, however, in the detailing of this non-sequential evolution, we find in the work of the poets a momentum that is dedicated to providing a poetry that is true to the language and true to the age. Of the hundreds of little magazines that have appeared in Canada, perhaps only a dozen can be considered landmark publications. But each magazine, simply by virtue of its existence, has contributed something to the creation of a vital literary climate. The cumulative result of all these publications is that there now exists a healthy environment for poetry in Canada, one that allows for diverse work to develop and to constitute contemporary Canadian writing. Poet bpNichol asserts that different forms release new contents. The Canadian poet today is in possession of, or at least proximate to, a body of Modernist aesthetics filled with infinite possibilities. Out of this ferment, new poetries will continue to emerge, with new little magazines serving as their initial gathering place and continuing forum.

Footnotes

I

1 Robert Kroetsch, "A Canadian Issue," *Boundary 2*, 3, No. 1 (Fall 1974), p. 1.
2 Malcolm Bradbury and James McFarlane, "The Name and Nature of Modernism," *Modernism* (New York: Penguin, 1976), p. 25.
3 Louis Dudek, *Technology & Culture* (Ottawa: Golden Dog, 1979), pp. 87–88.
4 Bradbury and McFarlane, p. 25.
5 Bradbury and McFarlane, p. 22.
6 Bradbury and McFarlane, p. 27.
7 Bradbury and McFarlane, p. 46.
8 Bradbury and McFarlane, pp. 34–35.
9 Monroe K. Spears, *Dionysus and the City* (New York: Oxford Univ. Press, 1970), p. 15.
10 William Pratt, ed., *The Imagist Poem* (New York: Dutton, 1963), p. 13.
11 F.S. Flint, "Imagisme," rpt. in *Imagist Poetry*, ed. Peter Jones (New York: Penguin, 1972), p. 129.
12 Frederick J. Hoffman, Charles Allen, and Carolyn F. Ulrich, *The Little Magazine: A History and a Bibliography* (Princeton, N.J.: Princeton Univ. Press, 1946), p. 4.
13 Hoffman, p. 4.
14 Hoffman, pp. 4–5.
15 Louis Dudek, *Literature and the Press* (Toronto: Ryerson/Contact, 1960), p. 140.
16 Hoffman, pp. 1–2.
17 Hoffman, p. 4.
18 Hoffman, p. 6.
19 F. R. Scott, "...It is the Heart that Sees," *Athanor*, 1, No. 2 (Feb. 1980), 5.

[20] Louis Dudek, "The Role of the Little Magazine in Canada," in *The Making of Modern Poetry in Canada* (Toronto: Ryerson, 1967), p. 206.

[21] James Doyle, "Canadian Poetry and American Magazines, 1885–1905," *Canadian Poetry: Studies, Documents, Reviews*, No. 5 (Fall-Winter 1979), p. 74.

2

[1] Louis Dudek and Michael Gnarowski, "The Precursors: 1910–1925," in *The Making of Modern Poetry in Canada* (Toronto: Ryerson, 1967), p. 3.

[2] Dudek and Gnarowski, p. 4.

[3] Dudek and Gnarowski, p. 4.

[4] Dudek and Gnarowski, "The Little Magazines," in *The Making of Modern Poetry in Canada*, p. 203.

[5] Tessa and John Lavery, "An Afternoon with F. R. Scott," *Cyan Line*, Fall 1976, p. 13.

[6] "Editorial," *The McGill Fortnightly Review*, 1, No. 1 (21 Nov. 1925), 2.

[7] Michael Gnarowski, "The Role of 'Little Magazines' in the Development of Poetry in English in Montreal," in *The Making of Modern Poetry in Canada*, p. 216.

[8] Lavery, p. 13.

[9] *The McGill Fortnightly Review*, 1, No. 2 (5 Dec. 1925), 9–10.

[10] F. R. Scott's sense of time is a bit off here. By 1925 Eliot had been known in England and America for close to ten years, had already written and published *The Waste Land*, and, in that year, published "The Hollow Men." Similarly, D. H. Lawrence's work had been appearing regularly since 1911.

[11] Lavery, pp. 13–14.

[12] A. J. M. Smith paraphrasing W. B. Yeats in "Symbolism in Poetry," *The McGill Fortnightly Review*, 1, No. 2 (5 Dec. 1925), 16.

[13] Lavery, p. 18.

[14] Lavery, p. 15.

[15] A. J. M. Smith, "Contemporary Poetry," *The McGill Fortnightly Review*, 2, No. 4 (1926), 31.

[16] Smith, p. 31.

17 Smith, p. 31.
18 Smith, p. 31.
19 Smith, p. 31.
20 Smith, p. 31.
21 *The Canadian Mercury*, 1, No. 1 (Dec. 1928), 3.
22 Leo Kennedy, "The Shrouding Revisited," in *The Shrouding* (Ottawa: Golden Dog, 1975), p. xix.
23 Leo Kennedy, "The Future of Canadian Literature," *The Canadian Mercury*, 1, Nos. 5–6 (April-May 1929), 99.
24 *Mercury*, p. 99.
25 *Mercury*, p. 100.
26 *Mercury*, p. 100.
27 F. R. Scott, "Wild Garden," *The Canadian Mercury*, No. 7 (June 1929), p. 140.
28 Peter Stevens, *The McGill Movement* (Toronto: Ryerson, 1969), pp. i–ii.
29 Joan McCullagh, *Alan Crawley and Contemporary Verse* (Vancouver: Univ. of British Columbia Press, 1976), p. xxii.
30 McCullagh, p. xxii.
31 McCullagh, p. xxii.
32 A. J. M. Smith, "A Rejected Preface," *New Provinces* (Toronto: Univ. of Toronto Press, 1976), p. xxvii.
33 Leo Kennedy, "Direction for Canadian Poets," *The McGill Movement*, pp. 12–13, 19.

3

1 Joan McCullagh, *Alan Crawley and Contemporary Verse* (Vancouver: Univ. of British Columbia Press, 1976), p. xxvi.
2 Floris McLaren, transcribed in "Alan Crawley & Contemporary Verse," prepared by George Robertson, *Canadian Literature*, No. 41 (Summer 1969), p. 88.
3 McCullagh, p. 4.
4 McCullagh, p. 12.
5 Louis Dudek, "The Role of Little Magazines in Canada," *The Making of Modern Poetry in Canada* (Toronto: Ryerson, 1967), p. 208.
6 McCullagh, p. 17.
7 Alan Crawley, *Contemporary Verse*, 1, No. 1 (Sept. 1941), 2.

8 Alan Crawley, "Editor's Note," *Contemporary Verse*, 1, No. 4 (June 1942), 3.

9 A.J.M. Smith, *The Book of Canadian Poetry* (Toronto: Gage, 1948), p. 32.

10 McCullagh, p. 16.

11 John Sutherland, "The Past Decade in Canadian Poetry," *The Making of Modern Poetry in Canada*, p. 119.

12 McCullagh, pp. 40–41.

13 Alan Crawley, "Foreword," *Contemporary Verse*, No. 36 (Fall 1951), p. 4.

14 Crawley, p. 4.

15 Alan Crawley and Floris Clark McLaren, "A Special Notice," *Contemporary Verse*, No. 39 (Fall-Winter 1952), p. 1.

16 McCullagh, p. 52.

17 Michael Gnarowski, *An Index to "Direction"* (Québec: Culture, 1965), p. 4.

18 *Preview*, No. 1 (March 1942), p. 1.

19 Patrick Anderson, "Ourselves," *Preview*, No. 11 (Feb. 1943), p. 11.

20 P.K. Page, "Canadian Poetry 1942," *Preview*, No. 8 (Oct. 1942), p. 8.

21 F.R. Scott, "A Note on Canadian War Poetry," *Preview*, No. 9 (Nov. 1942), p. 4.

22 Scott, p. 3.

23 Neufville Shaw, "The Maple Leaf Is Dying," *Preview*, No. 17 (Dec. 1943), p. 1.

24 Shaw, p. 3.

25 Shaw, p. 3.

26 Patrick Anderson, *Preview*, No. 21 (Sept. 1944), pp. 2–3.

27 Anderson, p. 3.

28 John Sutherland, "Introduction to *Other Canadians*," *The Making of Modern Poetry in Canada*, p. 59.

29 Sutherland, p. 59.

30 Wynne Francis, "Montreal Poets in the Forties," *Canadian Literature*, No. 14 (Autumn 1962), pp. 21–22.

31 John Nause and J. Michael Heenan, "An Interview with Louis Dudek," *The Tamarack Review*, No. 69 (Summer 1976), pp. 30–31.

32 John Sutherland, *First Statement*, 1, No. 1 [1942], 1.

33 Sutherland, 1, No. 2 [1942], 9.

34 Sutherland, "On a Story Published in *Preview* Magazine," *First Statement*, 1, No. 1 [1942], 5.

35 Sutherland, 1, No. 12 [1943?], 1.

36 Nause and Heenan, p. 34.

[37] Sutherland, 1, No. 12, pp. 1–3.

[38] *First Statement*, 1, No. 13 [1943?], 10.

[39] Louis Dudek, "Geography, Politics, and Poetry," *First Statement*, 1, No. 16 [1943?], 3.

[40] Wynne Francis, "Montreal Poets in the Forties," *Canadian Literature*, No. 14 (Autumn 1962), p. 27.

[41] Dudek, p. 3.

[42] Irving Layton, "The Modern Poet," *First Statement*, 1, No. 16 [1943?], 4.

[43] John Sutherland, "The Writing of Patrick Anderson," *First Statement*, 1, No. 19 [1943?], 4.

[44] Sutherland, p. 5.

[45] John Sutherland, "Literary Colonialism," *First Statement*, 2, No. 4 (Feb. 1944), 3.

[46] Dorothy Livesay, rev. of *News of the Phoenix*, by A. J. M. Smith, *First Statement*, 2, No. 6 (April 1944), 19.

[47] Livesay, p. 19.

[48] John Sutherland, rev. of *The Book of Canadian Poetry*, by A.J.M. Smith, *First Statement*, 2, No. 6 (April 1944), 20.

[49] Neil H. Fisher, *First Statement 1942–1945: An Assessment and an Index* (Ottawa: Golden Dog, 1974), pp. 23–24.

[50] William Goldberg, "The Beginning," *Direction*, No. 1 (Nov. 1943), p. 1.

[51] *Direction*, No. 1 (Nov. 1943), p. 1.

[52] Raymond Souster, "The Present State of Canadian Literature," *Direction*, No. 1 (Nov. 1943), p. 2.

[53] John Sutherland, "Great Things and Terrible," *Direction*, No. 9 (Nov. 1945), p. 2.

[54] Raymond Souster, *Direction*, No. 6 (Nov. 1944), p. 8.

[55] Raymond Souster, "A Letter: From the Other Side of the Fence," *Direction*, No. 6 (Nov. 1944), p. 8.

[56] Nause and Heenan, p. 34.

[57] "Editorial," *Northern Review*, 1, No. 1 (Dec.-Jan. 1945–46), 2.

[58] A. J. M. Smith, "Nationalism and Canadian Poetry," *Northern Review*, 1, No. 1 (Dec.-Jan. 1945–46), 42.

[59] Nause and Heenan, pp. 34–35.

[60] *Northern Review*, 2, No. 1 (Oct.-Nov. 1947), 40.

[61] John Sutherland, "Critics on the Defensive," *Northern Review*, 2, No. 1 (Oct.-Nov. 1947), 23.

[62] John Sutherland, *Northern Review*, 3, No. 1 (Oct.-Nov. 1949), 3.

[63] Harold Horwood, "Number Ten Reports," *Northern Review*, 4, No. 2 (Dec.-Jan. 1950–51), 21.

⁶⁴ Horwood, pp. 18–19.
⁶⁵ John Sutherland, "The Past Decade in Canadian Poetry," *Northern Review*, 4, No. 2 (Dec.-Jan. 1950–51), 43–44.
⁶⁶ Sutherland, pp. 44–45. For complete quotations see pp. 46–47.
⁶⁷ Sutherland, p. 45.
⁶⁸ Sutherland, p. 47.
⁶⁹ *Northern Review*, 5, Nos. 3–4 (Feb.-March & April-May 1952), cover.
⁷⁰ John Sutherland, "The Great Equestrians," *Northern Review*, 6, No. 4 (Oct.-Nov. 1953), 21.
⁷¹ "Editorial," *Here And Now*, 1, No. 1 (Dec. 1947), 6.
⁷² *Here And Now*, p. 6.
⁷³ *Index*, 1, No. 1, 1.
⁷⁴ *Index*, p. 1.

4

¹ Raymond Souster, in a letter to Louis Dudek in his possession, dated at Swansea (Toronto), 23 June 1951. Reprinted in *Contact 1952–1954* (Montreal: Delta Canada, 1966), p. 3.
² Souster to Dudek, dated at Toronto, 6 Oct. 1951. *Contact 1952–1954*, p. 4.
³ Michael Gnarowski, *Contact 1952–1954*, p. 5.
⁴ Raymond Souster, "Some Afterthoughts on *Contact* Magazine," *Contact 1952–1954*, p. 1.
⁵ *Contact*, 1, No. 1 (Jan. 1952), 1.
⁶ *Contact*, 1, p. 1.
⁷ *Contact*, 1, p. 1.
⁸ Gnarowski, p. 8.
⁹ *Contact*, 1, No. 3 (May-July 1952), 15.
¹⁰ *Contact*, 1, No. 4 (Aug.-Oct. 1952), 15.
¹¹ Charles Olson, "These Days," *Contact*, 2, No. 1 (Nov.-Jan. 1952–53), 6.
¹² Gnarowski, p. 11.
¹³ *Contact*, No. 8 (Sept.-Dec. 1953), p. 12.
¹⁴ *Contact*, No. 8, p. 13.
¹⁵ *Contact*, 2, No. 2 (Feb.-April 1943), 13.
¹⁶ *Contact*, No. 10 (March 1954), cover.

[17] Louis Dudek, "The Making of *CIV/n*," *Index to CIV/n* (n.p.: n.p., n.d.), p. 3.
[18] Louis Dudek, *CIV/n*, No. 2 [1953], p. 18.
[19] Neil Compton, "Cerberus," *CIV/n*, No. 2 [1953], p. 22.
[20] Ezra Pound, in *Dk/Some Letters of Ezra Pound*, ed. Louis Dudek (Montreal: DC, 1974), p. 101.
[21] Louis Dudek, in *Dk/Some Letters of Ezra Pound*, p. 103.
[22] Dudek, p. 110.
[23] Pound, in *Dk/Some Letters of Ezra Pound*, p. 102.
[24] *CIV/n*, No. 5 [1954], no pag.
[25] *CIV/n*, No. 5, p. 24.
[26] *CIV/n*, No. 5, p. 24.
[27] *CIV/n*, No. 7 [1954], p. 26.
[28] *Yes*, No. 1 (April 1956), p. 1.
[29] *Yes*, No. 3 (Dec. 1956), pp. 2–3.
[30] *Yes*, No. 17 (Oct. 1969), inside front cover.

5

[1] *Talon*, No. 1 (1963), p. 2.
[2] *Talon*, 4, No. 3 [1967], inside front cover.

6

[1] Frank Davey, *From There to Here* (Erin, Ont.: Porcépic, 1974), p. 107.
[2] Northrop Frye, "The Archetypes of Literature," *Fables of Identity* (New York: Harcourt Brace and World, 1963), p. 9.
[3] Northrop Frye, *Anatomy of Criticism: Four Essays* (Princeton: Princeton Univ. Press, 1957), p. 11.
[4] Frye, *Anatomy*, p. 12.
[5] Frye, *Anatomy*, p. 14.
[6] Frye, *Anatomy*, pp. 15–16.
[7] Frye, *Anatomy*, p. 16.

8 Frye, *Fables*, p. 12.
9 Frye, *Anatomy*, p. 71.
10 Frye, *Anatomy*, p. 99.
11 Frye, *Anatomy*, p. 99.
12 Frye, *Fables*, pp. 12–13.
13 Frye, *Fables*, pp. 15–16.
14 Frye, *Fables*, p. 17.
15 Frye, *Fables*, p. 18.
16 Frye, *Anatomy*, p. 97.
17 Davey, p. 110.
18 Margaret Atwood, "Eleven Years of *Alphabet*," *Canadian Literature*, No. 49 (Summer 1971), p. 62.
19 Atwood, p. 61.
20 *Alphabet*, No. 1 (Sept. 1960), p. 3.
21 *Alphabet,* No. 1, p. 3.
22 *Alphabet*, No. 1, p. 4.
23 *Alphabet*, No. 1, p. 4.
24 *Alphabet*, No. 1, p. 3.
25 *Alphabet*, No. 1, p. 3.
26 Richard Stingle, "To Harpooneers," *Alphabet*, No. 1 (Sept. 1960), p. 6.
27 Jay Macpherson, "The Woods No More," *Alphabet*, No. 1, p. 25.
28 Margaret Atwood, "Eleven Years of *Alphabet*," p. 61.
29 *Alphabet*, No. 2 (July 1961), p. 2.
30 *Alphabet*, No. 4 (June 1962), p. 3.
31 *Alphabet*, No. 8 (June 1964), p. 5.
32 *Alphabet*, No. 8, p. 5.
33 *Alphabet*, No. 16 (Sept. 1969), p. 3.
34 Atwood, "Eleven Years of *Alphabet*," p. 62.
35 Atwood, pp. 62–63.

7

1 Louis Dudek, "Lunchtime Reflections on Frank Davey's Defence of the Black Mountain Fort," *The Writing Life: Historical & Critical Views of the Tish Movement*, ed. C. H. Gervais (Coatsworth, Ont.: Black Moss, 1976), pp. 129–30.
2 Robin Mathews, "Preface," in *Poetry and the Colonized Mind: Tish*, by

Keith Richardson (Oakville/Ottawa: Mosaic Press/Valley Editions, 1976), p. 7.

3 Mathews, "Preface," p. 7.

4 Robin Mathews, "Poetics: The Struggle for Voice in Canada," *CV/II*, 2, No. 4 (Dec. 1976), 6.

5 Mathews, "Poetics," p. 6.

6 Mathews, "Poetics," p. 7.

7 Dudek, p. 133.

8 Martin Duberman, *Black Mountain: An Exploration In Community* (New York: Dutton, 1972), pp. 386–87.

9 Duberman, p. 389.

10 "Robert Creeley in Conversation with Charles Tomlinson," *Contexts of Poetry: Interviews 1961-1971* (Bolinas, California: Four Seasons Foundation, 1973), pp. 13–14.

11 David Ossman, "An Interview With Robert Creeley," *Contexts of Poetry*, p. 5.

12 George Bowering, "How I Hear Howl," *The Writing Life*, p. 216.

13 Duberman, p. 390.

14 Charles Olson, "Projective Verse," *The Poetics of the New American Poetry*, ed. by Donald M. Allen and Warren Tallman (New York: Grove, 1973), p. 147. Subsequent references are noted in the text.

15 Warren Tallman, "Wonder Merchants: Modernist Poetry in Vancouver During the 1960s," *The Writing Life*, p. 52.

16 George Bowering, "The Most Remarkable Thing About Tish," *Tish*, No. 20 (Aug. 1963), rpt. in *Tish No. 1-19*, ed. Frank Davey (Vancouver: Talonbooks, 1975), p. 423.

17 Frank Davey, "Introduction," *The Writing Life*, pp. 22–23.

18 Tallman, "Wonder Merchants," p. 30.

19 Warren Tallman, "Poet in Progress: Notes on Frank Davey," *Canadian Literature*, No. 24 (Spring 1975), pp. 24–25.

20 Frank Davey, "Introducing *Tish*," *The Writing Life*, p. 152.

21 Davey, p. 150.

22 Davey, pp. 153–54.

23 Tallman, "Wonder Merchants," p. 54.

24 Frank Davey, "Editorial," *Tish No. 1-19* (Vancouver: Talonbooks, 1975), p. 13.

25 Davey, p. 14.

26 *Tish No. 1-19*, p. 17.

27 *Tish No. 1-19*, p. 19.

28 *Tish No. 1-19*, p. 23.

29 *Tish No. 1-19*, p. 26.

30 *Tish No. 1–19*, p. 19.
31 Frank Davey, "Watch," *Tish No. 1–19*, p. 23.
32 Fred Wah, "A Tale," *Tish No. 1–19*, p. 24.
33 *Tish No. 1–19*, p. 31.
34 *Tish No. 1–19*, p. 83.
35 *Tish No. 1–19*, p. 71.
36 *Tish No. 1–19*, p. 67.
37 *Tish No. 1–19*, p. 68.
38 *Tish No. 1–19*, p. 68.
39 *Tish No. 1–19*, p. 68.
40 *Tish No. 1–19*, p. 91.
41 *Tish No. 1–19*, p. 155.
42 Davey, "Introduction," p. 23.
43 Robin Mathews, "Poetics: The Struggle for Voice in Canada," *CV/II*, 2, No. 4 (Dec. 1976), p. 6.
44 *Tish No. 1–19*, p. 221.
45 *Tish No. 1–19*, p. 201.
46 Robert Creeley, *Tish No. 1–19*, pp. 251–52.
47 Robert Duncan, "For the Novices of Vancouver," *Tish No. 1–19*, p. 253.
48 Duncan, p. 254.
49 *Tish No. 1–19*, p. 423.
50 *Tish No. 1–19*, p. 424.
51 Richardson, *Poetry and the Colonized Mind: Tish*, p. 55.
52 George Bowering, "A Note or Justification," *Imago*, No. 1 (March 1964), p. 2.
53 *Open Letter*, No. 1 (1965), p. 1.
54 *Open Letter*, No. 1, p. 3.
55 *Open Letter*, No. 1, p. 3.
56 George Bowering, *Open Letter*, No. 1, p. 10.
57 *Open Letter*, No. 1, pp. 17–18.
58 *Open Letter*, No. 2 (March 1966), p. 6.
59 *Open Letter*, No. 2, p. 18.
60 *Open Letter*, No. 2, p. 3.
61 *Open Letter*, No. 4 (June 1966), p. 7.
62 *Open Letter*, No. 5 (Nov. 1966), p. 18.
63 William Carlos Williams, *Island*, No. 1 (Sept. 1964), p. 47.
64 *Island*, No. 7–8 (May 1967), p. 2.
65 *Is*, No. 1 (1966), inside front cover.

8

1 bpNichol in an unpublished interview [1978] conducted by the author, in his possession, p. 3.

2 This is the key idea in Louis Dudek's essay "The Meaning of Modernism," in *Technology & Culture: Six Lectures* (Ottawa: Golden Dog, 1979), pp. 78–96.

3 Ezra Pound, "A Few Don'ts By an Imagiste," *Imagist Poetry*, ed. Peter Jones (Harmondsworth: Penguin, 1972), p. 130.

4 Judy Rawson, "Italian Futurism," *Modernism*, ed. by Malcolm Bradbury and James McFarlane (New York: Penguin, 1976), p. 246.

5 Rawson, p. 247.

6 Rawson, p. 247.

7 G. M. Hyde, "Russian Futurism," *Modernism*, pp. 264–65.

8 Hyde, p. 263.

9 Lucy R. Lippard, *Dadas on Art* (Englewood Cliffs, N.J.: Prentice Hall, 1971), p. 8.

10 Steve McCaffery, "Sound Poetry: A Survey," *Sound Poetry: A Catalogue*, ed. Steve McCaffery and bpNichol (Toronto: Underwhich, 1978), p. 6.

11 McCaffery, pp. 7–8.

12 Hyde, p. 265.

13 Hyde, p. 265.

14 Hugo Ball, *Flight Out of Time* (New York: Viking, 1974), p. 57.

15 Ball, pp. 67–68.

16 Ball, pp. 70–71.

17 McCaffery, pp. 8–9.

18 McCaffery, p. 9.

19 McCaffery, p. 11.

20 John Sharkey, "Introduction," *Mindplay: An Anthology of British Concrete Poetry* (London: Lorimer, 1971), pp. 9–10.

21 Emmett Williams, "Introduction," *Anthology of Concrete Poetry* (New York: Something Else, 1967), pp. vi–vii.

22 bill bissett, a letter to the author, dated 27 Nov. 1979 at Vancouver.

23 bissett.

24 bissett.

25 bissett.

26 *Blew Ointment*, unnumbered issue (1970), inside back cover.

27 *Ganglia*, No. 4 (June 1966), p. 97.

28 *Ganglia*, No. 4, p. 98.

29 *Ganglia*, No. 4, p. 98.

30 *Ganglia*, No. 4, p. 99.

31 Ken Norris, "An Interview With bpNichol," *Essays on Canadian Writing*, No. 12 (Fall 1978), p. 247.

32 Norris, p. 250.

33 Norris, pp. 248–50.

34 *GrOnk*, I, No. I (Jan. 1967), front cover.

35 bpNichol in an unpublished interview conducted by the author, in his possession, p. I.

36 Nichol, p. I.

37 *GrOnk*, 3, No. I (April 1969), n. pag.

38 *GrOnk*, 6, No. 2–3, back cover.

9

1 Al Purdy, "The Ego Has It Both Ways: Poets in Montreal," *Northern Journey*, Nos. 7 and 8 (1976), p. 142.

2 *Moment*, No. I [1960], p. I.

3 *Moment*, No. 4 [1960], p. 5.

4 *Moment*, No. 4, p. 5.

5 *Moment*, No. 4, p. 5.

6 *Moment*, No. 4, p. 5.

7 *Moment*, No. 4, p. 6.

8 *Moment*, No. 6, p. I.

9 *Moment*, No. 6, p. 2.

10 *Moment*, No. 6, p. 2.

11 *Cataract*, No. 2 (Winter 1962), p. [16].

12 Louis Dudek, "Patterns of Recent Canadian Poetry," *Selected Essays and Criticism* (Ottawa: Tecumseh, 1978), p. 109. This essay originally appeared in *Culture*, 19 (1958), 399–415.

13 *Cataract*, No. 2, p. 26.

14 *Cataract*, No. 2, p. I.

15 *Cataract*, No. 3, p. 42.

16 *Cataract*, No. 3, p. 44.

17 *Intercourse*, No. 8 (Aug. 1968), p. I.

18 *Moongoose*, No. 4 (Nov. 1972), n. pag.

19 *Booster & Blaster*, I, No. 2 (Dec. 1972), I.

[20] *Booster*, 1, No. 2, inside front cover.
[21] *Anthol*, No. 2 (Winter 1972–73), p. 1.
[22] *CrossCountry*, No. 1 (Winter 1975), p. 2.
[23] *Hh*, No. 2 (1977), inside front cover.
[24] *Montreal Journal of Poetics*, No. 1 (Winter 1978–79), p. 1.
[25] Stephen Morrissey, "The Purpose of Experimental Poetry," *Montreal Journal of Poetics*, No. 1 (Winter 1978–79), p. 5.
[26] Tom Konyves, "Videopoetry," *Montreal Journal of Poetics*, No. 1 (Winter 1978–79), p. 13.
[27] Konyves, pp. 14–15.
[28] Konyves, p. 14.

10

[1] *Northern Light*, No. 3 (Winter 1976), p. 3.
[2] *Northern Light*, p. 6.
[3] *CV/II*, 1, No. 1 (Spring 1975), 2.
[4] *NMFG*, No. 1, inside front cover.
[5] *NMFG*, No. 18, inside front cover.
[6] *The Front*, No. 6 (May 1979), p. 1.

Bibliography

THE LITTLE MAGAZINES

The Alchemist, 1, No. 3. Montreal, 1976.
Alphabet, Nos. 1 to 19. London, Ontario, 1960–71.
Anthol, Nos. 1 to 4. Montreal, 1972–1975.
Atropos, No. 2. Montreal, Spring 1979.
Blew Ointment, irregularly numbered. Vancouver, 1963–80.
Booster and Blaster, 1 and 2. Montreal, 1972.
The Canadian Mercury, 1, Nos. 1 to 7. Montreal, Dec. 1928–June 1929.
The Capilano Review, Nos. 7 to 17. Vancouver, 1975–80.
Catapult, Nos. 1 and 2. Montreal, 1964.
Cataract, Nos. 1 to 3. Montreal, 1962.
CIV/n, Nos. 1 to 7. Montreal, 1953–54.
Combustion, Nos. 1 to 15. Toronto, 1957–60.
Contact, Nos. 1 to 10. Toronto, 1952–54.
Contemporary Verse, Nos. 1 to 39. Vancouver, 1941–52.
CrossCountry, Nos. 1 to 12. Montreal/New York, 1975–80.
CV/II, 1 to 4. Winnipeg, 1975–80.
Davinci, Nos. 1 to 6. Montreal, 1973–79.
Delta, Nos. 1 to 26. Montreal, 1957–66.
Direction, Nos. 1 to 10. Montreal–Port Aux Basques, 1943–46.
Elan, No. 1. Montreal, Feb. 1946.
Evidence, Nos. 1 to 10. Toronto, 1960–67.
First Statement 1 to 3. Montreal, 1942–45.
The Front, Nos. 5 and 6. Kingston, Ont., Oct. 1978; May 1979.
Ganglia, Nos. 1 to 5, 7. Toronto, 1965–67.
GrOnk, 1 to 8, Nos. 1–64. Toronto, 1967–72.
Here and Now 1, Nos. 1 to 4. Toronto, 1947–49.
Hh, Nos. 1 and 2. Montreal, 1976–77.

Imago, Nos. 1 to 20. Calgary–London, Ont.–Montreal–Vancouver, 1964–74.

Index, 1, Nos. 1 and 6. Montreal, March 1946; Aug. 1946.

Ingluvin, Nos. 1 and 2. Montreal, 1970–71.

Intercourse, Nos. 1 to 17. Montreal, 1966–71.

Is, Nos. 1 to 20. Toronto, 1966–77.

Island, Nos. 1 to 8. Toronto, Sept. 1964–May 1967.

Jaw Breaker, Nos. 1 to 3. Montreal, 1971–72.

Kontakte, 1, No. 2. Toronto, Dec. 1976.

Le Chien D'or / The Golden Dog, Nos. 1 to 4. Montreal, 1972–74.

Los, Nos. 4 and 5. Montreal, 1976–77.

Maker, Nos. 1 to 3. Montreal, 1976–78.

Matrix, Nos. 1 to 10. Lennoxville, Quebec, 1975–80.

The McGill Fortnightly Review, 1 and 2. Montreal, 1925–27.

Moment, Nos. 1 to 7. Montreal–Toronto, 1960–62.

Montreal Journal of Poetics, Nos. 1 to 3. Montreal, 1979–80.

Montreal Poems, Nos. 2 and 4. Montreal, 1975–78.

Montreal Writers' Forum, 1, Nos. 1 to 12; 2, Nos. 1 to 7. Montreal, Oct. 1978–April 1980.

Moongoose, No. 4. Montreal, Nov. 1972.

Mountain, Nos. 1 to 4. Hamilton, Ont., May 1962–Oct. 1963.

Mouse Eggs, Nos. 1 to 13. Montreal, 1975–77.

NMFG, Nos. 1 to 26. Vancouver, Feb. 1976–June 1979.

Northern Light, No. 3. Winnipeg, 1976.

Northern Review, 1 to 7. Montreal–Toronto, 1945–56.

Open Letter, 1 to 4. Victoria–Toronto, 1965–80.

P.M., 1, No. 2. Vancouver (no date).

Preview, Nos. 1 to 23. Montreal, 1942–45.

Process, Nos. 1 to 4. Montreal, 1975–78.

Reading, Nos. 1 to 3. Toronto, 1946.

Salt, Nos. 15 to 17. Moose Jaw, Fall 1976–Winter 1977.

Sum, Nos. 1 to 7. Albuquerque, New Mexico–Buffalo, New York, 1964–65.

Talon, 1 to 5. Vancouver, 1963–67.

Teangadoir, 5, Nos. 1 to 5. Toronto, July 1961–May 1963.

Tide, Nos. 1 to 7. Montreal, 1968–71.

Tish No. 1–19. Ed. Frank Davey. Vancouver: Talonbooks, 1975.

Versus, Nos. 1 to 4. Montreal, Summer 1976–Winter 1978.

Waves, 5 to 8. Toronto. 1977–80.

what is, Nos. 1 to 14. Montreal, 1973–75.

Yes, Nos. 1 to 19. Montreal, 1956–70.

SECONDARY SOURCES

Anthology of Concrete Poetry. Ed. Emmett Williams. New York: Something Else, 1967.

Atwood, Margaret. "Eleven Years of *Alphabet*." *Canadian Literature*, No. 49 (Summer 1971), pp. 60–64.

Ball, Hugo. *Flight Out of Time*. New York: Viking, 1974.

bissett, bill. A letter to the author, in his possession, dated 27 Nov. 1979.

Bowering, George. "How I Hear Howl." *The Writing Life: Historical & Critical Views of the Tish Movement*. Ed. C. H. Gervais. Coatsworth, Ont.: Black Moss, 1976, pp. 216–29.

Bradbury, Malcolm, and James McFarlane. "The Name and Nature of Modernism." *Modernism*. Ed. Malcolm Bradbury and James McFarlane. New York: Penguin, 1976, pp. 19–55.

Creeley, Robert. *Contexts of Poetry: Interviews 1961–1971*. Bolinas, California: Four Seasons Foundation, 1973.

Davey, Frank. *From There to Here*. Erin, Ont.: Porcépic, 1974.

———— "Introducing Tish." *The Writing Life: Historical & Critical Views of the Tish Movement*. Ed. C.H. Gervais. Coatsworth, Ont.: Black Moss, 1976, pp. 150–61.

———— "Introduction." *The Writing Life: Historical & Critical Views of the Tish Movement*. Ed. C.H. Gervais. Coatsworth, Ont.: Black Moss, 1976, pp. 15–24.

Dk/Some Letters of Ezra Pound. Ed. Louis Dudek. Montreal: DC, 1974.

Doyle, James. "Canadian Poetry and American Magazines, 1885–1905." *Canadian Poetry: Studies, Documents, Reviews*, No. 5 (Fall-Winter 1979), pp. 73–82.

Duberman, Martin. *Black Mountain: An Exploration in Community*. New York: Dutton, 1972.

Dudek, Louis. *Literature and the Press*. Toronto: Ryerson/Contact, 1960.

———— "The Little Magazine." *English Poetry in Quebec*. Ed. John Glassco. Montreal: McGill Univ. Press, 1965, pp. 59–64.

———— "Lunchtime Reflections on Frank Davey's Defence of the Black Mountain Fort." *The Writing Life: Historical & Critical Views of the Tish Movement*. Ed. C. H. Gervais. Coatsworth, Ont.: Black Moss, 1976, pp. 128–33.

———— and Michael Gnarowski, ed. *The Making of Modern Poetry In Canada*. Toronto: Ryerson, 1967.

——— "The Meaning of Modernism." *Technology & Culture: Six Lectures*. Ottawa: Golden Dog, 1979, pp. 78–96.

——— "Patterns of Recent Canadian Poetry." *Selected Essays and Criticism*. Ottawa: Tecumseh, 1978, pp. 94–110.

——— "The Role of the Little Magazine in Canada." *The Making of Modern Poetry in Canada*. Ed. Louis Dudek and Michael Gnarowski. Toronto: Ryerson, 1967, pp. 205–12.

——— *Selected Essays And Criticism*. Ottawa: Tecumseh, 1978.

Fisher, Neil H. *First Statement 1942–1945: An Assessment and an Index*. Ottawa: Golden Dog, 1974.

Flint, F.S. "Imagisme." *Imagist Poetry*. Ed. Peter Jones. New York: Penguin, 1972, pp. 129–30.

"Four of the Former *Preview* Editors: A Discussion." *Canadian Poetry: Studies, Documents, Reviews*, No. 4 (Spring-Summer 1979), pp. 93–119.

Francis, Wynne. "The Expanding Spectrum: Literary Magazines." *Canadian Literature*, No. 57 (Summer 1973), pp. 6–17.

——— "Literary Underground: Little Magazines in Canada." *Canadian Literature*, No. 34 (Autumn 1967), pp. 63–70.

——— "The Little Magazine/Small Press Movement and Canadian Poetry in English Since 1950." *Laurentian University Review*, 10, No. 2 (Feb. 1978), pp. 89–109.

——— "The Little Presses." *Canadian Literature*, No. 33 (Summer 1967), pp. 56–62.

——— "Montreal Poets of the Forties." *Canadian Literature*, No. 14 (Autumn 1962), pp. 21–34.

Frye, Northrop. *Anatomy of Criticism: Four Essays*. Princeton, N.J.: Princeton Univ. Press, 1957.

——— "The Archetypes of Literature." *Fables of Identity*. New York: Harcourt Brace and World, 1963, pp. 7–20.

Ganglia Press Index. Ed. bpNichol. Toronto: Ganglia, 1972.

Gnarowski, Michael. *Contact 1952–1954*. Montreal: Delta Canada, 1970.

——— *Contact Press 1952–1967*. Montreal: Delta Canada, 1970.

——— *Index to CIV/n*. N.p.: n.p., n.d.

——— *An Index to Direction*. Quebec: Culture, 1965.

——— "The Role of the 'Little Magazines' in the Development of Poetry in English in Montreal." *The Making of Modern Poetry in Canada*. Ed. Louis Dudek and Michael Gnarowski. Toronto: Ryerson, 1967, pp. 212–22.

Hoffman, Frederick J., *et al. The Little Magazine: A History and a Bibliography*. Princeton, N.J.: Princeton Univ. Press, 1946.

Hyde, G. M. "Russian Futurism." *Modernism*. Ed. Malcolm Bradbury and James McFarlane. New York: Penguin, 1976, pp. 259–73.

The Imagist Poem. Ed. William Pratt. New York: Dutton, 1963.

Imagist Poetry. Ed. Peter Jones. New York: Penguin, 1972.

Kennedy, Leo. "Direction for Canadian Poets." *The McGill Movement*. Ed. Peter Stevens. Toronto: Ryerson, 1969, pp. 11–19.

Kennedy, Leo. *The Shrouding*. Ottawa: Golden Dog, 1975.

Kroetsch, Robert. "A Canadian Issue." *Boundary 2*, 3, No. 1 (Fall 1974), pp. 1–2.

Lavery, Tessa and John. "An Afternoon with F. R. Scott." *Cyan Line*, No. 2 (Fall 1976), pp. 11–21.

Layton, Irving. *Engagements: The Prose of Irving Layton*. Ed. Seymour Mayne. Toronto: McClelland and Stewart, 1972.

Lippard, Lucy R. *Dadas on Art*. Englewood Cliffs, N.J.: Prentice Hall, 1971.

The Little Magazine in America: A Modern Documentary History. Ed. Elliott Anderson and Mary Kinzie. Yonkers, New York: Pushcart, 1978.

Mathews, Robin. "Poetics: The Struggle for Voice in Canada." *CV/II*, 2, No. 4 (Dec. 1976), 6–7.

McCaffery, Steve. "Sound Poetry: A Survey." *Sound Poetry: A Catalogue*. Ed. Steve McCaffery and bpNichol. Toronto: Underwhich, 1978, pp. 6–18.

———— "Text-Sound Composition & Performance in Anglophone Quebec." *Sound Poetry: A Catalogue*. Ed. Steve McCaffery and bpNichol. Toronto: Underwhich, 1978, pp. 60–61.

McCullagh, Joan. *Alan Crawley and Contemporary Verse*. Vancouver: Univ. of British Columbia, 1976.

McCutcheon, Sarah. "Little Presses in Canada." *Canadian Literature*, No. 57 (Summer 1973), pp. 88–97.

Mindplay: An Anthology of British Concrete Poetry. Ed. John Sharkey. London: Lorimer, 1971.

Modernism. Ed. Malcolm Bradbury and James McFarlane. New York: Penguin, 1976.

Nause, John, and J. Michael Heenan. "An Interview with Louis Dudek." *The Tamarack Review*, No. 69 (1977), pp. 30–43.

New Provinces: Poems of Several Authors. Toronto: Univ. of Toronto Press, 1976.

New Wave Canada. Ed. Raymond Souster. Toronto: Contact, 1966.

Nichol, bp. An unpublished interview conducted by the author in December of 1979, in his possession.

Norris, Ken. "Interview with bpNichol: Feb. 13, 1978." *Essays on Canadian Writing*, No. 12 (Fall 1978), pp. 243–50.

―――― "The Little Magazines." *Essays on Canadian Writing*, No. 10 (Spring 1978) pp. 88–96.

―――― "Montreal Poetry in the Seventies." *CV/II*, 3, No. 3 (Jan. 1978), 8–13.

―――― "The Vital Necessity for Experimentation & Regionalism." *Essays On Canadian Writing*, No. 11 (Summer 1978), pp. 204–10.

Olson, Charles. "Projective Verse." *The Poetics of the New American Poetry*. Ed. Donald M. Allen and Warren Tallman. New York: Grove, 1973, pp. 147–58.

Other Canadians. Ed. John Sutherland. Montreal: First Statement, 1947.

Pound, Ezra. "A Few Don'ts by an Imagist." *Imagist Poetry*. Ed. Peter Jones. Harmondsworth: Penguin, 1972, pp. 130–34.

Purdy, Al. "The Ego Has It Both Ways: Poets in Montreal." *Northern Journey*, Nos. 7 and 8 (1976), pp. 127–47.

Rawson, Judy. "Italian Futurism." *Modernism*. Ed. Malcolm Bradbury and James McFarlane. New York: Penguin, 1976, pp. 243–58.

Richardson, Keith. *Poetry and the Colonized Mind: Tish*. Oakville/Ottawa: Mosaic Press/Valley Editions, 1976.

Robertson, George. "Alan Crawley and Contemporary Verse." *Canadian Literature*, No. 41 (Summer 1969), pp. 87–96.

Scott, F. R. "...It is the Heart That Sees." *Athanor*, 1, No. 2 (Feb. 1980), 5–10.

Smith, A. J. M. *The Book of Canadian Poetry*. Toronto: Gage, 1948.

―――― "A Rejected Preface." *New Provinces: Poems of Several Authors*. Toronto: Univ. of Toronto Press, 1976, pp. xxvii-xxxii.

Spears, Monroe K. *Dionysus and the City*. New York: Oxford Univ. Press, 1970.

Stenbaek-Lafon, Marianne, and Ken Norris. "Curiouser and Curiouser: An Interview with George Bowering." *CrossCountry*, No. 5, pp. 12–19.

Stevens, Peter. "Experimental Poetry Since 1950." *Laurentian University Review*, 10, No. 2 (Feb. 1978), 47–61.

―――― ed., *The McGill Movement*. Toronto: Ryerson, 1969.

Sutherland, John. "Introduction to *Other Canadians*." *The Making of*

Modern Poetry in Canada. Ed. Louis Dudek and Michael Gnarowski. Toronto: Ryerson, 1967, pp. 47–61.

—— "The Past Decade in Canadian Poetry." *The Making of Modern Poetry in Canada*. Ed. Louis Dudek and Michael Gnarowski. Toronto: Ryerson, 1967, pp. 116–22.

Tallman, Warren. "Wonder Merchants: Modernist Poetry in Vancouver During the 1960's." *The Writing Life: Historical & Critical Views of the Tish Movement*. Ed. C. H. Gervais. Coatsworth, Ont.: Black Moss, 1976, pp. 27–70.

Tovell, Vincent. "The World for a Country: An Edited Interview with Frank Scott." *Canadian Poetry: Studies, Documents, Reviews*, No. 2 (Spring-Summer 1978), pp. 51–73.

Watt, F. W. "Climate of Unrest: Periodicals in the Twenties and Thirties." *Canadian Literature*, No. 12 (Summer 1962), pp. 15–27.

Wilson, Ethel. "Of Alan Crawley." *Canadian Literature*, No. 19 (Winter 1964), pp. 33–42.

CANADIAN POETRY: THE BACKGROUND

The Arts in Canada. Ed. Malcolm Ross. Toronto: Macmillan, 1958.

Atwood, Margaret. *Survival: A Thematic Guide to Canadian Literature*. Toronto: House of Anansi, 1972.

Birney, Earle. *Spreading Time: Remarks on Canadian Writing and Writers, Book I, 1904–1949*. Montreal: Vehicule, 1980.

Bourinot, Arthur S., ed. *At the Mermaid Inn*. Ottawa: privately printed, 1958.

Brown, E. K. *On Canadian Poetry*. Ottawa: Tecumseh, 1977.

Canadian Anthology. Ed. C. F. Klinck and R. E. Watters. Toronto: Gage, 1966.

Canadian Literature Today. Canadian Broadcasting Corporation. Toronto: Univ. of Toronto Press, 1938.

Collin, W. E. *The White Savannahs*. Toronto: Univ. of Toronto Press, 1975.

Contexts of Canadian Criticism. Ed. Eli Mandel. Toronto: Univ. of Toronto Press, 1971.

The Culture of Contemporary Canada. Ed. Julian Parks. Toronto: Ryerson, 1957.

Eggleston, Wilfrid. *The Frontier & Canadian Literature*. Toronto: Ryerson, 1957.

Figures in a Ground. Ed. Diane Bessai and David Jackel. Saskatoon: Western Producer Prairie, 1978.

Frye, Northrop. *The Bush Garden: Essays on the Canadian Imagination*. Toronto: House of Anansi, 1971.

Gnarowski, Michael. *A Concise Bibliography of English-Canadian Literature*. Toronto: McClelland and Stewart, 1978.

Innis, Harold Adams. *The Strategy of Culture, with Special Reference to Canadian Literature—a Footnote to the Massey Report*. Toronto: Univ. of Toronto, 1952.

Jones, D. G. *Butterfly on Rock*. Toronto: Univ. of Toronto Press, 1970.

Klinck, Carl F., *et al. Literary History of Canada*. Toronto: Univ. of Toronto Press, 1965.

Leading Canadian Poets. Ed. Walter Pillings Percival. Toronto: Ryerson, 1948.

Logan, John Daniel, and Donald G. French. *Highways of Canadian Literature*. Toronto: McClelland and Stewart, 1924.

MacMechan, Archibald. *Headwaters of Canadian Literature*. Toronto: McClelland and Stewart, 1974.

New, William H. *Articulating West*. Toronto: new, 1972.

Pacey, Desmond. *Creative Writing in Canada*. Toronto: Ryerson, 1952.

——— *Essays in Canadian Criticism 1938–1968*. Toronto: Ryerson, 1969.

——— *Ten Canadian Poets*. Toronto: Ryerson, 1958.

Pierce, Lorne Albert. *An Outline of Canadian Literature (French and English)*. Toronto: Ryerson, 1927.

——— *Unexplored Fields of Canadian Literature*. Toronto: Ryerson, 1932.

Rashley, R. E. *Poetry in Canada: The First Three Steps*. Ottawa: Tecumseh, 1979.

Ricou, Laurence R. *Vertical Man/Horizontal World*. Vancouver: Univ. of British Columbia Press, 1973.

Smith, A. J. M., ed. *Masks of Poetry*. Toronto: McClelland and Stewart, 1962.

——— *On Poetry and Poets*. Toronto: McClelland and Stewart, 1977.

——— *Towards a View of Canadian Letters: Selected Essays 1928–1971*. Vancouver: Univ. of British Columbia Press, 1973.

Stevenson, Lionel. *Appraisals of Canadian Literature*. Toronto: Macmillan, 1926.

Watters, Reginald Eyre. *A Check List of Canadian Literature and Background Materials 1628–1950*. Toronto: Univ. of Toronto Press, 1959.

────── and Inglis Freeman Bell. *On Canadian Literature 1806–1960*. Toronto: Univ. of Toronto Press, 1966.

Woodcock, George. *A Choice of Critics*. Toronto: Oxford Univ. Press, 1966.

────── *Odysseus Ever Returning*. Toronto: McClelland and Stewart, 1970.

────── *Poets and Critics: Essays from Canadian Literature 1966–1974*. Toronto: Oxford Univ. Press, 1974.

CrossCountry

No. 3/4

Special Issue: Montréal

NUMBER FOURTEEN   JULY, 1945

Contemporary
Verse

A Canadian Quarterly

ONE DOLLAR A YEA
TWENTY-FIVE CENTS A COP

---

do not drive on paved shoulder   Ramp speed 25

Beeeeeeeeeep   **bump**

left lane must exit

right lane must exit

alphabet

stop   maximum 30 ahead
maximum 30 ahead

rail ing cross way   rail cross ing way
rail ing cross way   rail cross ing way

radar enforced R*RrrRrrRrrr*Rrr
RrrRrrRrrr

Construction zone ahead   **RATA-RATA**
RATATATA   Construction zone ends

No exit   No stopping   No left turn   Do not pass   No parking

YIELD

DELTA

(CANADA)

POETRY   •   ARTICLES   •   REVIEWS

New Roads To Peace

RESOLVED: That the next war should be fought on the moon.

RESOLVED: That atomic scientists should be transfe work on love potions.

RESOLVED: That this poetry magazine be made req
reading in all armies and military academies

FIRST STATEMENT

15 CENTS A COPY

CIVn

6

NADIAN PROSE & POETRY

THE CANADIAN MERCURY

VOL. I No. 1   DECEMBER 1928

Holy Night
Jean Burton

The Problem of Canadian Literature
Stephen Leacock

On Funeral and Other Homes
B. K. Sandwell

nts a Copy $2.00 a Year

BLEWOINTMENTPRESS
OCCUPATION
ISSEW

IF YOU REALLY ARE AN EAGLE
YOU CAN FLY THE COOP WITH ME